THE
COOK
YOU
WANT
TO BE

EVERYDAY RECIPES TO IMPRESS

THE COOK YOU WANT TO BE

ANDY BARAGHANI

PHOTOGRAPHS BY GRAYDON HERRIOTT

LORENA JONES BOOKS
An imprint of **TEN SPEED PRESS**
California | New York

For my mom and dad

CONTENTS

Grains, Pastas, Cheap Happiness   197

Soup Obsessed   229

Fish, I Love You   247

Meaty Things   267

Sweet Spot   303

Acknowledgments   320

Index   321

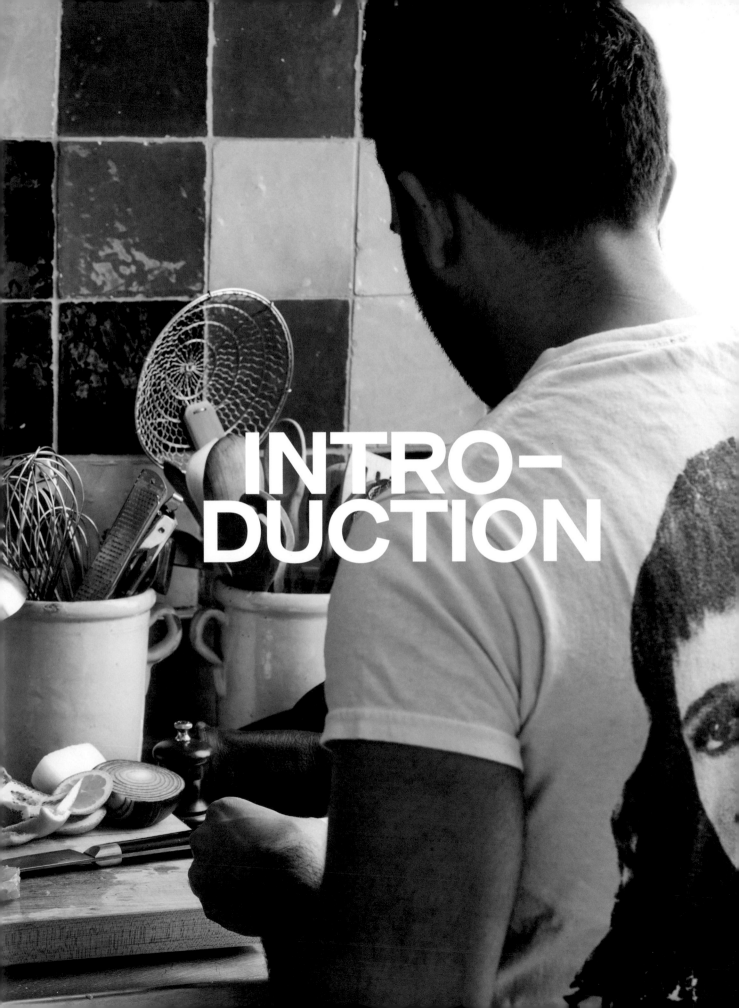

INTRO-
DUCTION

I really tried to not be a cook. I mean, this little gay Persian boy imagined he was going to be the next Al Pacino. Then, I thought I might be an anthropology professor. After I ghosted that idea, I put in a couple of years in the fashion world but grew tired of the lack of food in that industry.

Just because you love something deeply, I thought, doesn't mean you should make it your career. I think I feared that if I worked in kitchens, the job would suck the joy out of what was always more than a hobby—more like an obsession—to me.

Thing is, I don't remember a time when I was *not* obsessed with food. I remember going on a family trip to Paris when my sister and I were kids and we were each allowed to get one souvenir. She wanted a pair of leathery strappy black stilettos. I wanted a fancy restaurant meal with as many courses as I could get (I got five).

2

Eventually, I took one restaurant job that led to another. And over the years (15 now!), after putting in the time in and out of restaurants and editorial test kitchens, traveling around the world to (mostly) eat, and still constantly thinking about what I would cook for dinner, I've learned a lot that I'm excited to finally share in this book. I learned how to prep two buckets worth of onions lightning fast and to break down a whole lamb. I learned how pork shoulder, generally a tough cut of meat, will fall apart at the touch of a fork after gentle braising over low heat. I learned how to buy spices whole and toast them to get their fullest flavor. I picked up the habit of constantly tasting while I cook. I became an encyclopedia of ingredients. I may have even become slightly better than my mom (!) at making Persian rice. I now know that if the chicory I'm buying is small, tender, and barely bitter, it would be perfect in a salad. But if it's large and unruly, and so bitter it would make your mouth pucker, it should be browned in butter and gently cooked with a bit of stock. And I know there's still so much more for me to learn.

All of these experiences have helped me discover my own cooking style—a style that took time to develop. I crave simple, delicious cooking rather than dishes that are overly complicated. Generally, I keep a pretty tight pantry but I do admit to having a large collection of spices. I am picky about rice because it can have major mood swings compared with how pasta behaves. I want my food to look beautiful and to impress—not just your friends but yourself!

I know that my food may be a touch too lemony for some. And that I use what has been called a ridiculous amount of herbs. I prefer vegetables to meat. (But I still love meat!) I have an aversion to many kitchen tools and would rather do most tasks with my hands so I can slow down and relax a bit. I know that if I can't efficiently make a recipe in my tiny home kitchen, then I won't develop it.

The recipes that follow were formed by the lessons I've learned over time. Some are deeply personal; these are recipes inspired by the Persian food I grew up with, the restaurants I've worked at, or dishes I've tasted while traveling. I want you to make and love the recipes, and REALLY use this book until it is beautifully turmeric-stained all over. Maybe you're here to find some dinner inspiration. I got you. But these recipes will also teach you a few tricks, answer questions you may have about a technique, or lead you to discover that maybe you're not *that* into parsley (But are you sure??)

There are a few cooking rules I live by and think you should too:

RULE NO. 1: COOK THE UNFAMILIAR

If you see an ingredient you've never seen before, whether a sheep's milk cheese, an uncommon citrus, or an olive you've never tasted, buy it if it's in your budget! So much of the joy of cooking is exploring and learning about new ingredients. Don't ever get too comfortable.

RULE NO. 2: KEEP IT ORGANIZED

Look, I wouldn't give myself a 10 in cleanliness but my score is pretty good. I'm not telling you to do dishes in between cooking, but rather to keep things organized and tidy so you don't get overwhelmed and forget your next move. I like organized chaos. I find it facilitates the best kind of cooking.

RULE NO. 3: LOSE THE GADGETS

Certain tools are essential to becoming a great cook—a sharp knife, a well-seasoned pan, a durable cutting board. I am wary of tools for specific tasks and technology that take the joy out of cooking. You will not find a garlic press in my kitchen and never will I own an Instant Pot.

RULE NO. 4: TRY AGAIN

If you screw up a recipe and you're traumatized from undercooked chicken (if you do, just see page 232 and make chicken broth) and never want to face it again, well, don't give up so fast. Make it again and learn from what went wrong. Repetition makes you a better, more evolved cook.

4

RULE NO. 5: WHEN IN DOUBT, REACH FOR SALT OR ACID

I've heard from so many home cooks that their food doesn't taste right. Most of the time it's because the dish is missing salt—the flavors are hiding there, waiting to come out. Or it happens because there's so much going on in the dish that the flavors are all jumbled up; a hit of acid (citrus or vinegar) will clear things up.

RULE NO. 6: DON'T OVERTHINK

This rule could probably be useful in life to most people. I try to be effortless in my cooking. If a piece of fruit is perfectly ripe and doesn't need much else but some salt and a squeeze of lemon, I go with it.

RULE NO. 7: FLAKY SALT EQUALS MAGIC

Flaky salt just makes everything look a touch more fancy.

RULE NO. 8: KEEP IT SHARP

I am not one to advocate for spending a small fortune on a chef's knife. However, I do think it's essential to keep whatever brand of chef knife you have sharp. Honing it? Sure, a good quick fix. Using a whetstone? You get a gold star. Sending it out to a professional? Do whatever you gotta do.

RULE NO. 9: WATER WORKS

It can fix a broken aioli. Along with a handful of aromatics, it can be the base for soup or stew instead of stock. A splash will loosen a thick sauce. It keeps you and your plants alive! Love it, drink it . . . and cook with it.

RULE NO. 10: ALWAYS BE TASTING

I taste a dish a minimum of three times before it gets plated. I'll snack on some of the raw ingredients while I'm doing the prep, again halfway through when the dish is coming together, and then once more when it's almost finished. I might adjust the salt and fat each time, so whatever I'm cooking tastes right before I serve. Nevertheless, some people are still going to ask you to pass the salt and pepper. Live with it!

My goal is not just for you to love the recipes in this book—I do want that—but to take these nuggets of info and integrate them into your daily cooking routine. I want you to be excited by a spice mix and feel empowered to use it on another ingredient that I might have not suggested. I also want you to apply a technique you learned—whether from me or elsewhere—to other recipes you make. Air-fry my meatballs?! I won't tell.

If you come to understand the recipes and techniques in this book, you'll recognize the flavors and textures you're drawn to and be able to determine what tastes good to you. And between all that cooking and eating, you'll become the cook *you* want to be.

GET STOCKED AND STARTED

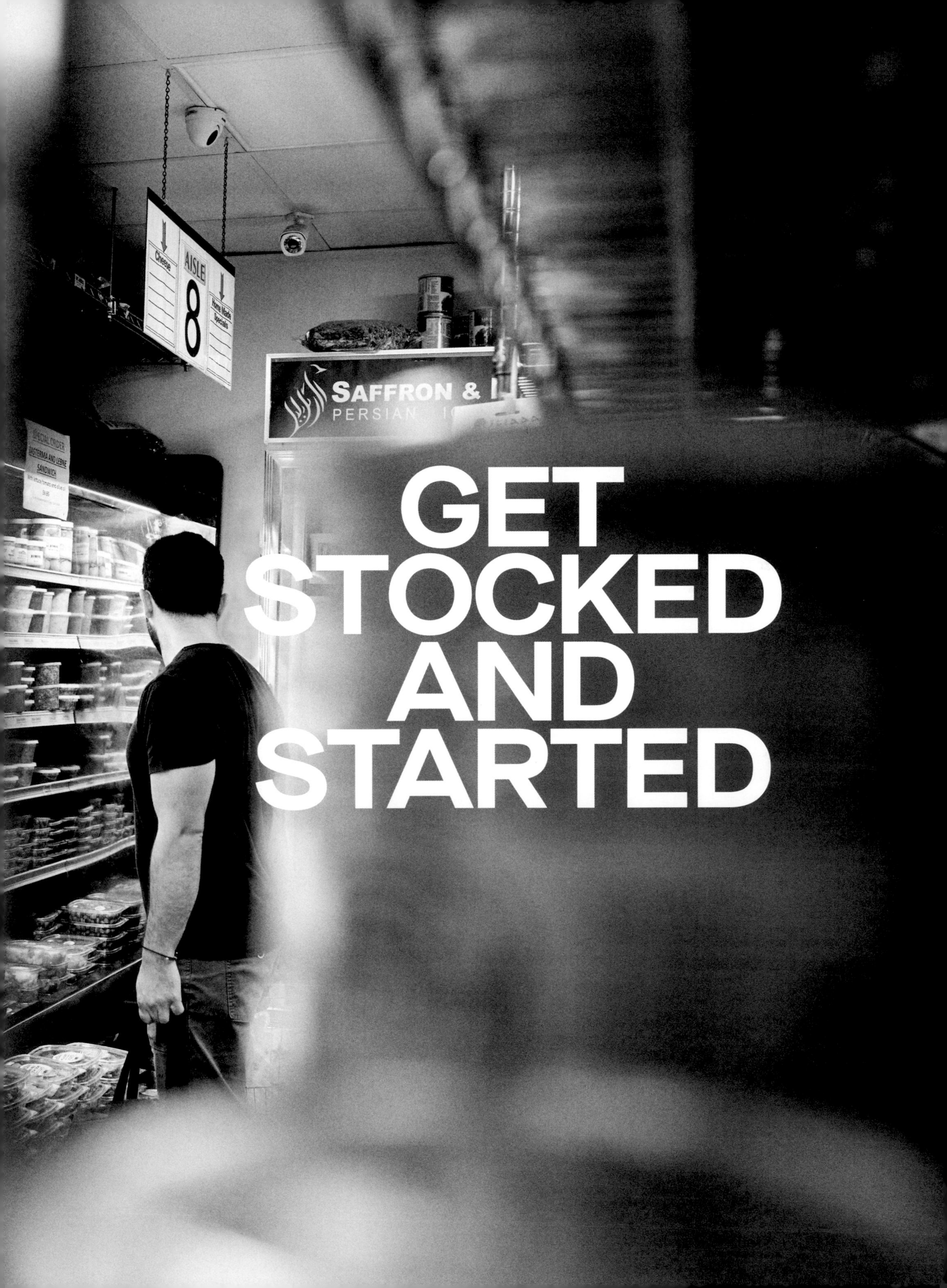

10

**People think I'm
a fussy person.**

And I *am* fussy about how my
T-shirts fit, playlists for long car
rides, and my skincare routine.
But when it comes to cooking, my
tools are relatively minimal. With
fewer tools, I can focus on the
dish and the project at hand. I wear
my worn-to-death sneakers and
an old white T-shirt in the kitchen.
When I'm cooking for myself,
I don't typically use measuring
cups or spoons. Gadgets take up
space and cloud your judgment.
You don't need a tomato knife;
you need a *sharp* knife. You don't
need a juicer; you have hands.
Use them. Less is more.

Tools
I Like

Hey, I'm assuming you have a big pot and a skillet or two. This isn't a full rundown of every kitchen tool that you'll need to cook from this book. These tools aren't super-fancy, they're all less than $20 (minus the Thermapen), and they'll ensure consistency. Frankly, these tools will enable you to cook with confidence and also elevate your cooking, as they did mine.

Cast-Iron and/or Black Carbon-Steel Pans

The recipes in this book mostly refer to the old stand-by, the cast-iron skillet. If you want to upgrade, buy a carbon-steel pan, which has less carbon and more iron than cast iron and weighs a lot less. I have yet to see any pan other than cast iron or carbon steel give me the deep sear that forms such a defined crust on a steak that it makes a *noise* when you cut into it. See what I mean when you make the perfect steak: A Proper Steak (Plus Brown Butter–Fried Onion Rings), on page 298.

Cheap Kitchen Towels

You want a stack of old kitchen towels at the ready. A BIG stack. I'm not a paper-towel guy—I only use them to blot meat or drain oil from just-fried things. I use kitchen towels to wipe the counters, to carry a hot pot of water, to clean off the cutting board, to stabilize a bowl for aioli, to wipe my knife between tasks. I need two towels when I'm cooking. Once they're stained with turmeric that just won't go away . . . I keep using them. When they REALLY break down and tear, then I recycle them.

Fish Spatula	This tool shouldn't be called a *fish* spatula. I use it to flip fillets of fish, yes, but I also use it to turn crispy potatoes on a cast-iron griddle, scraping and flipping 'em and pretending I work at an old-school diner with a cigarette smoke–stained ceiling. Use this spatula to flip roasted vegetables on a baking sheet or to transfer them to plate. A fish spatula is incredibly versatile and gets *under there* in ways a rubber spatula or wood spoon physically can't—but don't use it on a nonstick surface or it'll scratch the coating.
Japanese Mandoline	The Benriner. Always. It's lightweight plastic. Fancier mandolines have multiple parts that confuse the hell out of me. This tool is fast, efficient, and consistent in ways that the greatest chef's knife can't be. I use it to slice perfect rounds of radishes and cucumbers. Use a mandoline for dense, stubborn-to-cut ingredients—beets, carrots, daikon, fennel, potatoes—all robust vegetables that can quickly dull your knife.
Kunz Spoon	If there's one, *Uh, Andy, why you gotta be so extra?* tool, it's the Kunz spoon. It's the perfect spoon, with the perfect bowl, for ladling a pool of sauce or broth. I use this spoon to taste everything I cook. This spoon also happens to be the ideal size to collect foamy melted butter to spoon over steak or pork chops when basting. It costs about $12. Order it now.
Microplane Rasp Grater	I'm constantly grating garlic. Sliding an ingredient back and forth on a Microplane grater, you get the purest, most concentrated form of that thing: garlic, nutmeg, ginger, bright citrus zests. It turns hard cheeses, like Parm, into feathery, airy toppings. If you've cooked through one of my recipes, you'll notice how often I call for this tool. I use a Microplane grater every day, multiple times a day. You will likely only need one (I need two), but remember to use the whole Microplane, otherwise it goes dull in the one area you use repeatedly. When the grater you have is no longer doing the job, get a new one. Tools should make your kitchen tasks easier, not make you do most of the work.
Mortar and Pestle	A mortar and pestle is my most beloved tool. (On page 10 you see only part of my collection!) I don't even know how many I have at this point. My love for the mortar and pestle started at home because my mother had a tiny brass one she used to break down saffron to make saffron water for rice. At Chez Panisse, we used them for pulverizing herbs, crushing nuts, and turning garlic into paste to stir into aioli. At Estela, we ground chile flakes to release all their oils. There's no other tool in the world that requires the cook to be so active, and that so completely breaks down an ingredient, and there's no electricity required. The best food processor can't do what a mortar and pestle does.

14

Old T-Shirts (or an Apron)

Often an apron is too stiff and serious. For those times, I have twenty-something white T-shirts. I buy old shirts that feel comfortable and that are worn in nicely, without any holes—I want to control for that, so they get further worn in by me. I take them to the finish line. But dress however you want. It's your kitchen.

Oven Thermometer

I'm sorry to say this but I have to: Don't trust your oven. It doesn't matter how new or old it is. I've learned the hard way many, many, many times. I get so many DMs from people about how recipes they've cooked that took longer/shorter than what I wrote. That's your oven's fault. And every oven is calibrated differently. Invest the few dollars in an oven thermometer, hook it onto the center rack, halfway back, and let it just hang there. It's accurate and it'll give you peace of mind (and an accurate reading) the next time you go to bake, braise, roast, or toast something.

Rimmed Baking Sheets

These are essential for your roasting and baking needs, which is why you'll want to invest in more than one. Go for a large baking sheet (known as a half-sheet) and make sure it has a rim or lip, so things don't slide off. I use the quarter-size pans for toasting things such as nuts and coconut flakes, and the bigger pans for slow-roasted potatoes, fish, and chicken (SHOUT OUT to the recipes on pages 180, 265, and 278). If you wanna bake cookies on it, you can, but you're not gonna find cookies in this book. (I prefer that people give cookies *to* me.)

Sharp Things

You need three knives: a chef's knife, a paring knife, and a serrated bread knife. I use a chef's knife to prep and serve almost everything—to chop onions, carve chicken, slice cabbage. I use the side of the blade for making garlic paste. The paring knife is for smaller (less exciting) tasks, such as coring a tomato, dicing a shallot, or breaking cheese into nuggets for salad or to marinate for a snack. The bread knife is for the loaf of crusty miche, or sourdough, that's almost always on my counter. But I also use the bread knife to break open a spiky pineapple.

Spice Mill

You can crush spices in a mortar and pestle, but I like a spice mill for larger quantities, such as a spice mix for a roast. I'm not going to toast and grind multiple batches of fennel seeds in a mortar and pestle. If you have a coffee grinder, that's your spice mill (but you can't use just one mill to grind your coffee *and* your spices, or both are gonna be annoyed with you).

Thermapen

This will completely. Change. The. Way. You. Cook. IT'S SO EXACT. It's about time to stop with the guessing game. And when you're inserting the long, sharp probe into a big cut of meat or roast, don't jam it down in there so it touches bone—you want it in the center.

15

Timer
(Not Your Phone)

There are too many distractions on your phone. (Go ahead and ignore the messages from the person who didn't message you for weeks and, now, suddenly is.) A timer (or two) keeps me aware of what's going on *in my kitchen*. Click, reset. Click, reset. You'll be shocked how much more efficient and successful you'll be when you use a timer. In mere seconds, whatever you're cooking can go from peak golden toasty brown to straight-up burnt.

Wire Rack

This piece of equipment was a game changer when I started working at restaurants. You can cool cookies on it, sure. But I use it for seasoning big pieces of meat. I season the cut all over with salt and then air-dry it on a wire rack over a baking sheet in the fridge, which allows the salt to flavor all sides while water from the meat is pulled out and pools in the pan beneath. That gives you the deepest possible caramelization when you sear the meat in a hot pan.

Y-Shaped
Vegetable Peeler

I grew up using the peelers that look like pens, which give you these short little peels. The Y-peeler is, you know, shaped like a Y. Buy a pack of three. You get long strips of whatever you're peeling in broad strokes. It's so much more efficient. Why was I using that rubber thing before?

Ingredients I Can't Live Without

If I'm a minimalist with tools, I veer toward being a maximalist with spices. My pantry is constantly changing and growing, and yours should too. Mine went from plastic shakers of generic pizza-place red pepper flakes to Aleppo pepper and ground ancho chile, then on to Urfa biber and Maras pepper. Now, I have gochugaru and nine different ground peppers. Evolve, expand.

You'll see the ingredients that I call for over and over in the recipes. Not a day goes by when I don't use them. These are the building blocks of dishes in this book. Hopefully, you will love them as much as I do and bring them into your pantry. Play with them and you'll find the ones *you're* drawn to.

There are no preserved lemons or dried shiitakes on this list—I love them, and they do show up in my recipes, but what I need most often are anchovies, chiles, fish sauce, citrus, and kosher salt. And herbs. In. Every. Single. Way. From cilantro with a little bit of curl when it's young to the smallest, bitsiest parsley to chives that'll leave your breath too stinky to kiss. I *need* them all.

Canned/Tube Tomato Products

I use only two forms of canned tomatoes: whole peeled tomatoes and tomato paste in a tube. The whole peeled tomatoes are for long-cooked tomato sauce, or when I need tomato flavor in a soup or braise or pilaf. But tomato paste has a more concentrated flavor, so a squeeze of that goes a long way . . . though, sometimes, I'll use half a tube. I cook it down in fat, which darkens it a shade and turns it speckly, split, and spotty in the oil. Like a lava lamp. It gives dishes the developed-flavor taste that comes from having cooked a lot longer. In herby meatballs with spicy brothy tomatoes (see page 291), I combine tomato paste and fresh tomatoes for a dynamic, prominent tomato flavor.

Tangles of spaghetti sprinkled with Parmesan. Piles of corned beef cloaked in melted Swiss. Thick, glossy yogurt studded with sour cherry jam. Buttered toast! It's nearly impossible for me to go a day without dairy. Meat? Sure, I occasionally play double Dutch with the idea of going vegetarian (won't likely happen). Even in today's world, when the alternative-dairy section is likely to become bigger than the actual dairy aisle, there is no substitute for what dairy adds to a dish. Those tiny cheese crystals in Parmesan will always make me smile.

Butter

I use olive oil more frequently than butter, but I do use butter for desserts and pastries, and I finish almost every pasta dish with it. And I add it to rice. There's no substitute for a pat of butter melting into a fluffy bowl of rice. All the recipes in the book use unsalted butter because, well, I like controlling the amount of salt that goes into my food—and you should too.

Cheese

I tend to use hard cheeses: gruyère, Pecorino Toscano, and I can get behind a Manchego (a sheep at the table isn't exactly my thing, but a grassy barn I'm okay with). If there is one cheese I always have on hand, it's Parmigiano-Reggiano. I'll slice a few pieces and drizzle them with spicy olive oil and a few cracks of pepper. I fold in the finely grated stuff to finish all my pasta dishes. I like torn burrata with sliced persimmon/apple/pear. I love seared and squeaky Halloumi (try the combination with honey and sesame salt on page 108.) Oh, and FETA. I love its briny wetness. It's not a hard, salty cheese, it's a *wet* salty cheese. And it's essential to the snack on page 107. I sprinkle Parm on kale leaves and roast them into chips that I mix with raw kale—it's a textural green frico. You need the Parm's salty, lactic funk against the tangy mustard dressing for the full effect.

Yogurt

Very few things don't benefit from a big dollop of yogurt. I go through a quart of it every two days. I prefer my yogurt savory, and I prefer full-fat Greek yogurt. It's tangier and thicker than the American stuff, and you can thin it with water, lemon juice, vinegar, or olive oil. Again, fat is flavor. This is not the 1990s. Don't be afraid of fat.

Chiles

I'm not sure where my taste for the spicy stuff came from. Both my parents have a low tolerance but it's difficult for me to not make most of what I cook just a tad spicy. I always have fresh chiles, as well as dried (both whole and ground) and pickled, in my kitchen. Each has its own unique flavor, texture, and heat level. Just wash your hands thoroughly after working with chiles, and especially before you go to the bathroom. Learn from my mistakes.

Dried

I go to dried chiles when I want gentle-tingle-in-the-back-of-the-throat heat that'll smack me in the face 15 seconds later. I use them in two forms: whole and ground. I sneak them into stews or a pot of beans. Or I toast them first and then hydrate, puree, and add to a braise in which the chile flavor is FULLY a part of the dish, up-front and center. I use dried ground chiles to finish dishes and spice up dressings and sauces. I bloom them in oil to bring some heat to a dish. A straight-up red pepper flake, with garlic and oil, gives that in-your-face slap of heat, but not a lot of complexity and a rather neutral flavor. Urfa pepper has an almost leathery scent and deep, dark color. I also like a milder, fruity chile, such as Aleppo or gochugaru. I'll use it in a spice mix to season meat, and to finish roasted vegetables.

Fresh

Sometimes I need a vegetal, fresh chile, with a fruity in-your-face perfume. A Scotch bonnet can be almost melonlike with a heat that lasts, whereas others are less complex. A jalapeño is vegetal, grassy, and hot. With serranos, you never know what you're gonna get heat-wise. I tend to cook with Fresno, serrano, jalapeño, Holland, and bird's eye chiles, but I like to play around with others, especially in the summer when I'll find all kinds of chiles at the farmers' market. If you're sensitive to heat, an easy way to tame a chile is to split it and cut out the veiny interior ribs and the seeds.

Pickled

Pickled chiles have my three favorite flavors: salty, spicy, vinegary. Those three words describe so much of the food I make. I'll eat a few pepperoncini out of the jar before I put them in a salad or chop them finely and them add to a salsa verde. And I need with my In-N-Out burger. I take a bite of my Double-Double, a bite of pickled chile, and moan with happiness. They're the perfect condiment. In the first chapter, I'll show you how to make quick pickled chiles rather than buying them (but either works).

Citus

Lemons are my favorite. Regular ol' lemons. Maybe it's the Cali boy in me, but I love their tart juice, bitter pith, fragrant zest, and even the whole thing chopped up (like in the sauce on page 36). There is about 3 tablespoons per lemon, 2 tablespoons per lime, ¼ cup per orange, and ½ cup of juice per grapefruit. (I know this because I've squeezed *a lot* of citrus.) Use one hand to squeeze, the other to catch the seeds—no tools necessary.

Bitter grapefruit is my number-two favorite. I would never make a citrus salad without grapefruit (otherwise, it's just a plate of sweet fruit). And grapefruit pairs so well with seafood (like the recipe on page 253). You'll see limes and oranges used in these recipes too. But there are so many other exquisite members of the citrus family: Buddha's hand, finger limes, kishu mandarins, kumquats, yuzu. Zesting all this citrus is what dulls my Microplane.

Fish Sauce

I get these intense cravings for fish sauce. It's a salty pantry ingredient that can be quite assertive. A little goes a long way. It gives a lip-smacking quality to a dish that very few ingredients can. When I was traveling in Vietnam, I went to the Red Boat factory in Phú Quõc, where they make some of the best fish sauce I've ever tasted. I remember seeing their vast wooden barrels, three times the size of me, filled with anchovies and stacked on each other. The fish are periodically salted and pressed until they've aged, fermented, and transformed into a glossy amber liquid. I like Red Boat's fish sauce and I also cook with Squid brand (it's just a name—there's no squid in it). Look for two ingredients in fish sauce: anchovies and salt. If there's anything else in there, don't take it home to your kitchen.

Herbs

If there's an ingredient that's most associated with my cooking, it's fresh herbs. Herbs are in my DNA. Although the foods I ate at my parents' house varied while my sisters and I were growing up, there was one dish on the table every single night: sabzi khordan, which is a platter of raw herbs. The platter had up to eight herbs, including scallion tops, radish tops, basil, Persian basil, and savory. It's traditional to eat herbs with Iranian food to cleanse the palate and help digestion—a mouthful of herbs cuts through the buttery rice and rich stews. If my family went to another house for dinner and they had only two or three herbs, it was as if they had plastic covers on their furniture. Not a good look.

I want my food to feel fresh and alive. Herbs do that. Whether finely minced, chopped, torn, or left whole . . . the finer the chop, the more concentrated the flavor. I usually keep about five different herbs in my fridge at once. I don't think there's an herb that I don't like, but parsley is essential: it adds an airy, sweet grassiness to whatever it touches.

I can tell if an herb will taste good. A good bunch of chives should be able to stand tall when held upright and only slightly give a bow at the very top. Rosemary stems shouldn't be brown; the leaves should almost flare—and they shouldn't be as woody as you think. Rosemary should be tender enough to bite with your front teeth. Now you know.

Herbs fall into two textural categories: hard and tender. Hard herbs are rosemary, thyme, sage, and bay leaves. Tender herbs are basil, parsley, cilantro, dill, mint, and tarragon (to name a few).

To store, scatter cleaned herbs on a damp paper towel or kitchen towel, then loosely roll it up into a log. Place in a resealable plastic bag and refrigerate for up to a week, pulling a few leaves whenever you need them.

Nuts and Seeds

I like a lot of sprinkles. Not the rainbow kind, but savory sprinkles made of black and white sesame seeds, hemp, nigella, and chopped toasted nuts. I've had to edit sesame seeds out of so many recipes because I put them on everything. I had to do the same with hazelnuts. Chopped nuts bring crunch and a bit of welcome irregularity. With my kind of sprinkles, you're adding another layer of texture to the dish you're preparing, which keeps your guests coming back for more. Plus, cooking with nuts and seeds adds another fat beyond the olive oil or ghee you're using.

Choose nuts and seeds that are raw and haven't been seasoned. You want to have real-time control over how they taste. Toasting them just before you use them will give a fresher toasty flavor. If I'm wet-toasting (cooking the nuts in some kind of fat, like oil or butter), those directions will be given in that specific recipe.

If a recipe calls for toasted nuts, this is the method: Preheat the oven to 350°F. Spread out the nuts in an even layer on a rimmed baking sheet and pop them in the oven. Tender nuts like pecans, pistachios, and walnuts will take 6 to 8 minutes to get to a good, toasty place. Denser nuts like almonds, hazelnuts, and macadamias will take 8 to 10 minutes to finish toasting. Trust your nose though. The nuts should smell fragrant but never burnt or acrid.

If a recipe calls for toasted seeds, this is the method: Add the seeds to a dry skillet and place over medium heat. Stir the seeds continuously as they toast, never taking your eyes off them, until they begin to look shiny and are fragrant, 1 to 2 minutes.

Oils and Fats

Fats are used throughout this book, as they do serious heavy lifting for so many recipes. Not only do they provide flavor—like a fresh, buttery olive oil, or the salty porky richness of bacon—fats also have the ability to completely transform other ingredients and create different textures; think puffy beer-battered fish, flaky piecrust, and soft jammy onions. I tend to choose my cooking fat based on the type of flavors I'm going for in the dish. If I'm making a tomato sauce, I'm reaching for olive oil because I want that flavor in that sauce.

Extra-Virgin Olive Oil

My food wouldn't be what it is without olive oil. I usually have two olive oils on hand. I need an everyday olive oil I can use for cooking that isn't too assertive, peppery, or spicy—I don't want it to dominate the dish. The second olive oil is for cold sauces, salsa verde, vinaigrette, and yogurt sauce. I want it to be flavorful, with a prickly bit of pepperiness, but not so much that it overpowers your mouth. Anything from the Liguria region of Italy is my favorite; that's where pesto is from, and their regional oils tend to be gentle and fruity. Taste the olive oil when you open it, then you'll know if you like the flavor (otherwise, why add it to your food?). Use liberally and often.

Neutral Oil

So many cultures don't use olive oil simply because olives don't grow there so they rely on other neutral-tasting oils. I can't live without neutral oil, such as grapeseed, sunflower, or canola, for my stir-fries, my Very Crispy Garlic-Chile Oil (page 54), or The Greatest Aioli (page 61). I prefer grapeseed and sunflower oil as they have a high smoke point but are less processed than canola and vegetable oil.

Other Fats

Animal fats! Bacon fat. Butter. Lamb fat (from the roast on page 282). Coconut oil. Ghee. Sesame oil. I want the sweet, toasty, and coconutty flavor of virgin coconut oil in the cauliflower (see page 191). I use ghee when cooking dishes with certain flavor profiles, such as the Masoor Daal with Salty Yogurt (page 240)—the high fat content of the ghee blooms and extracts the spices. A few drops of toasted sesame oil can make a dish intensely toasty with its smoky sesame flavor. I use it in dressings, drizzled over soup, in the Eggs in Spicy Tomato Curry on page 70, and in any stir-fry. Every fat has a purpose (which is also how I feel about sneakers).

Onion-y Things

Sliced, diced, brunoised, roasted, charred, cooked in butter until blond, confited, cooked 'til their walls collapse, 'til they shrink, are deeply brown, jammy, and reduced to an unctuous savory paste—that's how I like my alliums. All the ways. I use them throughout this book, so if you're a person who doesn't do onions, it's time to turn back. Things aren't going to work out between us.

Garlic

You will see garlic used in just about every way I can imagine in this book: fried into crispy chips, the heads cut in half to infuse a big pot of something brothy, crushed to a fine paste and stirred into sauces . . . I love it just about any way. It's a staple that I cook with daily. We see fully mature garlic year-round, even though garlic is actually quite seasonal. I find it best in the hottest months, when my fingers almost become a little sticky from trying to peel the papery skins off the cloves. And then there's green garlic (sometimes called young garlic) that shows up in the spring. Green garlic has this sweet, mild freshness and grassiness—you should buy as many bundles as you can before it's gone. Unlike when garlic matures and is dried, you can chop and use the whole green garlic stalk. Use it the same way you would use mature garlic. It doesn't get better than a green garlic scramble with plenty of butter and Parm. In the summer you'll see their twisted, snakelike garlic scapes in the stalks that grow from the bulbs. They have a firm texture and can be tossed in oil, thrown on the grill, and eaten like a sturdy green veg.

Leeks

They're more work to prep than onions because they're muddy, but it's worth the time it takes to clean leeks because they're sweeter than standard onions and a whole different experience to eat. I get them charred and smoky on the outside while they steam on the inside, creating smoky ash against a luscious interior (see page 261).

Onions

An onion can be pungent and spicy when raw but also sweet and tender when cooked for a long time. Onions can be tamed in ice water or perked up and added to a bowl of brothy beans or chili. Or sizzled until they're turned to wispy, lacy whiskers (which I like as a topping for stews and fluffy rice). Yellow is standard, but play with others. Keep a couple red onions on hand to pickle or macerate.

Shallots

I use shallots whenever I want a subtle onion-y moment (see Pomegranate Spoon Salad on page 131). And a small shallot might get sweated gently for a clam dish because its sweetness will cut through the brininess. I like them finely chopped for dressings in which they add a bit of texture. They're fried with garlic for the Sticky-Sweet Roast Chicken (see page 274). After making that, you'll come to find out that a crispy shallot is one of the greatest toppings.

Rice and Legumes

It's probably the Iranian in me, but I think rice and legumes—what many think of as sides, afterthoughts, the base of a Chipotle bowl—are life-sustaining staples. When I serve a rice or legume dish, I consider it a main event. It isn't a cup of rice, it's a *platter* of rice. I don't combine rice with water, cook it, and call it a day. There's a process of rinsing and combining the right ratio of water to rice (rinse, parboil, steam—I promise the result will be life-changing). And I have deep respect for these ingredients.

As for legumes, I don't know where to begin. I couldn't tell you how many cans of chickpeas I have in my pantry at any given time. They're one of the greatest staples. You can crisp them in oil with grated garlic, dried ground chiles, and lemon zest as a snack; dump them into a stew; or flatten them and make pancakes. Otherwise, I cook beans and lentils from dried. I'm a Rancho Gordo customer, but I also buy beautiful beans wherever I travel. But listen: more than recommending specific rice or beans, I want to emphasize that rice and legumes can stand on their own and warrant deep respect.

Salt (Flaky and Kosher)

When people tell me whatever they cooked didn't taste good, I know it's probably because they didn't add enough salt (or they're missing acid). Let's focus on the salt part: Salt is crucial, no matter the dish, to bringing out the flavors of the ingredients you're working with, from salads to desserts. I season a dish two or three times while I'm making it. Salting early allows the salt to penetrate whatever it touches—you're building the flavor foundation. I salt in the middle of the cooking process to continue building flavor. Then, toward the end, I adjust the salt to taste before sitting down to eat. Most of the time, I'm salting lightly—unless I'm seasoning a big fatty roast, in which case I'm getting that salt into every nook and cranny early on.

Flaky Sea Salt

Jacobsen is my go-to. Every single flake is perfect. I don't know what the equivalent diamond cut would be—princess cut?—but Jacobsen makes these little airy, crunchy diamonds. They add texture and a hint of saltiness. This salt isn't to be wasted on seasoning meats—it's a finishing salt for salads, seared steak, steamed cooked rice (like the Buttery Nori-Speckled Rice on page 200), and freshly cut melon. I also love the container, which ends up acting as a sacred storage place for any unused animal fats.

Kosher Salt

I use Diamond Crystal kosher salt, with its tiny pyramid-like salt crystals and delicate flavor that give you more control over the saltiness of a dish. It's the standard salt used in most restaurants. If you're using Morton or any other brand, cut the measurements in this book in half (yes, Morton is *salty*).

Spices

Either you grew up in a household that used spices or you didn't (or, if your family did use spices, it was limited to ground black pepper). In my mother's kitchen, spices were swirled and bloomed and stirred into so many dishes. They have the effect of making your mind feel as though it doesn't know what's happening in your mouth but in a very good way. So, if using more than one spice scares you, you need to check yourself. If I call for six spices, there's a reason. Trust me when I tell you the result will be worth it.

I insist you use whole coriander, cumin, and fennel seeds. These three taste ten times more like *themselves* than the ground versions. I toast the whole spices in a dry skillet over medium heat until my kitchen smells like a Marrakesh market. Do NOT turn on your vent! When the spice is fragrant, pour it into a spice mill or mortar and pestle to cool before grinding or crushing. In my recipes, ground spices get activated, bloomed, or cooked in fat—however you want to say it. However you do it, you're awakening their flavors.

Vinegars

Vinegars are finally getting the attention they deserve, even though olive oil has been the more popular kid for thousands of years. I have more vinegars on my shelf than fats. I use them in the obvious way—to make a vinaigrette—but also to bring acidity to caramelized vegetables, to balance a rich and fatty steak, to brighten a braise that has been simmering for hours. I use unseasoned rice vinegar as my multipurpose choice, it has a delicate sweetness and an almost nutty flavor. (Be sure to use *unseasoned*. Otherwise the vinegar contains salt and sugar and will throw your recipe off-balance.) I use it for stir-fries, quick pickling, and marinades. I like playing around with sherry vinegar; it's robust and woodsy and you *know* it's there. Use red and white wine vinegars for most dressings. Spend more than you thought you would on vinegars (more than $6). I promise it'll make your vinaigrette that much better.

28

MIGHTY LITTLE RECIPES

When I'm burned out from a workday of testing recipes and thinking about doing the dinner dishes, my mind and body crave something simple.

That's when my arsenal of flavor enhancers saves the day. Vinegar-spiked, spicy, sour, and creamy sauces; crunchy and savory sprinkles; and a few different herby green sauces are my lifesavers. I'm not going to tuck them into a basics chapter at the end of this book. They are as crucial to me as my well-worn white T-shirts. Oh, those dishes? Yeah, I'll get to them tomorrow.

All of these condiments add texture and brightness without weighing down any dish. They're a study in balance: When you have a heavy, meaty meal, you need to counter it with something light and green (meet crispy salsa verde). When you have something soft and tender, you need to keep it interesting with an explosion of crunchy and spicy (chili crisp does the trick). You'll see these recipes referenced in recipes throughout the book, but I hope you take them and do your own thing—they're flexible, foolproof, and irresistible.

A HIT OF ACID

The whole-lemon sauce, mustard dressing, and turmeric- and-black-pepper dressing are like my favorite children. I love acidic, tangy, mouth-puckering flavors. Most, but not all, of these recipes use citrus, and that's no accident. Citrus is crucial. It perks up a dish, and keeps people coming back for more. Many of my condiments use a combination of acids—lemon with vinegar, two types of vinegar, or citrus zest *and* juice—to add layers to a dish.

Each sauce has a different texture. The Fresh and Puckery Lemon Sauce (see page 36) is pebbly and piece-y. The Tangy Mustard Dressing (page 37) is luscious and rich (mustard is more acidic than you think). The thin Turmeric and Black Pepper–Citrus Dressing (page 40) is juicy and perfect on Fat Pieces of Citrus with Avocado and Caramelized Dates (page 128). The most acidic condiment of all is the Anything Pickles brine (page 38), which I can drink straight. But you can pickle some vegetables in it if you wish.

FRESH AND PUCKERY LEMON SAUCE

Here is a sauce for my fellow lemon lovers, who crave sinking their teeth into lemon wedges even though they know it could ruin their enamel. Using an entire lemon—skin, pith, and flesh—gives this sauce its tangy, bright, floral scent and lots of texture. The pith will lend some bitterness, but it's offset by the honey. It's a tad abrasive, but I wouldn't have it any other way. Feel free to change up the ingredients: Swap the ground pepper for a dried or fresh chile.

MAKES 1½ CUPS

2 small Meyer or regular lemons

1 small shallot, finely chopped

Kosher salt

⅔ cup extra-virgin olive oil

⅔ cup coarsely chopped parsley or mint

2 teaspoons runny honey

Freshly ground pepper

Trim and discard the knobby ends from the lemons (they're tough). Quarter each lemon lengthwise to get four wedges. Using a chef's knife, cut out the core and seeds. Thinly slice each wedge, including the pith and peel, then finely chop everything into bitsy pieces smaller than the size of a pea. You should end up with a messy pile of chopped lemon, with no large chunks remaining.

Scoop up the lemon mess and juices from the cutting board and transfer to a medium bowl. Add the shallot and a pinch of salt and let sit for 10 minutes to soften the shallot. Stir in the olive oil, parsley, and honey. Season with more salt and a few turns of pepper to taste. The sauce should be boldly lemony and tangy. The sauce keeps, covered and refrigerated, for up to 3 days.

WAYS TO USE

Stir into yogurt for a tangy dip.
Toss with just about any roasted veg.
As a marinade for fresh cheese, such as feta.
On top of braised meat or a rich stew.
Spoon over Butter-Slathered Whole Fish with Jammy Fennel (page 265).

TANGY MUSTARD DRESSING

This is my house vinaigrette. It's Frenchy, overly mustardy, garlicky, and the closest I'll get to a simple vinaigrette. (Simple isn't any fun, is it?) I prefer the pungency that garlic brings to the dressing, but you could use a small, finely chopped shallot or a sprinkling of chives instead.

MAKES 1¼ CUPS

1 garlic clove

1 small lemon

¼ cup Dijon mustard

¼ cup red wine vinegar

⅔ cup extra-virgin olive oil

Kosher salt

Freshly ground pepper

Using a Microplane, finely grate the garlic clove into a medium bowl. Finely grate the zest from the lemon into the bowl, then halve the lemon and squeeze about 2 tablespoons lemon juice into the bowl, catching any seeds with your other hand. Add the mustard and vinegar and then whisk in the olive oil until smooth and creamy. Season with salt and plenty of pepper. You want to taste a slight prickle. The vinaigrette keeps, covered and refrigerated, for up to 3 days. Bring to room temperature before using.

WAYS TO USE

Drizzle over warm boiled and smashed potatoes.
As a dressing for blanched leeks or asparagus.
Spoon over slow-roasted salmon.
Toss with Parmesan-Kale Chip Salad (page 147).

ANYTHING PICKLES

This is all you need to make homemade pickles of any kind. We're not sanitizing jars and going full pioneer here. This brine is a simple ratio of water, vinegar, salt, and sugar, which I use as my go-to method for quick pickling any kind of sturdy vegetable. Because these are not fermented pickles, they don't develop that funky flavor but they are faster to make and only require a day or two of curing before snacking.

MAKES 2 QUARTS

1¾ cups water

1¼ cups unseasoned rice vinegar

2 tablespoons kosher salt

2 teaspoons granulated sugar

2 pounds vegetables (such as whole kirby cucumbers, sliced red onions, small peeled carrots, cauliflower florets, and whole chiles—the possibilities are truly endless)

In a small saucepan over medium-high heat, combine the water and vinegar. Whisk in the salt and sugar and bring to a simmer, stirring occasionally, until the granules have completely dissolved (this will happen quickly), about 3 minutes.

Pack your prepped veg into two 1-quart jars with lids. Pour in the hot brine, making sure your veg is properly submerged in the brine and leaving ½ inch of headspace between the liquid and the rims of the jars. Let the jars cool for 1 hour at room temperature.

Screw on the lids and place in the fridge to chill and cure for 2 days. Do your best and be patient—wait the 2 days before snacking and using. I promise the wait will be worth it. Quick pickles keep for up to 1 month—they have a shorter lifespan than their fussy peacocking counterparts—but I have a thing for acid, so mine rarely last more than a week.

GO PICKLE

Giardiniera-Style Pickles: Replace the rice vinegar with red wine vinegar. Once the salt and sugar dissolve, add 1 teaspoon dried oregano, 1 garlic clove (smashed), and 1/3 cup extra-virgin olive oil.

Lemon-Fennel Pickles: Substitute white wine vinegar for the rice vinegar. Once the salt and sugar dissolve, add four 2-inch strips of lemon peel to the brine along with 1 teaspoon fennel seeds.

Spicy Turmeric Pickles: Once the salt and sugar dissolve, add 1 teaspoon coriander seeds, 1 teaspoon cumin seeds, ½ teaspoon ground turmeric, and 1 small chile to the brine.

Torshi (Persian Pickles): Replace the rice vinegar with apple cider vinegar. Once the salt and sugar dissolve, add 2 garlic cloves (thinly sliced), 2 teaspoons dried tarragon, 1 teaspoon dried mint, and ½ teaspoon red pepper flakes to the brine.

WHAT MAKES THE BEST PICKLE BRINE

I've eaten—and made—a lot of pickles, and here's what I've learned makes the best ones.

1. Go heavy on the acid: I prefer a brine that is almost equal parts vinegar to water.

2. Your brine needs to be seasoned properly for taste, but the salt also acts as a preservative. If you ever see a pickle recipe with 3 cups of brine and less than 1 tablespoon of salt, look the other way.

3. Sugar should provide balance to your brine rather than sweetness. (I'll admit this is personal preference, as I don't care much for sweet pickles.) Keep it minimal.

4. Boiling your brine dissolves the sugar and distribute the ingredients evenly, making a tasty bath for whatever you're pickling. Do the right thing and start by simmering.

5. Adding your ingredients to the hot brine will briefly cook them, but they will retain their crunch. If you add your ingredients to a cooled brine, they'll take an extra day or two to become tasty and soak up the seasoning.

6. This may go without saying, but: Whatever you choose to flavor your brine (spices, herbs, garlic . . .) will flavor the ingredient(s) you're pickling. So, if you don't like fennel seeds, you're probably not going to start liking their flavor in your pickles.

TURMERIC AND BLACK PEPPER– CITRUS DRESSING

You know those tiny jars of "tonics" at fancy gyms, made with berries that you've never heard of and a ton of ginger and cayenne, that cost $8 a swallow? I decided to make my own tonic that acts as a dressing, but I would gladly drink it on its own. (Yes, I'm aware there is ½ cup of olive oil in this recipe. I'm still sticking with my statement.)

MAKES 1 CUP

½ cup fresh lemon juice

2 teaspoons runny honey

2 teaspoons peeled, finely grated ginger

1 teaspoon ground turmeric

½ cup extra-virgin olive oil

Kosher salt

Freshly ground pepper

In a medium bowl, combine the lemon juice, honey, ginger, and turmeric and whisk to blend. While whisking continuously, stream in the olive oil until the dressing is smooth and assumes a color that makes you feel healthy. Season with salt and add as little or as much pepper as you like. The dressing keeps, covered and refrigerated, for up to 2 days. Bring to room temperature before using.

WAYS TO USE

As a marinade for grilled chicken legs or quick-cooking steaks, such as skirt or flank.
Toss with shredded cabbage and radishes for a citrusy slaw.
As a dressing for a grain or lentil salad.
Spoon over Fat Pieces of Citrus with Avocado and Caramelized Dates (page 128).

40

CRUNCHY
THINGS

Crunch should disrupt a dish, in a good way. You fool the palate for a moment and then you go back to the regularly scheduled programming—say, the creamy soup beneath. I use nuts and seeds as well as fried shallots or garlic, for texture. But it's not enough to throw a seed on a dish. I also use crunchy toppings to add flavor. Like pistachio za'atar with sumac, salt, and thyme. Breadcrumbs crisped up with anchovies. A sesame and chile–salt mixture you can jar and stash for months. And frizzled shallots that get lightly pickled—for pucker and crunch. You'll see more crunchy toppings in other recipes (I could fill a book with them), but I constantly rely on the ones in this section.

PISTACHIO ZA'ATAR

Each component in za'atar is essential: the sesame adds crackly nuttiness; the dried herbs give a floral, woodsy flavor; and the sumac brings that distinct tanginess. No two batches of za'atar are ever the same because everyone has their own ideal proportions of ingredients. And because the quality can vary, I tend to make my own.

My blend is a fresher version of the classic, using fresh thyme or oregano in place of dried. If you're adamant about using sesame seeds, go ahead, ¼ cup in place of the pistachios. If you want to make this into a pourable condiment, submerge the za'atar in ½ cup olive oil, which I love slicked onto hot bread. Make this the day you use it.

MAKES ABOUT ½ CUP

½ cup toasted pistachios, walnuts, or almonds (see page 24), finely chopped

2 tablespoons chopped thyme or oregano

2 teaspoons ground sumac

2 teaspoons finely grated lemon zest

Kosher salt

In a small bowl, combine the nuts, thyme, sumac, and lemon zest. Use your fingers to mix, making sure the lemon zest is evenly distributed and doesn't clump. Season with salt and set aside until ready to use.

WAYS TO USE

As a crunchy potato topper (za'atar fries are a thing).
On top hard-roasted veg, like carrots, brussels sprouts, or cauliflower.
Stir into yogurt as a savory dip.
Sprinkle over big, juicy wedges of summer tomatoes.
Spoon over Sweet-and-Sour Caramelized Squash (page 166).

COCONUT AND FRESH CHILE CRISP

This is a dry, crispy topping inspired by Filipinx condiment palapa but, well, it's not palapa, which has more of an oily-crisp consistency. It's sweet and toasty, yet spicy and crunchy, and somehow brings some excitement to anything it's sprinkled on. I favor unsweetened coconut flakes (preferably without the bark, but you can use grated coconut as well, it will just take less time to cook. If you're lucky enough to get your hands on freshly grated coconut, you get a gold star.

MAKES 1 CUP

2 tablespoons virgin coconut oil or extra-virgin olive oil

2 small serrano or bird's eye chiles, thinly sliced

1 cup unsweetened coconut flakes

1 teaspoon finely grated lime zest

Kosher salt

In a small skillet over medium heat, warm the coconut oil. Drop the chiles and coconut flakes into the skillet and cook, stirring occasionally, until the coconut is golden brown in spots, toasty, and smells sweet, 3 to 5 minutes. Remove the skillet from the heat and stir in the lime zest. Season with a bit of salt and give the pan a shake.

Let cool completely. Transfer to an airtight container and store in a cool place for up to 2 days.

WAYS TO USE

On top of crispy roasted broccoli.
Sprinkle over slow-roasted salmon.
As a textural topping for Masoor Daal with Salty Yogurt (page 240)
    or Perfect Cauliflower with Spicy Coconut Crisp (page 191).

SWEET AND TOASTY NUTS

These are exactly what they sound like. No candy thermometer needed. No need to make caramel or turn on the oven. When cooked down, the water in the honey starts to evaporate and the sugar crystallizes and clings to the nuts. A sweet little revelation. No need to thank me.

MAKES 1 CUP

1 cup raw pecans, walnuts, or cashews

2 tablespoons runny honey or maple syrup

1 teaspoon freshly ground pepper

Kosher salt

In a skillet over medium heat, combine the nuts, honey, and pepper. Cook, stirring constantly, until the honey reduces and crystallizes around the nuts, 5 to 8 minutes. They will look darkened and smell toasty and extra nutty. Remove the skillet from the heat and immediately season the nuts with salt. Transfer to a small, shallow bowl and let cool before breaking into large pieces or coarsely chopping. Transfer to an airtight container and store in a cool, dark place for up to 2 days.

WAYS TO USE

As a snack, obviously.
Sprinkle over cut-up stone fruit and torn burrata for a savory fruit salad.
Add crunch to a sweet roasted veg, like carrots, squash, or sweet potatoes.
In Super-Crunchy Celery Salad (page 135).

44

ANCHOVY BREADCRUMBS

After working in restaurants, I was so used to making my own breadcrumbs in the oven on a baking sheet. The problem is, you have to keep pulling the tray out of the oven and giving the crumbs a stir. I still have a few burn scars from that routine. The stove-top method is faster, and you get the added bonus of smelling the crumbs as they become toasty in the oil. Just stay attentive while making these. They can go from perfect to burned while you glance at your phone one more time. . . .

MAKES 1 CUP

3 tablespoons extra-virgin olive oil

4 oil-packed anchovies, drained

1 cup panko breadcrumbs

Kosher salt

Freshly ground pepper

In a skillet over medium heat, warm the olive oil until it looks shiny. Add the anchovies and, using a wooden spoon, stir them around until they've broken down and have speckled the oil, about 3 minutes. Add the breadcrumbs and continue cooking, stirring until the crumbs are deeply golden brown and getting real toasty, another 5 minutes. Don't worry if the breadcrumbs are a little uneven in color—it adds character and they're going to taste amazing. Transfer the breadcrumbs to a small bowl and season with salt and pepper while still warm. Use right away or cool completely, cover, and store at room temperature for up to 1 day.

WAYS TO USE

Sprinkle over sautéed garlicky greens.
Top a soft-boiled, over-easy, or poached egg—any egg, really.
Add crunch to a pot of beans with or without a spoonful of aioli.
Sprinkle over Fall-Apart Caramelized Cabbage Smothered in Anchovies and Dill (page 184).
Scatter over Little Gems with Green Goddess Yogurt and Tangy Shallots (page 144).

BREADCRUMB BONUS

Garlicky Breadcrumbs: Crush 3 garlic cloves and drop them into the skillet with the oil (sans anchovies). Cook the garlic until just golden, about 3 minutes. Add the breadcrumbs and cook until golden brown, about 5 minutes. Pluck out and discard the garlic. Proceed as directed.

Lemony Anchovy Breadcrumbs: Once the breadcrumbs are almost finished cooking, stir in 2 tablespoons finely chopped fresh parsley and 1 teaspoon finely grated lemon zest. Proceed as directed.

FRIZZLED PICKLED SHALLOTS

This showstopper of a topping was first introduced to me at now-closed Fung Tu, which was on the Lower East Side in New York City. The chef, Jonathan Wu, regularly blew my mind, and I was devastated when the restaurant closed. Jonathan marinated shallots in a mixture of black vinegar and sherry vinegar, then dredged and fried them. They were puffy and addicting, like Funyuns. I went with one vinegar for my version and added soy sauce to give them another salty layer.

MAKES ABOUT 1 CUP

¼ cup sherry vinegar
or red wine vinegar

2 tablespoons low-sodium
soy sauce

4 large shallots, sliced into
thin rings

⅓ cup neutral oil
(such as grapeseed)

¼ cup all-purpose flour

¼ cup finely ground cornmeal

Kosher salt

In a medium bowl, mix together the sherry vinegar and soy sauce. Add the shallots and let sit for 20 to 30 minutes to lightly pickle. Drain and discard the liquid and pat the shallots dry.

Pour the neutral oil into a skillet and place over medium heat. While the oil heats, in a shallow bowl (a pie pan also works well), whisk together the flour and cornmeal to combine. Dredge the shallots in the flour mixture, shaking off the excess coating. Line a plate with a paper towel (to soak up the excess oil, so skip using a kitchen towel this time).

Test the oil by dropping in one shallot slice. If the oil is ready, tiny bubbles will form around the edges of the shallot right away (if they don't, wait a minute and try again). Working in batches, add the shallots to the oil and fry, stirring occasionally. The tiny bubbles will form more rapidly. When the bubbles subside, that means moisture from the shallots has been drawn out, and they'll get deeply golden and crisp after about 3 minutes. Using a slotted spoon, transfer the fried shallots to the prepared plate and season with salt while still hot.

Let the shallots cool completely. Transfer to an airtight container and store at room temperature for up to 3 days.

WAYS TO USE

As a crispy topping for salads.
Sprinkle over nearly any egg.
Scatter over a stir-fry or noodle dish.
As a garnish for Ginger Chicken and Rice Soup with Sizzled Black Pepper (page 244).
Scatter over Black Pepper and Ginger Asparagus Stir-Fry (page 158).

A FEW GREEN SAUCES

Another green sauce? (Go ahead, you can roll your eyes.) Never enough green sauces! The sauces in this section get their green factor from a variety of herbs, so there's a freshness that'll wake up whatever they're dressing. The green tahini is loose and thin—use it generously. The zhoug is thick and potent—you only need a spoonful. And the salsa verde is somewhere between the intensity of chimichurri and herby potato chips; it's absolutely incredible on a perfectly basted steak.

HOT GREEN
TAHINI

This is the most versatile condiment in the book. It can be a dip, a sandwich spread, a marinade for chicken, a salad dressing, you name it. Important to note: You can't dump everything in a blender here and call it a day. The tahini will aerate and get too thick and pasty. Blend the garlic-lemon-oil mixture and then stir in the tahini for a luscious consistency. And be flexible. You could use only parsley instead of a combination of herbs. And you could slip in some anchovies, never a bad idea.

MAKES ABOUT 1 CUP

2 serrano or jalapeño chiles, coarsely chopped

2 garlic cloves, crushed

2 cups mixed tender fresh herbs (such as parsley, mint, and dill)

2 large lemons

¼ cup extra-virgin olive oil

½ cup tahini

Kosher salt

In a blender, combine the chiles, garlic, and herb leaves. Finely grate the zest of one lemon into the blender jar, then halve both lemons, squeeze out and measure ½ cup juice, catching any seeds with your other hand, and pour in the juice, along with the olive oil. Blend until mostly smooth; a few flecks of herbs are okay. Pour the herb oil into a medium bowl, then whisk in the tahini until smooth. Season with salt to taste. This keeps, covered and refrigerated, for up to 4 days. Bring to room temperature before using.

WAYS TO USE

Marinate a roast chicken (great decision).
As a dressing for leafy salads (works well for Bibb, cabbage, chicory, and iceberg).
As a dip for crunchy veg or flatbread.
As a spread on sandwiches.

ZHOUG

The Yemenite condiment zhoug (pronounced "zoog") has many variations, and although the green version is the most popular, it can also be red. No matter the color, it should be brilliantly hot. If you want a mild sauce, that's not zhoug. I make this in a mortar and pestle but you can also hand chop everything into almost a powder (I'm kidding! . . . kind of), but I'll look away if you need to pull out the food processor. It's a thick, powerful sauce, so although this recipe yields just ½ cup, a dab goes a long way.

MAKES ABOUT ½ CUP

1 garlic clove

Kosher salt

2 serrano or jalapeño chiles, finely chopped

¼ cup finely chopped parsley

¼ cup finely chopped mint

1 teaspoon ground coriander

1 teaspoon ground cumin

¼ cup extra-virgin olive oil

2 teaspoons fresh lemon juice

In a mortar and pestle, pound the garlic a few times. Add a pinch of salt, then continue to mash the garlic until it turns into a paste. Add the chiles and keep mashing until they have mostly broken down and your paste has taken on a greenish hue. Add the parsley and mint and get into the groove, mashing and stirring, back and forth, until the herbs have bruised and slightly darkened. Stir in the coriander, cumin, olive oil, and lemon juice to get a thick green paste and then season with salt. Get a taste by dipping your pinkie into the sauce. Wait 15 minutes and taste again. See how the flavor transformed? Patience. Use the zhoug soon after you make it.

WAYS TO USE

Plop spoonfuls onto hummus.
Dab onto scrambled or fried eggs.
Drop a spoonful into a pot of beans.

CRISPY HERB SALSA VERDE

I can't tell you how many times I burned the sage and rosemary when I was learning how to make this salsa years ago. That's why I make you fry the herbs separately here. Serve it over a fatty braise, to which it will add a touch of texture and green brightness.

MAKES ABOUT 1½ CUPS

½ cup neutral oil
(such as grapeseed)

1 cup sage leaves

½ cup rosemary leaves

1 small garlic clove, finely grated

½ cup finely chopped parsley

½ cup extra-virgin olive oil

2 teaspoons red wine vinegar

Kosher salt

Freshly ground pepper

Line a large plate or baking sheet with a paper towel. Set the plate next to the stove and grab a slotted spoon or spider spatula. You'll be frying, with no time to walk away from the stove, so you need your station all set up before you start.

Pour the neutral oil into your smallest saucepan and place it over medium heat. When the oil begins to look glossy, after a few minutes, drop the sage leaves into the oil and fry until the sizzling subsides, 30 to 40 seconds. Using the slotted spoon or spider, scoop the sage from the oil and place it on a cutting board. Repeat with the rosemary leaves, using the same oil and transferring the rosemary to the cutting board when done. Remove the saucepan from the heat. Let the oil cool and then discard.

Chop the sage and rosemary. In a medium bowl, combine the garlic, parsley, olive oil, vinegar, and herbs. Season with salt and pepper. The salsa verde keeps, covered and refrigerated, for up to 2 days. Bring to room temperature before using.

WAYS TO USE

Spoon over torn burrata (with some toasted bread).
Spoon over a roasted starchy winter veg, like squash or sweet potato.
For dipping boiled, creamy potatoes.
Spoon over a steak; see A Proper Steak (Plus Brown Butter–Fried Onion
    Rings), page 298.

50

HOT AND NOT-THAT-HOT SAUCES

I'm here for the heat. A spicy sauce can bring a slow burn or a pop of assertiveness and immediate zing. Dried and fresh chiles work differently to make that happen. It's rare for me not to add something spicy to whatever I'm eating, which is why my cabinet is a mess of hot sauces and why I buy fresh chiles by the fistful. The heat wakes up my senses and makes me feel alive. The heat also slows me down (I'm a fast eater) and keeps things interesting. I like a little pain with my pleasure.

CRUNCHY ROMESCO

This is the only recipe in this book that uses red bell peppers as an ingredient because I only like them when they are roasted to hell and back, transformed into something smoky, sweet, and silken . . . and then blended. This interpretation of romesco is pretty true to the version from Spain's Catalan region, where the sauce originates. But some can veer orange-brown, so I keep the nuts and red pepper base separate, then combine at the last minute, so the nuts retain their crunch and the sauce stays vividly colorful.

MAKES 2 CUPS

1 cup drained jarred roasted red peppers

1 garlic clove, finely grated

⅓ cup extra-virgin olive oil

⅓ cup raw hazelnuts, coarsely chopped

1 teaspoon sweet paprika

½ to 1 teaspoon red pepper flakes (depending on how spicy you like it)

1 tablespoon sherry vinegar or red wine vinegar

Kosher salt

In a food processor, pulse the roasted peppers until you achieve a saucy (but not smooth!) consistency. Alternatively, you can chop the peppers but they won't be as saucy. Transfer the peppers to a medium bowl and add the garlic.

Pour the olive oil into a small skillet and add the hazelnuts. Cook over medium heat, stirring often, until the hazelnuts become golden brown, about 3 minutes. Slide the skillet off the heat and add the paprika and red pepper flakes. Pour the spiced hazelnuts and olive oil into the bowl with the peppers. Stir until well mixed. Add the vinegar and season with salt. Use the romesco soon after you make it.

DO AHEAD

The roasted red peppers and garlic can be prepped up to 2 days ahead. Cover and chill. Bring to room temperature and stir in the spiced hazelnuts and other ingredients before using.

WAYS TO USE

Spoon over cold (or warm) boiled and smashed potatoes.
As a sauce for just about any grilled meat (especially white fish and
    lamb chops).
As a sandwich spread.
With good oiled and toasted bread.

52

GARLICKY HOT VINEGAR

This sauce always reminds me of taking the BART train from Berkeley to San Francisco, where my mom worked. During her lunch break, we would frequent a Thai restaurant, called King of Thai, that had bowls of condiments on every table. My favorite was a spicy vinegar with slices of green chile and garlic floating in it. More than a spoonful and the vinegar would ruin any dish, but a few drops would lend brightness, heat, and a sensation that made me go back for bite after bite.

I stick with bird's eye chiles that pack quite a bit of heat but, really, any chile works. You can puree the whole thing for a smooth, thicker sauce, but I prefer the texture you get from the pieces of chile, garlic, and onion.

MAKES A LITTLE MORE THAN 2 CUPS

8 to 10 bird's eye chiles, stemmed, thinly sliced, seeds left in (if you're feeling frisky)

4 garlic cloves, thinly sliced

½ small red onion, or 1 large shallot, thinly sliced

4 teaspoons granulated sugar

2 teaspoons kosher salt

2 teaspoons freshly ground pepper

2 cups unseasoned rice vinegar or distilled white vinegar

Drop the chiles, garlic, onion, sugar, salt, and pepper in a 1-quart jar with a lid.

In a small saucepan over medium-high heat, bring the vinegar to a gentle simmer. Pour the hot vinegar into the jar with the chile mixture and let cool to room temperature, about 30 minutes.

Screw on the lid and refrigerate for at least 1 hour before using, so the flavors can play nice together. The chile vinegar keeps, tightly sealed in the fridge, for up to 3 months.

WARNING: While this vinegar is quite spicy, I promise it has a lot going on besides burn. Give it a chance to interact with different dishes.

WAYS TO USE

Dab over crunchy cucumber and finish with a big pinch of salt.
Sprinkle on any fried savory dish—trust me on this.
For Salt-and-Pepper Crispy Rice with Garlic-Fried Eggs (page 89).

VERY CRISPY GARLIC-CHILE OIL

There is no chance that I'm eating at a Chinese restaurant without a side of la-yu (chile oil). It's the vicious, precious red oil that comes in countless variations, homemade and store-bought. It's commonly served with dumplings or noodle dishes, but it improves everything it touches, like the cucumber salad on page 136.

In its most basic form, chile oil can simply be oil that is heated and poured over dried chiles so their fire and flavor can be fully released. Peanut oil, which has a high smoking point, is most often used to make chile oils but any neutral-flavored oil will work. I tend to change it up a bit with each batch, adding sesame seeds or peanuts, a cinnamon stick or a few star anise pods, a sprinkle of mushroom powder and MSG, but this recipe is the foundation that I always build on. It's up to you to make it your own.

MAKES 1 CUP

2 teaspoons soy sauce

½ teaspoon kosher salt

½ teaspoon granulated sugar

¼ cup ground Chinese chile flakes or gochugaru, or 2 tablespoons red pepper flakes

1 teaspoon freshly ground pepper

1 cup neutral oil (such as grapeseed)

6 garlic cloves, thinly sliced

1 tablespoon peeled, finely chopped ginger

In a small heatproof bowl, stir together the soy sauce, salt, and sugar until mostly dissolved (it will fully dissolve once you add the hot oil). Add the chile flakes and pepper and set aside.

In a small saucepan over medium heat, combine the neutral oil, garlic, and ginger. Cook, swirling the pan occasionally, until most, but not all, of the garlic is lightly golden, 4 to 6 minutes. The garlic will continue to darken once the oil is pulled from the hot stove, so keep an eye on it.

Immediately pour the hot oil over the chile flake mixture and watch it sizzle. The oil will bubble for a few seconds, warming the chiles and extracting their oils and colors. Stir, then let the chile oil cool completely to give the ingredients some time to get to know one another. The chile oil keeps, covered and refrigerated, for up to 1 month; but I promise you'll use it up sooner than that.

WAYS TO USE

Spoon over a jammy, scrambled, or nicely fried egg.
Serve with a perfect pot of steamed rice.
Drizzle over roasted sweet potatoes that have been slicked with
    a bit of lemony yogurt.
Drizzle over Juicy Chicken Breast and Antipasto Salad (page 270).

RICH, CREAMY THINGS

I like heavy cream and butter as much as the next person with a pulse, but my creamy things bring the creaminess without the cream itself. These dressings deliver—using yogurt, miso, egg whites, and tahini—but they also add brightness, plenty of garlic (in the case of toum), salt, and heat. And I dare you to not like the Tahini Ranch.

CREAMY
NUOC CHAM

While this starts by pulling the foundational flavor of nuoc cham—the bold, acidic, spicy Vietnamese sauce—cashews transform it into a deeply toasty, nutty sauce that can turn a mundane, predictable dish upside-down. My nut preference is cashews but this could easily work with toasted peanuts or pecans instead.

MAKES 1½ CUPS

½ cup roasted cashews

⅓ cup water

3 tablespoons fresh lime juice

2 birds eye chiles, chopped

2 garlic cloves, crushed

1 tablespoon fish sauce

2 teaspoons granulated sugar

Kosher salt (optional)

Put the cashews, water, lime juice, chiles, garlic, fish sauce, and sugar in a blender. Puree until smooth and then taste, seasoning with salt as needed. (Even though the sauce includes the salty fish sauce, it may need some added salt.) Use the sauce soon after you make it.

WAYS TO USE

Serve with anything you ever grill.
Toss over all roasted veg—from broccoli to sweet potatoes.
Use as a creamy, spicy salad dressing.

GREEN GODDESS YOGURT

Think of this as a simpler (and healthier) green goddess dressing, which is usually made with mayonnaise or sour cream and plenty of herbs. I go with Greek yogurt instead. Tarragon is essential to me but a combination of herbs, like chives, dill, parsley, and, if you're lucky to find it, chervil, work well and give the dressing its verdant color.

MAKES ABOUT 1 CUP

2 oil-packed anchovies, drained (optional)

2 cups mixed tender herbs (such as basil, dill, parsley, and tarragon—use your favorites)

½ cup full-fat Greek yogurt

3 tablespoons extra-virgin olive oil

2 tablespoons red or white wine vinegar

1 teaspoon finely grated lemon zest

1 tablespoon fresh lemon juice

Kosher salt

Freshly ground pepper

In a blender, combine the anchovies, herbs, yogurt, olive oil, vinegar, lemon zest, and lemon juice. Add a big pinch of salt and a few cranks of pepper, then puree until smooth and pale green. (You can use a food processor, but the dressing won't be as smooth.) Bring to room temperature before using. The dressing keeps, covered and refrigerated, for up to 2 days.

DO AHEAD

Because the flavor and quality of citrus juice decline when it's stored, give the dressing another squeeze of fresh lemon juice to zhoosh it before using.

WAYS TO USE

As a dip for crunchy veg, like endive, fennel, and radishes.
Slather on sandwich bread (loaded with avocado, cheese, and greens).
As a dressing for a cold chicken salad.

58

TAHINI RANCH

My affinity for ranch dressing is thanks to my older sister, who showed me the light when we were kids, smothering her pizza with those tiny capsules of takeout Hidden Valley. She's also the reason I listened to Taylor Dayne and loved the movie *Beaches*, but those are stories for another time.

Here, I've adapted that pizza-night ranch to something slightly healthier but just as zesty, using Greek yogurt and tahini. The tahini adds a nuttiness, and the lemon juice, a touch of maple syrup, fresh garlic, and plenty of salt bring the salty-sweetness that we expect from ranch dressing. As salad dressing, I like this to be a bit runny but still able to coat a spoon or a leafy green, as on the Veg Wedge salad (page 148). To use as a spread on sandwiches or as a dip, keep it on the thicker side by omitting the water.

MAKES 1 CUP

⅓ cup full-fat Greek yogurt or sour cream

⅓ cup tahini

3 tablespoons extra-virgin olive oil

2 tablespoons fresh lemon juice, or as needed

2 teaspoons maple syrup or runny honey

1 small garlic clove, finely grated

¼ cup cold water

Kosher salt

In a small bowl, whisk together the yogurt, tahini, olive oil, lemon juice, maple syrup, garlic, and water until smooth. Season with a big pinch of salt, add more lemon juice if you need more tang, and then taste with a spoon or using your finger. The dressing should be savory, lemony, and so delicious you could eat it with a spoon (or your finger!). The dressing keeps, covered and refrigerated, for up to 3 days; but here's your fair warning: the garlic becomes more potent as it sits.

WAYS TO USE

Toss with shredded cabbage for a creamy coleslaw.
Drizzle over roasted sweet veg, like carrots, sweet potatoes, or winter squash.
Dress the Veg Wedge (page 148).

59

THE GREATEST AIOLI

I think of aioli as the slightly chic cousin of mayonnaise. Its thick, creamy texture and deep garlic flavor get me every time. The technique hinges on emulsifying the egg yolk and oil, which you'll master once you make this recipe. Then you'll realize that everything you cook is improved by a spoonful of aioli.

I pair aioli with seafood (see pages 250 and 262), slather it on my Jammy Egg and Scallion Sandwiches (page 86), and stir it into bowls of beans (see page 235) and stews. Thin it with a splash of lemon juice or vinegar, and it becomes a salad dressing.

I call for two oils here—a neutral oil as well as an extra-virgin olive oil. This is because using only olive oil can make the aioli taste too peppery, depending on the brand. For the neutral oil, I prefer grapeseed or sunflower oil, but canola oil also works.

MAKES ¾ CUP

1 egg yolk

½ cup neutral oil
(such as grapeseed)

Water, as needed

¼ cup extra-virgin olive oil

1 small garlic clove, finely grated

Fresh lemon juice for seasoning

Kosher salt

Grab a dish towel and get it damp. Roll it up lengthwise and form it into a ring on the counter, then set a deep medium bowl in the ring. This will keep the bowl steady and secure on your work surface while one hand is whisking as the other hand streams in the oil.

Add the egg yolk to the bowl and whisk until it turns a shade lighter and you see a few tiny bubbles. That's when it's time to start adding the oils. Slowly drizzle in the neutral oil, just a trickle at first. (If you pour in too much at the start, the egg and oil might not emulsify properly.) Keep adding neutral oil until the mixture starts to look ribbony and pulls away from the sides of the bowl. Your wrist might be tired at this point, but don't worry, you're almost done. The yolk will have begun to reach the point where it has absorbed the maximum amount of oil it can, so add a few drops of water to loosen it.

Carry on whisking as you continue streaming in the rest of the neutral oil and then the olive oil—you can speed up the pour now—until all the oil is mixed in and the aioli looks luscious and smooth and clings to a spoon. Add the garlic and a few drops of lemon juice and whisk once or twice to incorporate. Taste, season with salt, and give another stir with the whisk. The aioli keeps, covered and refrigerated, for up to 2 days.

AIOLI SHORTCUT

While not TRUE aioli, if you want to cut a corner, you can combine 1 cup mayo doctored with 1 tablespoon lemon juice and 1 grated garlic clove instead of making the aioli from scratch.

BONUS AIOLI

Caesar Dressing: Smash 3 anchovy fillets in a mortar and pestle or use the side of the blade of a chef's knife until you have a paste. Stir the anchovy paste into the aioli, along with 2 tablespoons fresh lemon juice, 2 tablespoons finely grated Parmesan cheese, and 1 teaspoon coarsely ground pepper. If the dressing looks thick, thin it with 1 to 2 tablespoons water. Obviously great on lettuce, Caesar also does wonders for grilled vegetables such as carrots and zucchini.

TOUM

Toum is for my garlic lovers, which better be everyone reading this book. it is a Lebanese condiment, found throughout the Levant, that has an intensely pungent flavor and an almost fluffy, cloudlike texture. I've enjoyed toum on so many occasions at shawarma shops, where it gets swiped onto pita stuffed with heavily spiced meat, but I especially love it with crispy potatoes.

MAKES 2 CUPS

4 garlic cloves

2 egg whites

2 tablespoons fresh lemon juice

1½ cups neutral oil (such as grapeseed)

¼ cup cold water

1½ teaspoons kosher salt

Drop the garlic, egg whites, and lemon juice into a food processor. Pulse a couple of times until the garlic has broken down completely and things are looking a little foamy. With the food processor running, gradually stream in half of the neutral oil. Take some time. The oil will emulsify with the egg whites and garlic, and the mixture will start to thicken. Stop and scrape down the sides of the processor bowl with a rubber spatula. Continue to process while gradually streaming in the remaining oil, along with the water to thin things out. The toum is ready when it easily clings to a spoon. Season with the salt and pulse again to combine. Toum keeps, covered and refrigerated, for up to 3 days.

DO AHEAD

Toum loses some of its pizzazz when stored. Add a squeeze of fresh lemon juice to bring it back to life.

WAYS TO USE

Spread underneath or serve on or alongside roasted sweet potatoes.
As a marinade for roast chicken (I use ½ cup for a 3½- to 4-pound bird).
Serve with Shawarma-Spiced Lamb Chops with Pickle Salad (page 281).

EXTRA-SESAME DRESSING

I want to drench *everything* with this sesame sauce, usually served on the Japanese spinach dish gomae. It has so many things I love. Layers on layers of flavors. Miso and soy sauce add saltiness, each in their own way. Tahini makes the sauce creamy, and the sesame oil brings a potent nuttiness. Then, there are the two types of acidic zing—from the lemon and ginger. It's second nature to me to combine two like-minded ingredients in this way. This sauce is something special.

MAKES ¾ CUP

¼ cup tahini

1 teaspoon finely grated lemon zest

3 tablespoons fresh lemon juice

2 tablespoons white miso

2 tablespoons extra-virgin olive oil

1 tablespoon soy sauce

1 teaspoon runny honey

1 teaspoon peeled, finely grated ginger

1 teaspoon toasted sesame oil

2 to 3 tablespoons water

Kosher salt (optional)

In a small bowl, whisk together the tahini, lemon zest, lemon juice, miso, olive oil, soy sauce, honey, ginger, and sesame oil to combine. The sauce will look thick, like a nut butter, at this stage. Thin it with the water to get a pourable, smooth consistency. Taste for salt—you probably don't want any more since you have the soy and miso, but you might need to add a smidge. The dressing keeps, covered and refrigerated, for up to 2 days. Bring to room temperature before using.

WAYS TO USE

Toss with boiled and drained ramen noodles.
Smother torn, roasted sweet potatoes in it.
Drizzle it over a pile of sliced cucumbers.
For Long Green Beans with Creamy Sesame (page 187).

63

START (OR END) YOUR DAY WITH AN EGG

I've been known to slick on black lipstick and perform Alanis Morissette in grungy drag, but even that act is no match for the ways that eggs can morph. Nothing can transform like an egg.

You can whisk egg whites into stiff peaks for meringues, fold them into airy angel food cake, or emulsify the yolks into silky, garlicky aioli, and that's a few of their best performances. Eggs have a lot of looks but I prefer them the simplest ways. So the recipes here aren't about flaunting technique (except for the oil-basted fried eggs, see page 73, which you must make) but about showing off the egg itself. These are my favorite ways to eat eggs. Jammy Egg and Scallion Sandwiches (page 86), one of the best recipes in this entire book, will ruin deli egg salad for you forever (sorry). The fluffy kuku is wrapped up in so much personal history that I had to write an essay about it (see page 75). And Eggs in Spicy Tomato Curry (page 70) is all I want when it's eggs-for-dinner night. I'll never get tired of eggs. I start every morning with four eggs, softly scrambled with a side of avocado and hot sauce. And please don't worry about my cholesterol—it's *very* low.

EGGS IN SPICY TOMATO CURRY

Eggs and tomatoes are a pairing found in many parts of the world—and a combination I crave. But unlike, say, shakshuka, I prefer a dish in which the tomatoes don't dominate, and that's where coconut cream comes in. It makes this dish luxurious, saucy, and creamy. Everything is cooked on the stove top, in a covered pan so the eggs steam, which sets the whites and creates a perfectly runny yolk that mixes in with the curry.

SERVES 4

3 tablespoons virgin coconut oil or neutral oil (such as grapeseed)

1 or 2 red chiles (such as Fresno or Holland), halved, seeded, and thinly sliced

1-inch piece ginger, peeled and thinly sliced

3 garlic cloves, thinly sliced

1 teaspoon ground coriander

½ teaspoon ground cardamom

½ teaspoon ground turmeric

2 pints cherry tomatoes

Kosher salt

¼ cup unsweetened coconut cream or heavy cream

4 eggs

Basil, or whichever tender herb you like, for scattering

Fluffy (and Crisp) Flatbread (page 111) or a nice store-bought one, warmed for serving

In a large skillet over medium heat, warm the coconut oil. Add the chiles, ginger, and garlic and give things a stir until everything in the pan starts to get a little soft but hasn't taken on any color, about 2 minutes. Add the coriander, cardamom, and turmeric and stir so the spices coat everything and become fragrant—this happens in seconds.

Drop the tomatoes into the pan, season with a bit of salt, and let cook, stirring occasionally and squashing the tomatoes, so they burst and release their juices, 12 to 15 minutes. You want the tomatoes to soften so the sauce will thicken. Stir in the coconut cream and give the sauce a taste. It'll probably need another pinch of salt (don't we all).

Using the back of a spoon, make four little nests in the mixture, one for each egg. Crack an egg into each nest and season it with salt. Cover the skillet with a lid (a baking sheet works as well if you don't have a lid that fits) and cook until the egg whites are set but the yolks are still runny, about 3 minutes. Remove the skillet from the heat and scatter the basil over everything. Serve the eggs and sauce straight from the skillet with the flatbread to scoop and mop.

WHY AREN'T WE BAKING THOSE EGGS?

I am consistently disappointed by baked eggs. And I'm suspicious of any recipe that claims a perfect result. When you bake eggs, the yolks get hard before the whites are set, which drives me wild, and then the whites become the consistency of something from inside your nostrils, all slimy and sluggish. Here, you cover the pan on the stove with a lid so the eggs can gently steam-cook.

CRISPY CHICKPEA BOWLS WITH LEMONY YOGURT AND CHILE-STAINED FRIED EGGS

A tub of yogurt, a carton of eggs, and cans of chickpeas—I always have the ingredients for this true pantry dish, and I'll never get bored of it. The fried egg is achieved by basting with hot oil. I learned this way of making fried eggs in Spain, where I saw them being cooked in what looked like a pool of oil. The egg whites would crackle and puff up while the yolks still managed to stay runny. That is the texture you want your egg whites to be, not flim-flam-floppy.

As with everything in life, I'm going to encourage you to play, experiment . . . take a chance! I like my chickpeas crisped up with lots of oniony things, my yogurt thick and extra tangy with juice and zest from lemons, and my eggs extremely fried until they are crackly and browned around the edges. Make it once my way and then change it up to your liking. Swap the yogurt sauce for Tahini Ranch (page 59) if you want a nutty flavor. Or skip the herbs (how dare you) and add more onions.

SERVES 2 TO 4

1 cup full-fat Greek yogurt

1 lemon

Kosher salt

¾ cup extra-virgin olive oil

1 large red or yellow onion, or 1 bunch scallions, thinly sliced

2 (15-ounce) cans chickpeas, drained and rinsed

Freshly ground pepper

3 tablespoons finely chopped parsley, dill, and/or cilantro

4 eggs

1 teaspoon sweet paprika

½ teaspoon red pepper flakes

Place the yogurt in a medium bowl. Using a Microplane, finely grate the zest from half the lemon into the yogurt. Cut the lemon in half and squeeze the juice from both halves into the bowl, catching any seeds with your other hand. Add a nice big pinch of salt and stir. Set aside.

Pour ½ cup of the olive oil into a large skillet and place the skillet over medium-high heat. Add the onion and give it a stir. Yes, it may look like a lot of oil at first, but the chickpeas will come in later and you'll need it to crisp them up. Cook the onion until it just begins to soften, 3 to 5 minutes. No need to get the onion brown. Dump in the chickpeas and season with salt and ground pepper. Cook, tossing or giving the chickpeas a stir occasionally until they have become a few shades darker, to a golden brown and have crisped up around the edges, 7 to 9 minutes. Depending on how well you drained your chickpeas, it may take a little longer to get them crisp.

Remove the skillet from the heat and stir in the herbs. Now, taste a chickpea. It should be crispy with an almost creamy interior and properly seasoned. Partially cover to keep warm.

Add the remaining ¼ cup olive oil to a large nonstick skillet or a cast-iron pan over medium heat. When the oil is hot and shimmering, one by one, crack the eggs into the skillet. The whites should make a big, splattery fuss, but don't mind them because you're in control. Season each egg with salt and cook, spooning some of the hot oil over the whites until the edges begin to get crispy, browned, and lacy, 3 to 5 minutes. Remove the skillet from the heat and scoot the eggs a bit to the edge, so you can sprinkle the paprika and red pepper flakes into the hot oil. Now, watch the flaming red oil begin to stain the whites.

Set out the crispy chickpeas, eggs, and yogurt for people to serve themselves. Or, if you're feeling generous, assemble individual bowls, but I'll leave that up to you.

ON BASTING

The word *baste* might make you think of a huge plastic bulb squirting hot stock over a nightmarishly gigantic turkey. That's not what we're doing here. To baste is to collect any excess fat using a spoon (I suggest a Kunz spoon, see page 14) and then dump it over whatever you're cooking. For the fried eggs in the chickpea bowls (on page 73), tilt the skillet, gather the hot oil, and pour it over the whites to fry the tops, which creates this puffy, incredible texture. We'll baste again, for the steak on page 298, with foamy brown butter and steak juices, so you'll get used to doing it.

There Are Many Kukus. This Is Mine.

Kuku sabzi was the first Persian dish that I felt confident making on my own. I had watched my mother make it for years: taking the herbs by the bunch, thoroughly washing them, picking the leaves, grabbing and bundling a tight fistful, and sliding her knife back and forth, back and forth, through them. After she had carpal tunnel surgery, she had me chop the herbs because I could do it more quickly. Then, we'd finish making the dish together. Kuku sabzi ties me to her, and to my Iranian heritage, more than any other recipe. I want to preserve its core and pass it on—but I also want to share my signature approach.

Kuku translates as any "egg-based" dish, whereas *sabzi* specifies "herbs." There are other types of kuku, but kuku sabzi was my childhood staple. A good kuku has a light, airy texture. It's not dense or weighed down by the eggs. The prep starts with a mound of fresh herbs that are finely chopped, almost to a powder, which bruises the herbs and releases their fragrance. Then, you combine the herbs with spices, chives, leeks, and/or garlic. A bad kuku is too heavily spiced, which causes it to lose its subtlety and delicacy.

It's easy to want to compare kuku to a frittata, but that makes it seem like a casual, thrown-together thing. There's formality here. Kuku requires patience and a tremendous amount of prep. It is a sacred dish. When I was able to share it with the *Bon Appétit* American audience, I was also introducing them to Iranian culture, which is rarely presented

in a positive light in the United States. So, no, kuku is not a frittata. It's a *kuku*.

I spent years refining my recipe, changing it up, and making embarrassing mistakes. When I developed the recipe for a Persian New Year story in *Bon Appétit*, I was annoyed by all the herb prep and did a bad job washing them. That kuku turned out almost crunchy from the sand left in the herbs. I've made that mistake more than once. I'm averaging a three-round rinse cycle now. (See my salad spinner note on page 81.) I played with the ratios of turmeric, fenugreek, and eggs until I had a finely calibrated formula in which the eggs bind all the ingredients without taking over. Even the ratio of herbs became a math equation. Equal parts parsley, dill, and cilantro was a grave error—the dill overpowers everything.

I had to listen to (and ignore) everyone else's kuku opinions, whether it was from my mother or my colleagues. Some people add walnuts and barberries and would call my kuku "naked" for not including them. That's not my style. It's a delicate food that requires a delicate hand. Like wearing a pearl necklace with drop earrings, together, with everything else, they aren't more but diminishing. (Go with the necklace or the earrings, not both.) What kuku best represents to me? Mine must have fenugreek, eggs, the three herbs, and turmeric. Those are the essentials, and I will fight to defend them, even if it's against a ninety-seven-year-old Iranian grandmother.

CONTINUED

Traditionally, kuku is cooked completely on the stove top. You slide it out of the pan and flip it. But, I finish cooking mine in the oven, which avoids the need to flip. Another reason I cook it in the oven is to avoid the dark brown crust that kuku develops on the stove. It goes from deep forest green to an earthy brown. Mine is bright and green because the heat from the broiler sets the eggs faster. Iranians tell me, "Your kuku is raw!" "It's *set*," I reply.

Dried fenugreek is where people get into arguments. Some people add up to ¼ cup. I believe that with too much fenugreek, whatever it touches becomes overwhelmingly bitter and pungent. (It comes out of your pores; you can smell it for days.) The right amount adds a sweet perfume, so I add 1 tablespoon. Many Iranians sprinkle in advieh (the go-to spice mix of Iran) or cinnamon, mace, dried rose petals, and other warm spices. I season with restraint and prefer an onion-y bite from the scallions.

The *Bon Appétit* Persian New Year story was a breakthrough for me, personally and professionally. I was showcasing Iranian food in a national magazine with a largely white audience. There was some hesitancy when we pitched the recipe to the video team, but, eventually, they went for it. When the video came out, in the time of peak Facebook video popularity, I received emails, calls from relatives, and DMs in Farsi that I had to have my mother translate. I received lots of feedback on those missing walnuts. It seemed like all of Iran had seen and shared the video on Facebook.

I was not the first Iranian American to cook Iranian food in a mainstream food magazine, but possibly the first young gay man seen cooking Iranian food—a rarity for the Iranian community. The success of the video shook things up a bit at work. It showed that the magazine could reach beyond its typical demographic. It instilled a level of confidence in me that was my turning point in media, telling me: *Keep going.* That Persian New Year story made me realize I always need to cook recipes that feel right for me. And nothing feels more right to me than kuku.

KUKU SABZI

When I think about the dishes that have stuck with me for most of my life, kuku is at the top. You'll see other kukus made with potato and scented with saffron and black pepper, a sweet version made with dates and rose petals that is typically eaten for breakfast with bitter bergamot tea, and one made with zucchini and turmeric. To me, kuku sabzi reigns supreme. Packed with an intimidating amount of herbs, it was one of the first Iranian dishes that I learned to cook when I was a preteen. The dish varies depending on which Iranian household you're in. I take a less-is-more approach with my kuku, letting the herbs be the star. Wash the herbs in batches. If you wash them all at once, you might end up with sand and dirt in your kuku.

SERVES 6

3 bunches cilantro

3 bunches parsley

2 bunches dill

2 bunches scallions, thinly sliced

1 tablespoon dried
fenugreek leaves

1½ teaspoons kosher salt

1 teaspoon freshly ground pepper

1 teaspoon baking powder

¾ teaspoon ground turmeric

5 eggs

¼ cup neutral oil (such as
grapeseed) or extra-virgin olive oil

Fluffy (and Crisp) Flatbread
(page 111) or a nice store-bought
one, warmed for serving

Persian liteh pickles for serving

Yogurt for serving

Trim about 4 inches off the stems of the cilantro, parsley, and dill. You want only the leaves and tender stems. Place about one-third of the herbs in a salad spinner and fill it with cold water. Agitate the herbs with your hands to get rid of any dirt, which will sink to the bottom of the spinner bowl. Lift the basket from the bowl of the salad spinner and dump out the water. Repeat this process until the water is clear, then spin dry and transfer the washed herbs to a large cutting board. Repeat with the remaining herbs.

Grab a large fistful of the herbs and, using your sharpest knife, finely chop. Repeat until you have chopped your whole mountain of washed herbs. You will have about 4½ cups.

Transfer the chopped herbs to a large bowl and add the scallions. Using your fingertips, pinch and grind the fenugreek, sprinkling it over the herb mixture. This really helps bring out the fenugreek's sweet smell and taste. Add the salt, pepper, baking powder, and turmeric. One at a time, crack the eggs into the bowl. Use a fork to break the yolks and then fully incorporate the eggs with the herb mixture. It may seem like not enough eggs, but you want *just enough* to bind the mixture. The batter should be *very* green and the consistency should be light and airy.

Place an oven rack in the top position and preheat the broiler.

Pour the neutral oil into a 10-inch nonstick skillet and place it over medium heat. When the oil begins to shimmer, give the kuku batter a final mix and then scrape it into the skillet. Using a spatula, spread the batter to the sides of the skillet. Cover and cook, rotating the skillet to ensure it cooks evenly, until the bottom has set and darkened to a very dark green, almost brown, color, 8 to 10 minutes.

Remove the skillet from the heat and remove the lid. The top of the kuku will still be a touch wet but very green. Transfer the skillet to the oven and broil, watching carefully (each broiler's strength is different), until the top is set, about 1 minute. Remove from the oven and slide the kuku onto a platter or cutting board. Slice and serve with flatbread and pickles and yogurt spooned over the top.

78

I HEART MY
SALAD SPINNER

There are a lot of questionable salad spinners out there. My favorite is the Zyliss salad spinner with the pull-cord. It dries greens *so* fast—faster than the ones with the button in the center or the hand crank. After one or two pulls, your herbs will be D-R-Y. Nothing kills the vibe like a wet, soggy salad.

FLUFFY PARMESAN SCRAMBLE

There was a point when I ate, more like, six eggs a day instead of four for breakfast, but we don't need to talk about that. I want them scrambled. I want a soft, fluffy consistency. (Some people like them runny and pourable. There's a time and place for that—keep reading.) These scrambled eggs take the opportunity to add fat at every turn because breakfast isn't a time to deprive yourself. The finely grated Parm makes them creamy while the thin prosciutto slices warm and meld with the scramble. Good morning.

SERVES 2

4 eggs

Kosher salt

2 tablespoons unsalted butter

½ cup finely grated Parmesan cheese, plus more for serving

4 paper-thin prosciutto slices, torn in half

Plenty of freshly ground pepper

2 to 4 pieces good toast (optional, but why not?)

Crack the eggs into a bowl and season with about ½ teaspoon salt. Using a fork, poke and break each yolk and then vigorously whisk until smooth and no streaks of white appear.

Drop the butter into a medium nonstick skillet and then place it over medium heat. (You don't want to add the butter to a hot pan, otherwise you'll likely end up with overly browned, or worse, burnt butter.) Tilt the pan so the butter coats the entire surface of the skillet.

Once the butter begins to foam, add the eggs and let cook, without fussing, until they begin to set around the edges and on the bottom. If the skillet is as hot as it should be, this will happen within 20 seconds. Sprinkle the Parmesan over the eggs and use a rubber spatula or wooden spoon to begin pulling the cooked outer edges of the eggs in toward the center of the eggs, continuously and gently. The wet spots will flood the area you just pulled in. Continue to pull the cooked eggs toward the center. In less than a minute, no more wet spots will spill over and the scramble will have collected into large fluffy curds. Remove the skillet from the heat when the eggs appear 80 percent fully cooked. They will be shiny and a little wet on top but the residual heat will finish cooking them.

Divide the eggs between two bowls or plates and drape a few pieces of prosciutto on top. Sprinkle with more Parm and pepper and serve with the toast.

FOR AN EXTRA-CREAMY (NOT FLUFFY) SCRAMBLE

Extra-creamy scrambled egg lovers, I know who you are, and I don't hold it against you. For those almost soupy, baby food–like scrambled eggs, you're trying to create the tiniest curds. Add another 1 tablespoon butter and turn the heat to low to cook the eggs, whisking constantly. Break up the eggs until they begin to thicken to a custard-like consistency but are still silky-wet looking. Add Parm, ground pepper, a drizzle of olive oil—and a dollop of caviar, if you *happen* to have any lying around.

84

JAMMY EGG AND SCALLION SANDWICHES

A few things about this sandwich make me happy: Thick slices of squishy white bread, like Japanese milk bread. The vinegary-zingy scallion sauce, which can be doubled and used to make scallion ramen noodles. And the perfectly timed 8-minute eggs (please leave this conversation if you boil eggs longer than 10 minutes).

SERVES 2 (BUT YOU CAN EASILY DOUBLE THE RECIPE)

4 eggs

4 scallions, thinly sliced

1 tablespoon toasted sesame seeds (see page 24)

2 teaspoons unseasoned rice vinegar

1 teaspoon soy sauce

1 pinch granulated sugar

Kosher salt

Freshly ground pepper

¼ cup The Greatest Aioli (page 61) or store-bought mayonnaise

1 tablespoon Dijon mustard

4 thick slices white sandwich bread, brioche, or milk bread

Pull the eggs out of the fridge to warm up while you do some prep, so they're less likely to crack while boiling. Fill a medium saucepan three-fourths full with water and bring it to a boil.

While the water comes to a boil, in a small bowl, stir together the scallions, sesame seeds, vinegar, soy sauce, and sugar with a pinch of salt and pepper. Use the back of a spoon to smash the scallions against the side of the bowl a bit to get them to break down. Set aside.

In another small bowl, stir together the aioli and mustard. Season with salt.

Fill a medium bowl with ice and add enough water so that the eggs will be submerged. Have your timer ready. Turn down the heat and bring the boiling water to a gentle simmer, then use a slotted spoon to carefully lower the eggs into the water. Boil for 8 minutes *on the dot*. Use the slotted spoon to transfer the eggs to the ice-water bath and let them sit for a minute or so. Then, one by one, whack each egg all over with the spoon and return it to the ice water. Cracking the shells and letting the eggs get one more stint in the ice bath helps loosen the shells from the egg whites, making them easy to peel. Peel the eggs, then slice them crosswise into thick rounds.

Slather the mustardy mayonnaise on all four slices of bread, then top two of the slices with the eggs. Spoon the scallion sauce over the eggs, then top with the remaining bread. Slice—or don't!—the sandwiches however you like, and serve right away.

SALT-AND-PEPPER CRISPY RICE WITH GARLIC-FRIED EGGS

Unless it's the holidays, I'm just not into leftovers. However, this feeling doesn't apply to leftover rice or grains, of which I usually make a larger batch so that I have an excuse to make fried rice the next day. This is a case in which you get a big payoff with only a few ingredients. By making a batch of garlic chips, you get a flavor-packed golden oil to fry up the grains and eggs, taking this "leftovers" meal to a much better place. And if you don't happen to have some leftover rice, just spread out freshly cooked rice on a baking sheet and chill it for a few hours, which will dry it out so that it can get more crisp when stir-fried.

SERVES 4

8 garlic cloves, thinly sliced

⅓ cup neutral oil
(such as grapeseed)

Kosher salt

3 cups day-old cooked white or brown rice, chilled

2 teaspoons toasted sesame oil

Freshly ground pepper

4 large eggs

1 cup coarsely chopped cilantro

Garlicky Hot Vinegar (page 53) or rice vinegar for serving

Set a fine-mesh strainer over a small bowl and set it near the stove. Put the garlic and neutral oil in a large nonstick skillet and place over medium heat. Cook, shaking the pan often, until the garlic is lightly golden and crisp, 3 to 5 minutes. Strain the oil through the strainer into the bowl. Dump the garlic chips onto a small plate and season with salt.

Pour half the garlic oil back into the skillet and place over medium-high heat. Add the rice and sesame oil and toss to combine. Season with salt and lots of pepper, then let it get crisp underneath, without fussing with it, 3 to 4 minutes. Once the rice begins to crisp up, give it a toss, then press down on it and cook until you get more golden crispy pieces underneath, another 2 to 3 minutes. Transfer the rice to a platter or plates.

Wipe out the skillet, pour in the remaining garlic oil, and place over medium heat. Crack the eggs into the skillet, being careful as they may spatter at first. Season each egg with salt and fry, rotating the pan to encourage even cooking, until the edges are lacy and crisp, whites are set, and yolks are still runny, 3 to 5 minutes.

Spoon some hot vinegar on top of the fried rice. Scatter the cilantro and garlic chips over. Top with the eggs and serve.

DO AHEAD

The garlic oil and chips can be made 1 day ahead. Store in separate airtight containers at room temperature.

I have a snack strategy. The food that I go for at any party, right away, is the bowl of cornichons or the toothpick-stabbed olives.

The acidity whets my appetite, makes me salivate, and builds some momentum, preparing me for the meal ahead. Look at fancy tasting menus: the amuse-bouche isn't rich and fatty, it's light and opens up the palate. Snacking is like stretching before a workout. I take it very seriously.

The snacks in this chapter cover carbs, cheese, and dips—the major snack food groups. If you've always gone to the same hummus, the tried-and-true salsa and chips, or had some alone time with a ripe wheel of Époisses, dive in here and try something new. These recipes are simple, but they elevate the usual appetizer round to something as exciting and worth looking forward to as dinner. You'll impress yourself, and others. You'll also get some key technique takeaways, such as the perfect, proper way to fry bread (the vessel for

three toasts on pages 113 to 118), how to make your own olive mix and nut mix (because this world deserves more than boring salted almonds), and how to transform an eggplant into a luscious smoky dip. Plus, a handful of throw-together snacks that begin with one ingredient: a credit card. You will become an expert snacker.

You can make a few snacks and turn it into dinner, something I do often (the anchovy toast on page 118 + the marinated artichokes on page 119 = made for each other). If you're hosting, buy some items you'd never, ever make to mix into the spread. (I always want those golden yellow potato chips from Spain.) I'm *never* going to make potato chips at home, no matter what. Have extra cheeses on board. Pile up some mortadella, which I'll get excited about forever. Just put the snacks that you made onto the center of the table. Those are the stars.

SPICY, CITRUSY OLIVES

When I was a teenager, the parents in my neighborhood occasionally hired me to cook for their dinner parties. Looking back, it was the best way to get my feet wet cooking for others in homes that felt safe and encouraging. I would present a few menus for them to choose from, and one of the snacks that always went over well were my "mixed olives," served warm. I wanted to show guests how good a freshly marinated olive could be—which I knew, from growing up in an olive-heavy Persian household—compared to mushy jarred olives that taste like lake water. I was so adamant about sourcing the best ingredients that I would barely break even, having blown my budget at the market. The compliments from the tipsy adults sipping their vodka martinis were enough compensation for me, at the time.

This is a highly customizable recipe. Sizzle some garlic, add more herbs, add some big chunks of feta or goat cheese. You can swap the spices for your favorites. The main objective is to gently bubble the olives with the flavored oil until their flesh is warmed through. You'll feel like you're in a restaurant. Kind of.

SERVES 6 (OR 4 GREEDY ONES)

1 orange

1 lemon

1 tablespoon coriander seeds

1 tablespoon fennel seeds

¼ cup extra-virgin olive oil

2 cups drained unpitted olives (Castelvetrano, Gaeta, Lucques, niçoise, and Picholine work well)

1 small handful bay leaves, rosemary sprigs, or thyme sprigs

2 dried chiles de árbol, or ½ teaspoon red pepper flakes

Using a vegetable peeler, work around the orange and lemon to remove wide strips of peel.

Give the coriander seeds and fennel seeds a light crush in a mortar and pestle. You want to break down the spices so they can scent the olives and add a subtle crunch but stay coarse enough that they don't burn.

In a medium pot, combine the olive oil, coriander, and fennel and then place it over medium-low heat. Let the spices begin to sizzle and become fragrant, 2 to 3 minutes, shaking the pot to keep them moving, so they don't burn. Add the olives, herbs, chiles, and citrus peels to the spices and cook, stirring occasionally, until the olives are warmed through, 8 to 12 minutes. The only way to find out if the olives are ready is to try one or two.

Spoon the olives into a serving bowl and serve warm or let them marinate a few hours at room temperature and then serve.

DO AHEAD

The olives can be made up to 5 days ahead and stored in the fridge, covered. Bring them to room temperature before serving.

COMMITTED TO UNPITTED

Yes, pitted olives are convenient, but they become a sad, literal shell of their former selves. The flavors are more intact when the pit is left in the meaty flesh. You wouldn't buy a pitted peach, would you? Exactly.

NUTS TO DRINK WITH

I want a nut mix that goes well with iced tea, beer, a glass of wine, vodka on the rocks, tequila, mezcal . . . you get it. It should be salty, spicy, and a touch sweet. These nuts are heavy on the garlic and salt and fragrant with lemongrass. I don't want candied nuts, which require making a caramel, finding a candy thermometer, that whole operation. I toss them with honey for a balanced sweetness. The key technique is keeping the oven heat low, so the water in the honey slowly evaporates, and all the ingredients stick without burning. When the nuts come out of the oven, squeeze some lime juice over everything and then squeeze the rest into your tequila.

MAKES 3 CUPS

2 lemongrass stalks, bottom third only (about 6 inches long), tough outer layers removed, finely chopped

6 garlic cloves, finely grated

¼ cup runny honey

2 tablespoons neutral oil (such as grapeseed)

1 tablespoon red pepper flakes

3 cups mixed raw nuts (cashews, hazelnuts, and pecans work well)

2 teaspoons kosher salt

Preheat the oven to 325°F. Line a rimmed baking sheet with parchment paper.

In a medium bowl, combine the lemongrass, garlic, honey, neutral oil, and red pepper flakes and, using a rubber spatula, stir until you have a thick, sticky paste. Add the nuts and sprinkle in the salt. Give the nuts a toss, so each one is happily coated.

Spread the nuts on the prepared baking sheet. Toast in the oven for 10 minutes and then toss. Continue toasting until they are golden brown and smell very nutty and garlicky, 10 to 15 minutes. Set aside to cool. If the nuts have formed into clusters, break them apart, but leave one cluster for a lucky someone.

Store in an airtight container at room temperature for up to 1 week. There's your snack for the week.

The Very End
of a Baguette

When I was too young to drive, my mother and I did weekly grocery errands together. My mom was a Lancôme lady for more than twenty years; I thought of her as the Isabella Rossellini of the Macy's counter. I'm biased, but my mother is beautiful, with just the littlest bit of an accent, like the face of Trésor, Isabella herself. In my mind, my mom spent her days off thinking about food and looking for the best ingredients, just as I do. Although, to her credit, she clearly had a lot more to worry about than what to cook.

On our errand days, after Mom picked up her coffee, we'd go to Monterey Market in Berkeley, one of the greatest grocery stores on the planet. There, you'd find half an aisle of wild mushrooms; herbs far beyond basil and parsley, like summer savory and flowering chives. They'd also stock twenty-plus varieties of citrus. In the store, we'd pick up a poppy seed–sesame baguette from Acme Bread. This started a silent race between us: Who was going to twist and tear off the tip of the baguette first? Whoever won would have it as a mini snack, right there in the grocery store. We never, ever spoke about it. And there was something else unspoken between us with our obsession with food so deeply ingrained: the understanding that to save the baguette for later would almost disrespect it. It was too good to ignore. It demanded our attention. Made me want to cook food with that kind of power.

We spent way too much time in Monterey Market, and even now, I can't go to a grocery store without stalking down every aisle the way my mom did. She bought bundles of herbs, onions, garlic, shallots, greens, and root vegetables. She also sampled quite a bit, which I'm pretty sure was without asking. I blame her for my sticky fingers. She would take a bite out of a plum and hand it to me to take the next bite. It was very maternal. I was once kicked out of the Bowery Whole Foods Market in New York City for "sampling" sushi (admittedly, I had a warning, and the next time they asked me to leave). I've unwrapped RXBARs and eaten them while I shopped. I've gnawed on sprigs of mint. I am my mother's son.

98

After shopping, Mom and I would pick up a few slices from the Cheese Board, our go-to pizza shop, and sit rebelliously in the median next to the sign that read KEEP OFF THE MEDIAN—very Berkeley—to listen to the violist or whichever ensemble was performing. No matter what the pizza of the day was—red onion, Fontina cheese, charred poblanos with corn and feta, or Gruyère and Parm with thin slices of potato and rosemary—we'd have Key limes to squeeze over our slices.

Occasionally, my mom would indulge me and we'd go to Masse's Pastries, where I'd get a wedge of passion fruit mousse cake. Or thumbprint cookies with fruit jellies. Or a dramatic tiramisu with big curls of chocolate, lined with a crown of ladyfingers. It felt indulgent, delicious, and kept me wanting to always taste more, order more.

I don't take it for granted that I grew up in the San Francisco East Bay, which is concentrated with people who have a deep love for food. Even though I didn't come from money, I was spoiled. The access to that food, those moments of median-eating pizza with my mom, laid the foundation for me to pursue cooking professionally. And maybe also to leading a life of crime.

FRESH FRUIT WITH SAVORY SPRINKLES

At my parents' house, every meal began and ended with fruit. My dad would sit at the table peeling, slicing, and seeding. He'd stab a piece of fragrant honeydew, a slightly bruised nectarine, or a crunchy Asian pear and point it at me. I'd reject his offer two or three times before he would implore, "You don't understand; fruit is nature's candy." I'd give in. My mom would sprinkle some salt over the fruit, making it a little more savory, allowing the juices to come through, and convince me to have one more bite.

These days, I need my fruit to be salty and savory. This sprinkle is influenced by my mother's orange wedges with salt, kind of, but also Mexican salt–chile mango, furikake, and my need to dress things up. What can I say—I want to make fruit, fruitier. There's texture, saltiness, brightness. It doesn't need much more.

SERVES 4

1½ pounds crunchy and/or fleshy fruit (melons, Asian pears, your favorite apples, oranges, pineapple, or mango)

1 sheet toasted nori

1 tablespoon toasted sesame seeds (see page 24)

2 teaspoons mild chile flakes (such as Aleppo), or 1 teaspoon red pepper flakes

½ lemon

1 teaspoon flaky sea salt

Cut the fruit into ½-inch-wide wedges, rounds, or however you deem fit. Set them aside while you make the sprinkles.

Tear the nori into small pieces, then pulse in a clean spice mill or blender until finely ground. Pour the nori powder into a small bowl and stir in the sesame seeds and chile flakes. Using a Microplane, finely grate the zest from the lemon half into the bowl, then mix with your fingers so it doesn't clump. Stir in the salt.

Squeeze the lemon over the fruit, catching any seeds with your other hand. Sprinkle the mixture over the fruit and serve.

DO AHEAD

You can mix the nori, sesame seeds, chile flakes, and salt 2 weeks ahead, cover, and store at room temperature. Add the lemon zest right before using.

NOW, ABOUT THAT NORI

I prefer to buy nori sheets untoasted, so I can slowly toast them on the stove, over an open flame, until they've got a slightly emerald-green sheen and give off a briny scent. But just buy them toasted. Then keep the rest of the nori in a resealable plastic bag and use it to make Buttery Nori-Speckled Rice (page 200). Think of it as seasoning and sprinkle it on top of brothy noodles or even fold it into your scrambled eggs.

SMOKY EGGPLANT DIP

Yes, we've got the baba ghanoush essentials here, but what's key is the technique. I broil the eggplant over the stove's flame, rotating every three minutes and watching as it turns darker and darker. It's so satisfying. It completely breaks down into a blackened shell with jammy custard inside, no longer the purple emoji it once was. (You can also broil or grill it.) Blending the eggplant flesh in a food processor aerates it in a way you couldn't pull off by hand, making it even lighter and more divine. Serve with your favorite snappy veg, flatbread, or as a side to Chile and Citrusy Yogurt–Brined Roast Chicken (page 278).

MAKES ABOUT 2½ CUPS

**2 globe eggplants
(about 1½ pounds total)**

**3 tablespoons extra-virgin
olive oil**

**2 tablespoons fresh lemon juice,
or as needed**

2 tablespoons tahini

Kosher salt

2 garlic cloves, thinly sliced

**1 teaspoon mild chile flakes
(such as Aleppo)**

**Pomegranate molasses
for drizzling**

Place each eggplant on a stove-top gas burner and turn the heat to medium-high. Once the skin begins to char and blacken, after about 3 minutes, use tongs to carefully turn the eggplants at the stem end, making sure you don't puncture the flesh. Continue to cook, turning every 3 minutes, until completely charred and the eggplant has collapsed onto itself, 12 to 15 minutes total. Remove the eggplants from the heat and let cool for 10 minutes. This will allow the flesh inside to steam and become soft and silky.

Halve the eggplants lengthwise and scoop the flesh into a food processor. Add 1 tablespoon of the olive oil, the lemon juice, tahini, and a generous pinch of salt. Pulse a few times until the eggplant has a light, almost whipped, texture. Taste and adjust with more lemon juice and salt.

Transfer the dip to a serving bowl and, using the back of a spoon, make some grooves here and there in the surface.

In a small skillet over medium heat, combine the remaining 2 tablespoons olive oil and the garlic. Cook, stirring often, until the garlic begins to turn golden and crisp, about 3 minutes. Remove the skillet from the heat, stir in the chile flakes, and spoon the mixture over the dip. Drizzle the pomegranate molasses in the grooves of the dip. Looks chic, no? Serve at room temperature.

DO AHEAD

The dip can be mixed up (without the garnish) to 2 days ahead, covered, and stored in the fridge. Just before serving, finish with the garlic-chile oil and molasses.

BORANI AKA THE QUEEN OF ALL YOGURT DIPS

Borani reminds me of hot hot hot California summer afternoons, my uncle grilling kabobs, mounds of rice, roasted tomatoes, and tubs full of borani that we kept cold in bowls of ice cubes because we made too much to fit in the fridge. Traditionally, borani is a deeply savory yogurt dip with cooked greens and onions. I skip the greens and go for shallots instead, plus a sunny turmeric oil that I drizzle on top.

Like all great yogurt dips, this one needs a good amount of salt to start and then you pick a direction. You can go all kinds of ways: thick and savory, or lighter and thinned with cucumber and lemon juice; textured with chopped raisins, currants, and pine nuts or pistachios; or brightly colored with roasted beets or sweet carrots. There's so much to explore—let this recipe be your starting point. Eat it with crunchy vegetables, Persian rice (see page 202), grilled meats, or whatever's on your plate.

MAKES 2 CUPS

⅓ cup extra-virgin olive oil

4 shallots, thinly sliced into rings

Kosher salt

½ teaspoon ground turmeric

2 cups full-fat Greek yogurt, labneh, or sour cream

1 teaspoon finely grated lemon zest

1 tablespoon fresh lemon juice

Freshly ground pepper

3 tablespoons coarsely chopped dill

Pour the olive oil into a large skillet and place it over medium heat. When the oil is shimmering, add the shallots, season with salt, and cook, stirring occasionally, until they're golden brown and begin to crisp, 4 to 6 minutes. Using a slotted spoon, scoop the shallots onto a small plate, leaving the oil in the skillet. Remove the skillet from the heat. Sprinkle the turmeric over the hot oil and give it a few stirs to bloom and wake up. Set aside.

In your chicest serving bowl, mix together the yogurt, lemon zest, lemon juice, and a big pinch of salt and pepper. Add most of the caramelized shallots to the yogurt (save some for a garnish). Stir and taste. It will be slightly sweet and onion-y from the shallots, creamy (obviously), and very delicious.

Drizzle the turmeric oil over the dip, then scatter the dill and reserved caramelized shallots on the surface. Top with more pepper, if you like, before serving.

DO AHEAD

The dip can be mixed (without the garnish) up to 2 days ahead, covered, and stored in the fridge. Just before serving, finish with the turmeric oil, dill, and caramelized shallots.

BROKEN FETA WITH SIZZLED MINT AND WALNUTS

In Farsi, *noon-o-panir* translates to "bread and cheese," but it's a translation that undermines the experience of noon-o-panir. Typically, it's a snack you put out when you're having a mehmooni (party): bowls of soft, tangy, sheep's milk cheese, typically feta, served with Persian flatbread, like barbari; a platter of raw herbs; and walnuts soaked in salty water to soften and season them. For the perfect loghmeh (bite), tear off a piece of hot bread and fold it around a piece of cheese, a walnut, and a few herbs, and squish everything together. Although you're more than welcome to make your own loghmeh, it's natural for Iranians to want to make the perfect bite for you. Now, allow me. This is a consolidated version of noon-o-panir but, in my humble opinion, it's just as delicious.

SERVES 4 (BUT YOU COULD EASILY DOUBLE THE RECIPE)

⅓ cup raw walnuts, finely chopped

¼ cup extra-virgin olive oil

2 teaspoons dried mint

Kosher salt

Freshly ground pepper

8 ounces feta (I like Bulgarian or French, but you're more than welcome to support the Greeks) or goat cheese

Barbari bread or Fluffy (and Crisp) Flatbread (page 111) for serving

Combine the walnuts and olive oil in a small skillet and place it over medium heat. Cook, stirring often, until the walnuts smell toasty and become a deeper golden brown, 2 to 3 minutes. Watch carefully; this happens quickly. Turn off the heat and immediately add the dried mint and watch it sizzle. Season with salt and lots of pepper.

Break the feta into 1-inch craggy pieces and put them on a platter. Spoon the walnut mixture over; there will be a happy pool of oil surrounding the cheese. Serve with bread to scoop it all up.

WHAT MAKES GOOD FETA

Feta can vary depending on the type of milk (sheep, goat, or cow), origin (Greece, France, or Bulgaria), and the way it's packaged (no negotiation here: It should always come in block form submerged in brine). Don't waste your money on the dry, pre-crumbled stuff. Bulgarian and French fetas are my favorites because they have a creamier texture than Greek feta, which makes them easy to slice into planks without crumbling too much. Bulgarian is saltier than French feta; whereas sheep's milk, the most common feta, is the sharpest. Try cow's or goat's milk feta to taste something milder.

HALLOUMI WITH LEMONY HONEY AND SESAME SALT

Fried cheese is one of life's greatest pleasures, and having experienced many of them, I feel confident saying so. Halloumi, usually a mixture of sheep's and goat's milk, is one of the rare cheeses that can be seared. It gets a deep golden, crackly crust. It oozes, spreads, and loses form. Delicious. It's also incredibly salty. To tame the salt, I add red pepper flakes and honey. The chives are extra, but I am who I am. Eat it while it's hot, as halloumi can get squeaky and rubbery as it sits (I'll still eat it).

SERVES 4

2 teaspoons toasted
sesame seeds (see page 24)

½ teaspoon red pepper flakes

Flaky sea salt

½ lemon

3 tablespoons runny honey

2 (8-ounce) packages
Halloumi cheese

3 tablespoons extra-virgin
olive oil, plus more for drizzling

1 tablespoon finely chopped
chives (optional)

In a mortar and pestle, crush the sesame seeds until some of them look powdery; or finely chop them. Scoop them into a small bowl and mix in the red pepper flakes and a pinch of salt. Using a Microplane, finely grate the zest from the lemon half over the bowl. Use your fingers to mix everything together, making sure the zest is evenly distributed and isn't clumpy. Set aside.

Squeeze the juice from the lemon half into another small bowl, catching any seeds with your other hand, and then stir in the honey. Set aside.

Halve each piece of Halloumi on a diagonal. Working with one piece at time, place the Halloumi, cut-side down, on a cutting board and slice it lengthwise into triangular planks to make eight pieces total. Pat dry with paper towels to remove any excess moisture, so the pieces will brown nicely.

Pour the olive oil into a cast-iron or nonstick skillet and place it over medium-high heat for about 1 minute, until hot. Lay the Halloumi pieces in the oil and cook, pressing down using a metal spatula to make sure the cheese is browning evenly on the bottom. The oil may pop, but don't be afraid. Sear the Halloumi, giving each piece a turn halfway through cooking, until deeply golden brown and crisp around the edges, about 4 minutes on each side.

Transfer the Halloumi to a serving plate and pour on the lemony honey while the cheese is still hot. Sprinkle the spicy sesame salt and chives over the Halloumi. Drizzle with a little olive oil and serve.

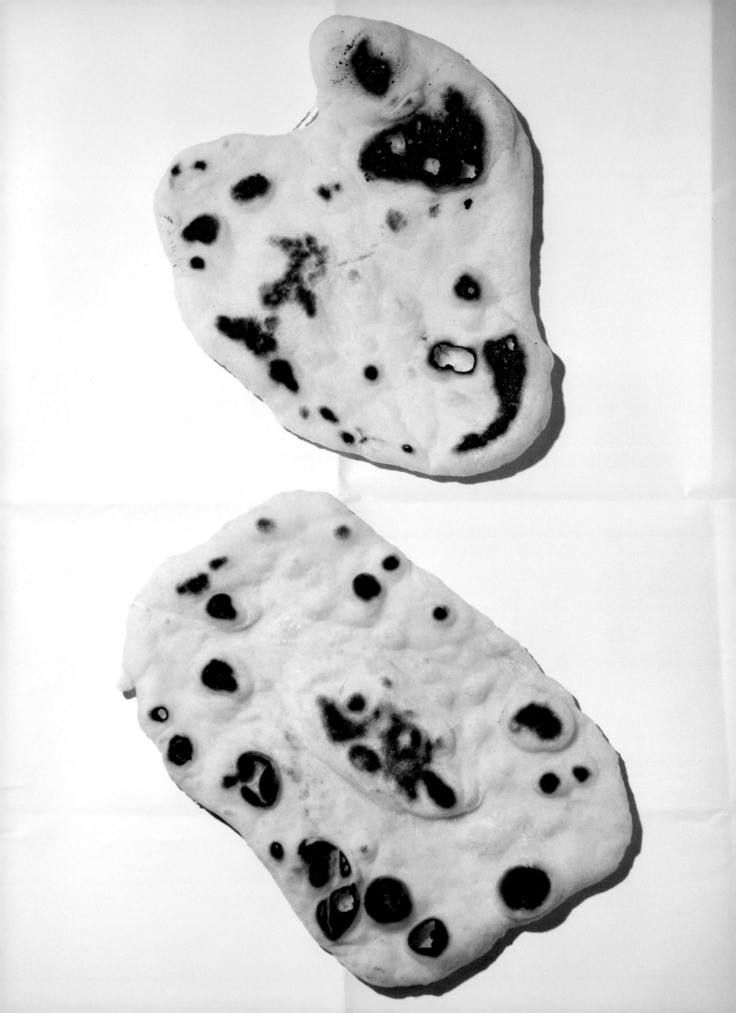

FLUFFY (AND CRISP) FLATBREAD

One day, I will nurture my very own sourdough starter, immerse myself in the art of bread baking, and show off my perfectly burnished loaves. Until then, I am going to stick with a category of bread that takes a lot less time and skill (let's be honest). This one is very easy and achieves both fluffy and, yes, crisp textures by letting the dough sit on an oiled baking sheet. It's the optimal blank canvas to dunk in creamy dips, mop any sauces on a plate, or act as a better bed for an avocado.

MAKES 8 FLATBREADS

¾ cup warm (but not hot!) water

2 teaspoons active dry yeast

1 teaspoon granulated sugar

2½ cups all-purpose flour, or as needed

½ cup full-fat Greek yogurt

2 tablespoons melted butter, ghee, or extra-virgin olive oil

2 teaspoons kosher salt

Pour the water into a large bowl and sprinkle the yeast and sugar over evenly. Let sit for 10 minutes for the yeast to activate and the surface to become foamy, about 10 minutes.

Add the flour, yogurt, butter, and salt to the bowl and mix until a shaggy dough forms and there are no more dry spots (I prefer to use my hands, but a wooden spoon works). The dough should feel tacky, but not overly sticky and should keep its shape when lifted. If the dough is too sticky, mix in a little more flour a tablespoon at a time.

Cover the bowl with a damp kitchen towel and place in a warm, dry spot to let the dough further hydrate and double in size, 60 to 90 minutes.

Lightly oil a few baking sheets and set aside. Turn out the dough onto a clean surface and divide into eight equal pieces using a knife or bench scraper. Working with one piece of dough at a time, form into balls by pinching and pulling the corners to the center. Roll out each ball into a 6-inch-ish round (no need to make them perfect rounds) about ¼ inch thick and transfer to the baking sheets in a single layer, flipping once so both sides are slicked with oil.

Place a large cast iron skillet over medium-high heat. Working with one dough circle at a time, lay the dough on the hot surface and cook until it starts to look dry around the edges and begins to bubble, about 1 minute. Flip and cook until the other side has blistered in spots underneath, 30 to 40 seconds. Continue to cook, turning often, until puffed and browned in spots on both sides, about 1 minute longer. Transfer to a wire rack to cool or wrap up in a kitchen towel to keep warm until ready to serve.

R-E-S-P-E-C-T THE SESAME SEED

As you cook through this book, you might notice that I have an affinity for—all right, an obsession with—sesame seeds. These tiny complex seeds are texturally interesting and pack so much flavor. I realize we're discussing a tiny seed; I could talk about them all day. I tend to use the white and black varieties interchangeably, but they are slightly different. The tear-shaped white sesame seeds have a sweet, toasty smell, similar to that of roasted peanuts and honey. Black sesame seeds tend to be fuller in shape, as their husks are still intact, and they have a pungent earthiness to them. Leave whole or crush them, as I love to do, with some seeds turned to powder and others remaining. The crushing activates their oils, creating concentrated nuttiness.

GARLICKY FRIED TOMATO TOAST

I want a big, fat, crunchy piece of toast. And the best method for making it that way is to fry it. The bread soaks up the oil and gets a deep char and incredible crunch, and yet retains a cushiony center. I want my slices fat (we're talking ¾ inch thick) and wide. I have to cut them myself because no pre-sliced bread comes sliced thick enough. The oil needs to get pretty hot, but not smoking, and the bread needs a generous pool of oil to soak up on both sides. It's ready when it's perfectly golden brown all over. That's your base, and there are so many ways to top it (see pages 116 and 118), but one of my favorite versions is this one, which stars summer tomatoes.

Even if you only topped your fried bread with some mayo and tomato slices, it would be terrific, but I add herbs and chile flakes (I can't *not*). One rule: Make this only during the hottest months with peak-season tomatoes. (Pictured on page 117.)

SERVES 2

GARLICKY FRIED TOASTS

¼ cup extra-virgin olive oil, or as needed

2 thick slices crusty whole-wheat sourdough bread (such as miche, bâtard, or even ciabatta)

1 garlic clove, halved

Flaky sea salt

———————

1 garlic clove, finely grated

¼ cup mayonnaise

½ lemon

2 firm but ripe heirloom tomatoes, sliced into ¼-inch-thick rounds

2 tablespoons finely chopped chives, mint, parsley, or tarragon

Chile flakes for sprinkling

Flaky sea salt

Extra-virgin olive oil for drizzling

To make the toasts: Pour the olive oil into a skillet large enough to fit both slices of bread comfortably and place over medium-high heat. Once you see that the oil is rippling and runny when you tilt the pan, gently place both pieces of bread in the skillet. The bread should start to sizzle and will soak up the oil right away. Cook, using tongs to press down on each slice occasionally, until they're crispy and jaw-droppingly golden brown, 30 to 45 seconds per side. If the pan looks dry after you flip the bread, add another tablespoon or two of oil. Using tongs, transfer both bread slices to a cutting board. While the bread is still hot, slide the halved garlic clove over each slice two or three times. The fried bread will start to melt the garlic. Sprinkle with flaky sea salt.

In a small bowl, mix together the grated garlic and mayonnaise. Squeeze a few drops of lemon juice into the bowl. Set the lemon aside.

Slather the mayonnaise over each piece of toast. Shingle the tomatoes over the mayo, covering as much of the toast as possible. Sprinkle with whatever herb you're using, chile flakes, and flaky sea salt. Finely grate some lemon zest from the reserved lemon over. Drizzle with olive oil and serve.

VINEGAR TOASTS

This was a happy accident during quarantine. I made slightly sad but delicious slow-cooked beans (there's a nicer version on page 235), and I needed something to go with them. I fried some toast, stabbed it all over with a paring knife, and then poured in this herby vinegar mixture. I haven't stopped thinking about it since.

SERVES 2

¼ cup finely chopped parsley

1 tablespoon finely chopped chives, mint, or tarragon (optional; I like two herbs in this, but it's not a must)

2 tablespoons red wine vinegar

½ teaspoon finely grated lemon zest

Freshly ground pepper

Kosher salt

2 pieces Garlicky Fried Tomato Toasts (see page 113)

Extra-virgin olive oil for drizzling

Dump the parsley and chives in a small bowl. Add the vinegar, lemon zest, and about 5 cranks of pepper. Sprinkle with salt and stir.

Using a paring knife, stab each slice of fried toast a few times, so the vinegar can really soak in. Spoon the herby vinegar over each slice and drizzle with olive oil. Let the toast sit for a minute or two, then serve. Swear your allegiance to fried bread, am I right?

ANCHOVY AND RADISH TOASTS

The goal here is to bite into butter. Anchovies out of the jar work, but I marinate them in olive oil to refresh them. Who knows how long they've been in that jar? (Pictured on page 117.)

SERVES 2

6 oil-packed anchovies, drained

2 tablespoons extra-virgin olive oil

1 teaspoon finely grated lemon zest

1 tablespoon fresh lemon juice

2 (¼-inch-thick) slabs cool butter (I use at least 4 tablespoons)

2 pieces Garlicky Fried Tomato Toasts (see page 113)

1 small radish, thinly sliced (optional)

Freshly ground pepper

In a medium bowl, combine the anchovies, olive oil, lemon zest, and lemon juice. Let them all hang out for a few minutes, so the anchovies revive.

Lightly smush the butter on the slices of fried bread. Place a few radish slices on top and spoon on the anchovies and all their oily mess. Sprinkle with pepper and serve.

SNACKS TO ASSEMBLE, NOT COOK

You don't always have time to char an eggplant before people come over. That's why these snacks require just one important ingredient—your wallet—and at-home assembly. Raid your nicest serving ware. Get out the fancy cocktail napkins. And take all the credit.

Burrata with Chopped Pepperoncini

Drain 2 (8-ounce) balls burrata and place in a serving bowl. Tear the burrata with your hands to release the creamy inside. Season with salt and stir. Finely chop 3 tablespoons of your favorite pickled chiles (mine are pepperoncini). Scatter the chiles over the burrata and top with olive oil. Serve with carbs.

Chaat Masala–Spiced Cukes

Slice 1 pound medium cucumbers lengthwise into spears that people can easily pick up. Toss the spears with the juice of 1 lime and season with salt. Let sit for 10 minutes and then drain and toss with 1 tablespoon chopped fresh dill or cilantro. Sprinkle with chaat masala and arrange on a tray, or stack them in a glass for people to grab.

Marinated Italian-Style Artichokes

Drain 2 jars of artichoke hearts. Pat dry and cut in half. In a shallow bowl, whisk ¼ cup olive oil, 3 tablespoons red wine vinegar, 2 tablespoons chopped fresh parsley, and ½ teaspoon red pepper flakes until blended. Add 1 shallot (sliced into rings) and the artichokes. Season with salt and let sit for 20 minutes before serving.

Nori Chip Dip

Give in to cravings for seasoned nori chips at the grocery checkout (kale chips also work). Crush about half a bag with your hands. Place 2 cups sour cream in a bowl and mix in the nori and the juice from 1 lemon. Serve with lettuce wedges to dip.

Open-Face Mortadella Bites

For a deconstructed sandwich, arrange 1 pound mortadella that has been sliced paper-thin (basically see-through) onto a platter. You want to drape the mortadella so it looks airy and is easier to pick up rather than having to painstakingly separate each slice. Cut a loaf of focaccia into small squarish bites and nestle them in with the mortadella. Grab your fancy small bowls and fill with cornichons, Dijon, and mayonnaise, then let your guests do the rest of the work to build their own snack.

Potato Chips with Caviar

Dump a bag of kettle-cooked potato chips (sturdy vessels to carry all the caviar) into a serving bowl. Pop open a tin of caviar and nest it in a small bowl of ice. Open something bubbly or pour vodka into lowballs over ice and add a squeeze of lemon. Cheers.

Radishes with Crème Fraîche and Furikake

Clean 2 bunches of radishes, then halve them, if large, or quarter them. I like leaving the stems on, but it's up to you. Arrange artfully on a platter. Spoon 1½ cups crème fraîche into a bowl, stir in salt to season, and top with a bit of olive oil. Serve with tiny bowls of furikake to sprinkle over.

SALAD
FOR
DAYS

When I was growing up, salad was never a sad dinner side. It was a task that my father took seriously.

Washing and drying the tender lettuce, occasionally sneaking in other, more pungent, bitter greens, like arugula or frisée. His dressing was simple and consistent: a delicate splash of balsamic and olive oil.

Cooking at restaurants completely changed my approach to what a salad can be. There, they took the best ingredients that they could find and did as little as possible to them. At both Chez Panisse and Estela, the salad stations were the hardest test for line cooks. They required intuition, confidence, and consummate multitasking. You didn't just make a salad, you composed one.

If I was salad conscious as a young boy, then it's safe to say I'm salad obsessed as an adult. Now, I want my salad to vary with each bite. I want crunch and pools of juice. There doesn't even need to be lettuce (try the spoon salad on page 131), though I can't help but snack on raw leaves like a rabbit as I put a salad together. When I plate the salad, I want it to look energetic and alive, because it *is*. Making salad is a moment to connect to your food, and where it came from, in a way that other dishes can't come close. It's raw, and right in front of you.

Not to brag, but I make *really* great salads. I could have filled this book only with salad recipes, but I'll save that for another time. Until then, I hope your biggest takeaways from this chapter are that you (1) fall in love/lust with Veg Wedge (page 148) and (2) put away your tongs and toss every leafy salad from now on with your hands. Get in there.

The Intern at Chez Panisse

I felt like a child, a little boy. I guess I was; I was just sixteen. My shoulders scrunched up to my ears, my voice cracking, I had wandered into the offices of Chez Panisse and asked, "Can I work here?"

My aunt and uncle had told me about this restaurant, which was a few blocks away from my home. "It's been around for decades!" they said, adding, "Very famous! Most famous in the country, if not the world." *In the world?* WHAT? On Shattuck Avenue? We lived across the bay from San Francisco, not in the city, where I thought all the good food was. They spoke about the woman behind the place. "The *woman*," my uncle said, as if unworthy of saying her name. My aunt gave me the *Chez Panisse Café Cookbook*. I fixated on it. I even remember the restaurant's website, designed as if it were an old French brasserie: violin music started playing when you opened the page, you'd press "enter," and see the daily menu. Even now, it's hard to explain how working at Chez Panisse felt like a calling. Without knowing much at all, I felt as though I belonged there.

I walked in one afternoon and interviewed with co-chef Beth Wells. We talked about what I was cooking, the influence of my mother's cooking. I was distracted by the art on the walls—stuff I'd never seen before in our home filled with Persian rugs— this antique art deco French iconography everywhere. Beth seemed confused about why I wanted to work there. "How old are you?" she asked. I didn't even have a driver's license. But I was eager (and free). By then, cooking was an addiction. I needed to cook. I couldn't turn it off. I was chasing a high that I wasn't even aware of. I knew this was what I was supposed to do. She said, "You can start next week."

I started interning at Chez on Fridays after school and on Saturdays starting at 7 a.m. I brought my own knives, which I'm embarrassed to think back on, like looking at old yearbook pictures with bad haircuts. A paring knife and a chef's knife, brands that any suburban mom would buy (but hey, those work). When I walked into the kitchen my first day, no one was there. I was hit with a smell that I will associate with the restaurant forever, of whole chickens submerged in fat and garlic, combined with bundles of herbs set aflame to clear the air.

124

The smell of home cooking, concentrated. Then, the sliding door of the walk-in opened, and out came a tall man with this wavy sun-kissed blond hair: head chef Cal Peternell.

Cal was incredibly nice. We talked; he had a teenage son around my age. He then showed me the locker room, where to store my stuff, even though I didn't have any stuff. My first task, and what would be my task for months, was to prep the onions. Cal asked if I knew how to cut an onion. I said I did. I was the boy who thought he could grill a steak properly, who made Mexican food for his family, who served roasted shrimp with green goddess dressing at neighbors' dinner parties. Cal watched as I sliced off about ½ inch from the core of the onion and then . . . "Hold up, let me show you," said Cal. "You don't want to cut off the root end too much, because it'll fall apart when the chefs are slicing and dicing. Keep it so that the petals stay attached. Cut it in half through the core. Then peel off the papery skin, sometimes the second layer, if it's tough, too, and drop it into the bucket." When two buckets were filled, I moved on to my next task.

The next lesson was toasting spices, something you'll see done throughout this book, and as natural to my cooking as salting. But at Chez, I burned those spices until I learned to toast them separately.

Each task had the same goal: Do just enough to preserve the ingredient's natural integrity. Don't remove too much onion when you peel it, but don't keep the layer on that'll only cause more inconvenience to the cooks. I was forced to think. Peel snap pea strings. Snap asparagus ends (my snaps were too big). Remove the dirt around turnips with a paring knife. Cal would ask, "Do you know how to make a . . . vinaigrette? Aioli?" In the beginning, I'd reply with an unconfident "*Yeah!*" Then it became, "No, can you show me?" Then it turned into "Yes I know, yes I know." I wish everybody could experience that progression in whatever they want to do in life.

There was nothing more delicious, more balanced, delicate, and perfectly assembled, than the food at Chez. It's refined home cooking. It's taking ingredients at their peak and doing just enough to let them shine. The food is subtle, gentle, not in-your-face. And the rustic plating, though not my style at this point—the carafe glasses, the jicama-colored ceramics—have a timelessness about it. I loved it. And I was so impressionable. It's the aliveness in the dishes at Chez, that unfussy yet incredibly delicious food that can completely open your eyes to a new ingredient, technique, or even culture, that I am constantly striving to carry out in my own cooking.

By 9 a.m., we'd go into the dining room and Cal would talk through the day's menu. I took notes. The day they changed the goat cheese in the garden lettuce salad, I remember thinking, "That's COOL." The salad was a signature dish of the café. This was such a big deal! Then Cal would ask, "What do you guys want to take?" And the cooks would split up the dishes they would cook. I never got a main; I was helping everybody. I did any work I was told to do—cutting carrots, celery, and onion (and burning them too many times). Removing pinbones from fish. Learning how to break down chicken, removing wings, legs, and breasts. Frenching duck legs and removing excess fat—but saving that fat to make duck confit. I remember learning to make aioli and hearing everybody's method, each slightly contradicting the other. Everyone, and I mean *everyone*, I encountered there had this presentness to them, this deep desire to be fully engaged in all their senses. To not only absorb those lessons in the kitchen, and in life, but also to be generous enough to share them.

When the shift would finish, all the cooks would have a drink, and I'd watch them talk. I was weird and awkward. I'd get an elderberry soda. The only time they gave me alcohol was a rosé sangria with basil, stone fruit, cognac, and bubbly wine; I still chase that memory.

CONTINUED

When I became more confident, I'd sneak into the back walk-in, where the fruit for the dessert station was kept. I'd take an itty-bitty candy-sweet kishu mandarin, peel it, and put the whole thing in my mouth, nearly swallowing it whole because I was so scared someone was going to come in. I remember these unbelievable mulberries that were like instant jams in your mouth. I pop, pop, popped so many mulberries! The cooks stopped putting the mulberries in that fridge because too many were being removed from the sheet trays, so I assume I wasn't the only one.

The salad station had so many components—different dressings for different salads, the tiniest ladles to pour them with. There were moving parts to each salad: it had to be properly dressed, have texture, no repetitiveness; you wanted it bright and acidic and not weighed down by fat. Whether leafy or crunchy or a savory fruit salad, you didn't want the dressing to pool. There were all these metal bowls that you cleaned and cleaned, constantly. You had to be thorough and neat. I remember watching staff cook Tamar Adler's hands at the salad station. Her movements were reasoned. Disciplined. There was a *reason* her hands would grab a blood orange and slice it into rounds.

On Valentine's Day, I heard the cooks saying that Alice Waters was going to have lunch at the café. I'd never seen her or interacted with her until that day—and I was shaking with anticipation. I carried a hotel pan of roasted beets in slow motion up the stairs, so worried I'd spill it all over my white chef's jacket. Everyone knew I was obsessed with Alice, whose name I said with the same reverence as my uncle saying, "the *woman*." I had read her cookbooks. I had watched nearly every video clip I could find of her. I now worked at her restaurant. And, at the moment, I knew, even in all my youth, that her influence meant so much to me without her even knowing.

She was sitting in a booth upstairs at the café, it was the end of lunch service, around 4:30 p.m., the restaurant was cleared of diners, and there were no cooks around. She looked at me and gestured at something and said an unknown-to-me French word. How would I know that? I looked around frantically, none of the cooks were to be found. I was mortified that she was asking me something and I had no idea what she was saying. I mumbled, "I'm sorry, what?" Eventually, a line cook returned to the kitchen, and handed her what she wanted. She smiled and thanked him—and me—and then I quietly left the restaurant. Outside, I started crying. Not because I was sad or disappointed. I was overwhelmed. This was the woman who had started it all. And I was just a kid.

126

FAT PIECES OF CITRUS WITH AVOCADO AND CARAMELIZED DATES

I don't think a dish could be more Californian than citrus and avocado on a plate. At Chez Panisse, I witnessed how transformative large pieces of citrus can be to a salad. In the dead of winter, we'd serve thick rounds of grapefruit with roasted beets—*delicious*. Tender spring leeks were dressed up with orange slices and crushed green olives. The pairing that I craved the most, though, was the bright mixed citrus with avocado. The tart, sweet flavors from the citrus would wake up the buttery avocado. I've re-created it here with a fluorescent turmeric dressing that takes it over the top and looks stunning, too. And those dates! Heating big, meaty Medjool dates in a little oil results in this chewy, caramelized butterscotch flavor that will have you thinking, *That Andy boy is clever.*

SERVES 4

1 tablespoon extra-virgin olive oil

6 Medjool dates, pitted and quartered

1 grapefruit

1 orange (navel, Cara Cara, or blood orange)

1 buttery-ripe avocado, halved and pitted

½ small white or red onion, thinly sliced into rings

Flaky sea salt

Freshly ground pepper

⅔ cup Turmeric and Black Pepper–Citrus Dressing (page 40)

In a small skillet over medium heat, warm the olive oil. Add the dates, turning occasionally, until darkened and caramelized in spots, about 2 minutes.

Cut off the ends of the grapefruit and orange, so they can stand upright. Cut away the peels and white pith, doing your best not to slice off much of the flesh. Slice the citrus into rounds or cut around the core, starting at the top, to get gemlike pieces. Pick out any seeds that come your way.

Arrange the citrus pieces and caramelized dates on a platter or plates. Using a spoon, scoop out the avocado flesh in big imperfect pieces and place them over the citrus. Scatter the onion on top. Season everything with flaky sea salt and plenty of pepper. Spoon the dressing over the salad, trying to not stain your shirt, and serve.

SO, YOU GOT LUCKY AND FOUND OTHER TYPES OF CITRUS

If you're using smaller citrus, such as tangerines, clementines, and/or kishu mandarins, use your hands to peel them and don't even bother using a knife to remove their pith, which is thin and not as bitter as grapefruit and orange pith.

POMEGRANATE SPOON SALAD

There are two things I look forward to in winter: the best movie releases and pomegranates. I use pomegranates to make a chopped salad similar to those you find across the Middle East and India that usually consist of a combination of finely diced tomato, cucumber, and onion. To me, those ingredients are the definition of a chopped salad—not the salad you stood in a line for as someone guillotined romaine lettuce into bits in a big metal bowl. These salads are based on sturdy ingredients that only get better as they bathe in their own juices.

To make this salad suitable for fall and winter, and slightly more textured than the usual tomato-based chopped ensemble, I swapped in pomegranate seeds for the tomatoes and added toasted walnuts. You'll devour it by the spoonful, the pops of pomegranate and flares of chile igniting your taste buds. No ingredient is filler or floppy. Sorry lettuce, but you're not always needed. This salad is great on its own, but also begs to be paired with rich and fatty mains like the Crushed Orange and Rosemary–Braised Lamb (page 282).

SERVES 4

1 shallot, finely chopped

¼ cup fresh lime juice

¼ cup extra-virgin olive oil

1 teaspoon runny honey or maple syrup

Kosher salt

1 large or 2 medium pomegranates

3 Persian cucumbers, finely chopped

1 Fresno or serrano chile, finely chopped, seeded for less heat, or ½ teaspoon chile flakes

2 cups mixed herbs (such as parsley, mint, and/or dill), coarsely chopped

1 cup toasted walnuts (see page 24), finely chopped

Place the shallot in a medium bowl. Stir in the lime juice, olive oil, and honey. Season with salt and set aside, so the shallot can soften.

Halve the pomegranate crosswise, along the equator. Working over a large bowl, hold a pomegranate half in your hand, cut-side down. Using a wooden spoon, smack the pomegranate skin, which will release the seeds from the shell and into the bowl. Repeat with the remaining pomegranate half. Pick out any pith that may have fallen into the bowl. Add the cucumbers, chile, herbs, and walnuts to the bowl.

Give the shallot dressing another stir before pouring it over the salad. Season with salt and toss with your hands (it'll feel great having all the tiny pieces raining through your fingers). I find that it's near perfect right away, but if you let it sit for 10 minutes before serving, you'll create a pool of spicy, salty liquid you can tip back and drink when the salad is gone.

CHOOSING POMEGRANATES

Back in California, I remember pomegranates growing to the size of softballs and being available only in fall, but now you can find them (often already seeded) year-round. I beg you to try to find them when they're in season, typically October to January. There should be all kinds of lumps and bumps where the skin is tightly encasing the seeds inside. The skin should be leathery with a few cracks, which indicates the fruit is ripe, sweet, and ready to burst.

131

PERSIMMONS WITH TORN BURRATA AND FRESH LEMON

This is a savory fruit salad that stimulates and intrigues in *all* the ways. I'll refrain from veering into the sensual with my description here, as this is a cookbook (and my sex book has yet to be written). All I'll say is the aroma of the inner flesh of a persimmon reminds me of something very distinct. Slice one open and you be the judge. Fuyu persimmons have a mild honey sweetness, and the milkiness of burrata takes it to a special place. It's sexy, fleshy, juicy, and a little messy. You'll need a napkin.

SERVES 4

1 small Meyer or regular lemon

3 tablespoons toasted pistachios (see page 24), chopped

1 tablespoon runny honey

Flaky sea salt

4 fuyu persimmons

2 (8-ounce) balls burrata or fresh mozzarella, drained

Extra-virgin olive oil for drizzling

Trim and discard the knobby ends from the lemon (they're tough). Quarter the lemon lengthwise, then slice out the core and seeds at an angle and discard. Finely chop each lemon piece, until they almost look like tiny tiles.

Transfer the lemon and any juices left on the cutting board to a medium bowl and add the pistachios, honey, and a pinch of salt. Stir together. The honey might make everything sticky at first, but the salt will bring out the juices from the lemon, which will loosen the whole thing up.

Pull off and discard the leaves from the persimmons, if necessary, then cut the persimmons into thin rounds. I don't mind the skin, but you should try a piece. If it's not your thing, just peel and slice the fruits.

When you're ready to serve, tear the burrata into big shaggy pieces and divide among shallow bowls or arrange on a platter. Scatter the persimmons over and sprinkle with some salt, then spoon on the lemon relish, drizzle some olive oil over, and serve.

CHOOSING PERSIMMONS

You'll most likely encounter fuyu and hachiya persimmon varieties. The fuyu (which I call for in this salad) is round and has a flat bottom. It can be eaten when it's firm and crunchy, but you can also let it soften slightly and it will become buttery and sweet. The hachiya is almost heart-shaped and tapers at the bottom. Its jelly-like, slippery texture makes it good for baking.

SUPER-CRUNCHY CELERY SALAD

This is the crunchiest salad that I could dream up. And, yes, it stars celery, that often unloved ingredient you forget about in your produce drawer. But celery is always there for you, and *I* love it. This salad shows its true potential and then takes it up a notch. As someone who's been cooking over half their life—and who unabashedly loves celery—this salad surprised even me. It's greater than the sum of its parts, but its parts are great: good blue cheese, crispy apple, quickly toasted candied nuts. The name of the game is to get a bite of everything on your fork. You'll find yourself coming back to this recipe again and again.

SERVES 4

6 celery stalks, with as many leaves as possible

1 crisp, tart apple (such as Granny Smith, Honeycrisp, or Pink Lady)

3 tablespoons lemon juice, or as needed

2 tablespoons extra-virgin olive oil, or as needed

Kosher salt

3 ounces mild blue cheese (such as Stilton) or a sharp cheddar (if you're one of those blue cheese haters), thinly sliced or crumbled

½ cup Sweet and Toasty Nuts (page 44), broken into large pieces or coarsely chopped

Freshly ground pepper

Pluck the leaves from the celery stalks, tearing any large leaves in two, and set aside. Thinly slice the celery on a sharp diagonal. (You're going for 2-inch-ish-long elegant slices.) Scoop up the celery and drop the pieces into a large mixing bowl.

Core and quarter the apple (like you would for an after-school snack), then thinly slice each piece. Add the apple to the bowl with the celery. Add the lemon juice and olive oil to the bowl and season with salt. Toss until the apple and celery are coated. Add the blue cheese, nuts, and celery leaves and toss once more. Taste a piece of celery. It should be bright and tangy. If it needs to be perked up a touch, add a dash more lemon juice, olive oil, and salt until it tastes delicious.

Transfer the salad to a platter or divide among plates. Finish with a lot of pepper and serve.

YOU DESERVE CRUNCHY CELERY

Celery gets wilted, flimsy, and floppy the longer it awaits its moment from your crisper drawer. A soak in ice water perks it back up, making it firm and crunchy again. This applies to lackluster lettuce too. Do the soak in your salad spinner so you can easily drain and spin it dry after. Just fill the bowl with ice water, place the celery in it, and leave to chill out for 5 minutes to 2 hours (hey, maybe you have errands to run). You'll notice that in the ice water, the celery almost curls and becomes beautiful again, but maybe that's just me.

EAT-WITH-EVERYTHING CUCUMBER SALAD

No matter which restaurant you're in, ALWAYS order the cucumber salad. It's a refreshing palate cleanser and truly goes with everything. Here, the dressing is potent with soy sauce and vinegar, and the cucumbers soak it up. So will you. Now, I'm not a stickler for how *you* cut the cucumbers, but *I* cut them into generous, irregular, angled pieces because I want to experience their snappy texture in every bite. If you're craving a creamy cucumber salad, follow these cutting-and-salting instructions and then top with Extra Sesame Dressing (page 63) and some toasted sesame seeds.

SERVES 4

6 Persian cucumbers, or 1 large English cucumber

Kosher salt

1 small garlic clove, finely grated

3 tablespoons unseasoned rice vinegar or fresh lemon juice

2 tablespoons soy sauce

1 teaspoon granulated sugar

1 teaspoon peeled, finely grated ginger

2 tablespoons toasted black sesame seeds (see page 24), lightly crushed in a mortar and pestle or left whole

Very Crispy Garlic-Chile Oil (page 54) or your favorite chile oil for drizzling (optional)

Halve each cucumber lengthwise, then slice on a steep diagonal into 2- to 3-inch pieces, but don't get the ruler out—imperfection is what we're after. Season with salt.

In a large serving bowl, whisk together the garlic, vinegar, soy sauce, sugar, and ginger. Add the cucumbers and toss to coat. Taste a cucumber and see if it needs a sprinkle more of salt. Top with the sesame seeds and spoon over the garlic-chile oil. Give another little toss and serve.

DO AHEAD

The cucumber salad can be made a day ahead and chilled. If you somehow don't eat it all at once, it'll really soak up the dressing and become even more delicious.

CHOOSING CUCUMBERS

I favor Persian cucumbers for their thin skin and tight, crunchy texture. If you're in the peak of summer, look for Armenian cucumbers that have furrowed green stripes or the Japanese variety that tangle and curl like pythons and don't have as many seeds. Please avoid (if you possibly can) the conventional garden cucumber with its thick, waxy skin and seedy flesh that has the texture of Styrofoam.

136

FENNEL SALAD WITH SPICY GREEN OLIVES AND CRUSHED PISTACHIOS

This fennel salad is slightly over the top. Do I really need the nuts and the cheese? (Yes, but it's up to you if you keep them.) Is this salad gonna be good if you don't have mint? Yep. Swap Planters cocktail peanuts you found in your pantry for the pistachios? Sure. What if you just use ground pepper and skip the red? Okay. The important step is eating this salad as soon as you dress the fennel. You want that full crunch experience. The crushed green olives should be big and fleshy, like a chunky relish to contrast the icy bite of the fennel. It's baroque and bright and briny. All that acidity in the salad begs to be paired with juicy pork chops (see page 288) or *the* steak (see page 298).

SERVES 4

1 cup green olives (Castelvetrano and Picholine are my favorites)

⅓ cup toasted pistachios (see page 24), finely chopped

⅓ cup extra-virgin olive oil, plus more for drizzling

¼ teaspoon red pepper flakes

1 lemon

Kosher salt

Freshly ground pepper

2 fennel bulbs, woody stalks and fronds trimmed

½ cup mint leaves, torn if large

2 ounces Parmesan, thinly sliced (about 1 cup)

2 tablespoons white wine vinegar

Using the side of a chef's knife or the bottom of a mug, crush the olives. Tear out the pits, leaving the olives a little craggy. Scoop them into a small bowl and add the pistachios, olive oil, and red pepper flakes. Using a Microplane, finely grate the zest of half of the lemon over the olive mixture, season with salt and ground pepper, and set aside. It should look like a chunky relish.

If you see brown jagged streaks on the fennel, remove an outer layer. Trim and discard about ½ inch from the root end of both fennel bulbs. Thinly slice the fennel bulb crosswise, starting from the base. It doesn't need to be paper-thin. You're going for about ¼-inch-thick slices. (This would be a good time to use the mandoline you bought.)

In a large bowl, combine the fennel, mint, cheese, and vinegar. Finely grate the zest of the remaining half of the lemon over the fennel salad. Halve the lemon and squeeze the juice into the bowl, catching any seeds with your other hand. Drizzle the salad with a little olive oil and season with salt. Toss until every piece of fennel is nicely coated. I like my fennel salad tangy, but you can add another tablespoon of oil if you want it less tart.

Spoon the olive relish onto a platter or plates and scatter the dressed fennel over it, trying to make it as architectural as you want (it's okay to play with your food). Serve immediately.

DO AHEAD

Go ahead and toast your nuts, pit your olives, and slice your cheese a few hours ahead—but don't assemble this salad until you're ready to serve it. The fennel will lose its crucial crispness if you dress it in advance.

CHOOSING FENNEL

You can find fennel year-round in most supermarkets, but it's happiest in fall or early spring, when its natural sweetness comes out. Even the shape is different: the farmers' market fennel has flared stalks and is more of a jadeite color, versus the stuff at the grocery store, which is bulbous and pearly white. When you're picking it out, the base should feel dense and tight, and the celery-like stalks should not be visibly dry or brown.

139

SPICY AND SOUR GRILLED CABBAGE WITH CHOPPED PEANUT VINAIGRETTE

Cabbage is my favorite vegetable and I doubt that'll ever change. It's almost blackened on the grill for this salad, getting near charred on the outside, like the ruins of an ancient volcanic eruption, while it steams inside and retains a good amount of crunch. While the grill is on, take advantage of it and throw on whatever onion-y ingredient you have on hand (scallions, shallots, or even a small sweet onion). Those go in the chopped dressing, which is not going for subtlety. It's spicy and sour, with some peanut crunch. The salad gets better as it sits; the mint will wilt, but the cabbage will get more delicious.

SERVES 4

1 small head purple or green cabbage

6 scallions

3 tablespoons neutral oil (such as grapeseed), plus ¼ cup

Kosher salt

1 garlic clove, finely grated

1 habanero, Fresno, or serrano chile, halved, seeded, and finely chopped

¾ cup toasted peanuts (see page 24), coarsely chopped

⅓ cup coarsely chopped mint

Finely grated zest of 1 lime

¼ cup fresh lime juice

Preheat the grill to medium heat.

Remove any floppy leaves from the cabbage. Quarter the cabbage through the core. Put the cabbage and scallions on a rimmed baking sheet and drizzle with the 3 tablespoons neutral oil. Season with salt and, using tongs, toss them around to get nicely coated.

Transfer the cabbage to the grill and cook until all sides are deeply charred (pretty much blackened), 8 to 10 minutes per side and about 25 minutes total. Throw the scallions on the grill during the last 2 minutes and let them cook, turning often, until tender and charred in spots. Transfer the cabbage and scallions back to the baking sheet.

Finely chop the scallions, scoop up the pieces, and place them in a large bowl. Add the garlic, chile, most of the peanuts (save a small handful to sprinkle on top), the mint, lime zest, lime juice, and remaining ¼ cup olive oil. Season with salt and give it a taste. It should taste exactly like its name—spicy and sour—with some crunch to it.

Coarsely chop the cabbage and throw it into the bowl with the dressing. Season with a big pinch of salt (cabbage can take a lot) and use your hands to toss and scrunch the cabbage a few times so it really soaks up the dressing. Serve as-is in the bowl or transfer to a pretty platter, sprinkle the remaining peanuts over, and wait for people to start asking, "Oh, what's that?!"

WANT TO SKIP GRILLING?

Although it's an entirely different experience, this salad can be made using raw cabbage and scallions. Thinly slice the cabbage as you would for slaw and season with ½ teaspoon salt (taste and adjust with more salt after you add the dressing). Use your hands to squish the leaves, as if you were giving a rather hard massage, to soften them a bit. Napa cabbage would also work here but, because it has a softer texture, keep the leaves in bigger pieces.

140

JUICY TOMATOES WITH ITALIAN CHILE CRISP

The truth is, most tomato salads don't need a recipe. Vinegar, olive oil, plenty of crunchy salt, and call it a day. If you have some herbs on hand, throw those in. What would a tomato salad look like if it *deserved* a recipe? Something like this. Very savory. Topped with a garlic-chile crisp and dressed with its delicious oil. Anchovies and fennel seeds heighten the tomato's flavor while bringing even more savory undertones. It's spicy, with the chile flakes. This isn't a simple caprese that you whipped up on a summer afternoon. It's still simple but steals the show.

SERVES 4

⅓ cup extra-virgin olive oil

5 garlic cloves, thinly sliced

4 oil-packed anchovies, drained

2 teaspoons fennel seeds, crushed or finely chopped

1 teaspoon red pepper flakes

2 pounds heirloom tomatoes (any size will do), some sliced and some cut into wedges, or small tomatoes (such as Sungold and/or cherry), some halved and some left whole

2 tablespoons sherry vinegar or red wine vinegar

1 cup basil leaves

Flaky sea salt

In a small skillet over medium heat, combine the olive oil, garlic, and anchovies. Cook, stirring often, until the garlic is barely golden and crisp and the anchovies have melted away, 3 to 5 minutes. Turn off the heat and stir in the fennel seeds and red pepper flakes.

Place the tomatoes on a large platter and splash with the vinegar. Spoon the chile crisp over and scatter the basil on top. Finish with plenty of salt and serve.

DO AHEAD

The chile crisp can be made up to 1 week ahead and stored, covered, in the fridge.

LITTLE GEMS WITH GREEN GODDESS YOGURT AND TANGY SHALLOTS

It feels right that the first salad dressing I learned to make was the regal and herbaceous green goddess. It was from a gardening book I had as a kid that featured recipes to go along with the produce you were growing. I was the proud father of a patch of mint (it spreads like a weed once planted), Persian cucumbers, and Early Girl tomatoes, which would all end up as a chopped salad that I'd eat like cereal.

I prefer to keep the typical mayonnaise out of my GG dressing and go with yogurt; this brings creaminess and tang at the same time. Quick-pickled shallots top the salad, and their pickling vinegar goes into the dressing, giving it an allium bite. If you don't have a blender or food processor, you can finely chop the herbs and stir everything together; you'll just have a slightly thicker and less green dressing, but it'll still be delicious. You can also double or triple the recipe and use it as a dip.

SERVES 4

2 tablespoons extra-virgin olive oil

½ cup panko breadcrumbs

Kosher salt

Freshly ground pepper

1 medium shallot, thinly sliced into rings

2 tablespoons red or white wine vinegar

4 to 6 heads Little Gem lettuce (about 1 pound total), or 2 large romaine lettuce hearts

⅔ cup Green Goddess Yogurt (page 58)

In a medium skillet over medium heat, warm the olive oil. Add the panko and cook, stirring often, so the crumbs toast evenly and turn deeply golden brown, 4 to 5 minutes. Transfer the breadcrumbs to a small bowl and season with salt and pepper while warm.

In a small bowl, combine the sliced shallot with the vinegar, and season with salt and pepper. Give the shallot rings a squeeze to help them start to pickle and set the bowl aside.

Trim and discard the cores from the lettuce heads and toss out any bruised or overly floppy leaves. Separate the leaves from each head. I like leaving the leaves whole to show off their crinkled texture, but if you're using romaine, go ahead and tear them into more manageable bites.

Drop the lettuce into a large bowl, pour in the green goddess yogurt, and season with salt and pepper. Using your hands, toss until each leaf is dressed nicely. Sprinkle with the toasted breadcrumbs and scatter the pickled shallot on top before serving.

USE YOUR HANDS

Your wooden fork-and-spoon salad tossers aren't going to have the sensory feel to know that every nook and cranny of the lettuce, every tip of each leaf, is properly dressed. Using salad tossers risks an over- or underdressed salad. Use your hands and get in there! Then taste the salad before serving and adjust: Add a drizzle more oil, a splash of vinegar, some salt and pepper. For leafy salads, the dressing should never pool at the bottom of the bowl.

144

PARMESAN-KALE CHIP SALAD WITH TANGY MUSTARD DRESSING

You're not going to do a kale salad, I told myself when I was writing this book. *It's been done. You've enjoyed them, you might enjoy them again, but the moment has passed.* Then I decided I wanted a salad with hearty greens, and I found kale staring back at me. I thought about how much I like crispy kale chips, and that's how I could bring another texture to this salad. You make kale chips sprinkled with an obscene 2 cups of Parmesan cheese. They become chewy-crisp as the cheese melts on the kale. There's also some raw kale in the salad (for the healthy folks), and an extremely creamy mustardy dressing to go along with it. This is now my favorite kale salad.

SERVES 4

2 bunches lacinato kale

1 tablespoon extra-virgin olive oil

Kosher salt

2 ounces Parmesan, finely grated (about 2 cups)

Freshly ground pepper

¾ cup Tangy Mustard Dressing (page 37)

½ cup toasted walnuts or other nuts (see page 24), finely chopped, or Anchovy Breadcrumbs (page 45)

Preheat the oven to 425°F. Line a baking sheet with parchment paper.

Pull the leaves from the kale stalks and discard the stalks. On the prepared baking sheet, toss half the kale with the olive oil and season with salt. Spread the kale in one even layer and then sprinkle the Parmesan over the leaves and top with a sprinkle of pepper. Bake until the leaves look crispy and shriveled, and the Parmesan has turned golden brown, 10 to 12 minutes.

While the kale chips are doing their thing, tear the remaining kale leaves into bite-size pieces and put them in a large bowl. Pour half the dressing over the kale and give the leaves a few good, mighty scrunches to soften them.

Arrange the raw leaves and crispy chips on a large plate or platter. Sprinkle the walnuts over the top and spoon more dressing over, if you'd like, or serve on the side for your guests to decide.

VEG WEDGE

Loyalists (to what? Blue cheese?!) will blast me for altering too many parts of the wedge salad with my version, but I'm not sorry. The classic wedge has a few issues. That dressing is always too thick and never properly enrobes the entire salad. The croutons are often stale. The occasional scattering of grape tomatoes always feels like a lazy afterthought that doesn't bring much to the table besides some underwhelming tomato energy. I don't have a problem with the bacon, as long as it's in the form of shards and not bits.

I felt compelled to come up with a recipe that solved my problems with the standard wedge. The cold, crisp, refreshing lettuce doesn't actually need much improving, but cutting it into smaller (read: cuter) pieces allows for more dressing to get between those wavy layers. My dressing is a garlicky tahini-based ranch that has the ideal drizzle consistency.

When it comes to the toppings, I admit that I go extra, and I think it's absolutely worth it. If you omit one or even two of the toppings, I won't be upset because you will still love this salad.

SERVES 4

1 head iceberg lettuce

1 small lemon

Kosher salt

1 cup Tahini Ranch (page 59)

2 small radishes, thinly sliced

½ small red or white onion, thinly sliced into rings

1 cup torn herbs (such as basil, cilantro, dill, and/or parsley)

2 tablespoons mixed toasted seeds (such as poppy, sesame, and/or sunflower)

1 teaspoon mild chile flakes (such as Aleppo; optional)

Flaky sea salt (optional)

Extra-virgin olive oil for drizzling

Remove any floppy or wilted outer leaves from the lettuce. Quarter the lettuce through the core, then cut each quarter into 3-inch-ish pieces. Arrange the iceberg wedges on a serving platter, pulling apart the leaves slightly, so dressing can easily get in there. Halve the lemon and squeeze its juice over the lettuce, catching any seeds with your other hand. Season each wedge with a bit of kosher salt.

Using a spoon, drizzle the ranch over the lettuce. (You can leave some on the side, depending on how much or how little dressing you want.) Scatter the radishes, onion, and herbs. Sprinkle the seeds, chile flakes, and flaky sea salt over the top. Finish with a drizzle of olive oil and then set out knives and forks and get to it.

CHICORY SALAD, WITH THANKS TO ESTELA

If there's a salad that changed my life, it's the endive salad at Estela, which is one of the Great Salads of the twenty-first century, rivaling the Waldorf, wedge, and Caesar. Before I had that salad, endive was merely a tiny boat for mayonnaise-laden crabmeat. So dated. And all the endive, walnut, and blue cheese salads in circulation were redundant. But Ignacio Mattos took those ingredients that go together and amplified them. The Estela endive salad starts with a pile of crispy bits: deeply toasted croutons and their crumbs mixed with crushed toasted walnuts. The dressing is mashed anchovies, garlic, vinegar, and good olive oil. You stab your knife into wedges of pecorino duro and Ubriaco Rosso cheese to release craggy nuggets onto a rimmed platter. The endive leaves get scattered in a mixing bowl with a few splashes of chardonnay vinegar, salt, orange juice, and a touch of olive oil and then tossed. Next, you arrange the leaves, cup-side up, on the platter and pour the juices from the bowl over them. To have the true experience, you have to go to the restaurant, but I've done my best to make an iteration for home cooks.

SERVES 4

1 small garlic clove

4 oil-packed anchovies, drained

½ cup toasted hazelnuts or walnuts (see page 24), crushed or coarsely chopped

3 tablespoons sherry vinegar or red wine vinegar

2 tablespoons extra-virgin olive oil, plus ¼ cup

4 ounces Manchego, pecorino, or an aged cheddar cheese

½ orange

Kosher salt

Freshly ground pepper

1 pound assorted chicory (use a combination of Belgian endive, Castelfranco, radicchio, Treviso, escarole, and/or Chioggia), leaves separated and torn if large

Runny honey for drizzling

In a mortar and pestle, crush the garlic until you have a coarse paste. Add the anchovies and mash until you have a smoother paste. (You can also do this by grating the garlic with a Microplane and mashing it with the anchovies, using your chef's knife.) Scoop the garlicky anchovy mixture into a medium bowl. Add the hazelnuts, 1 tablespoon of the vinegar, and the 2 tablespoons olive oil to the bowl.

Grab the cheese and use a paring knife to pierce and break into smallish irregular pieces (about ½ inch in size). Add the cheese to the bowl with the hazelnut mixture. Take the orange half, give it two swipes on a Microplane, and add the zest to the bowl. Keep that orange half close by. Season the hazelnut and cheese crumbles with salt and pepper and give it all a toss.

Put the chicory into a large bowl and pour in the remaining 2 tablespoons vinegar and remaining ¼ cup olive oil. Squeeze the juice from the orange half over the chicory. Season with salt and use your hands to toss the salad, making sure the dressing gets between each leaf. Add the hazelnut-cheese mixture and toss once more. Transfer the salad to a platter and drizzle with the honey. Grab a fork if you must, but I tend to use the thick chicory leaves to shovel all the crunchy bits into my mouth.

MIND
YOUR VEG

Seasonal vegetables. How groundbreaking, I know. But with this chapter, I want to show how just a little technique and a lot of flavor combinations can give you limitless versatility with vegetables in the kitchen.

Because this is my book, I included only my favorite vegetables: beets, cabbage, cauliflower, eggplant, fennel, and potatoes, to name a few. There's a noticeably minimal use of zucchini (other than for the recipe on page 209).

I blame it on the Californian in me, but vegetables excite me more than any other ingredient and provide the inspiration for whatever meal I'm cooking. The best cooks and the best kind of cooking subscribe to this philosophy, which, I'll admit, is certainly not a new concept. Farm-to-table and market cooking have become clichés (I wish they hadn't), so let's just call it *cooking*.

For each vegetable, I've chosen a technique that, to me, is the optimal way to cook that vegetable. Stir-fried asparagus cooks without turning to mush. Carrots, sweet potatoes, and winter squash need to be paired with sharp, spicy-textured ingredients to balance their sweetness. Cauliflower wants that hard, high-heat roasting to caramelize it and bring out those natural sugars hiding beneath its sulfuric stink. Steam-roasting beets concentrates their flavor while cooking them perfectly. You'll see what I mean when you dive in.

Some recipes are more technical, like Crispy Roasted Artichokes (page 195), whereas others are more of a template that you can riff on once you understand the process, like Fennel Buried in Cream (page 162). The whole point is to get you as excited about vegetables as I am about summer's first Early Girl tomatoes and Fairy Tale eggplants. Which is very. Don't let yourself get accustomed to what you see at the grocery store. Your goal as a cook should be to find the freshest ingredients and *fully* experience them.

COCONUT CREAMED CORN

Ninety percent of the time, I want my corn prepared as simply as possible: steamed or grilled and slathered with copious amounts of butter. The rest of the time, I find myself feeling I should let corn play with other ingredients. Because corn is sweet and crunchy, it can take on other flavors really well. I wanted to improve on creamed corn enough to erase the stuff in a can from your memory. Here, corn is prepared two ways: Some of it is cooked in a dry skillet, so the kernels can take on color and a roasted, nutty flavor that will fool you into thinking it's been on the grill. The remaining corn gets cooked with a double dose of coconut (oil and milk), turmeric (which gives it an extra-summery yellow color), and hazelnuts, which add crunch.

SERVES 4

4 ears corn

2 tablespoons virgin coconut oil, ghee, or neutral oil (such as grapeseed)

4 scallions, thinly sliced

4 garlic cloves, thinly sliced

1-inch piece ginger, peeled and finely chopped

Kosher salt

½ teaspoon ground turmeric

1 cup unsweetened coconut milk

⅓ cup toasted hazelnuts (see page 24), coarsely chopped

Generous pinch chile flakes

Chopped cilantro for serving

1 lime, cut into wedges

Shuck the corn, pulling away all of the pesky silky threads. Working with one ear at a time, position it in a large bowl (the wider the better), so that the ear angles down. Using a chef's knife, starting from the top, slice off the kernels into the bowl. You will have about 2 cups of kernels.

Place a large cast-iron skillet over medium-high heat for a few minutes. Add one-third of the corn kernels and cook, undisturbed, until lightly charred underneath, 1 to 2 minutes. A kernel or two may sizzle and pop out of the pan, but it's a small price to pay. Continue to cook, tossing occasionally, until the kernels have mostly browned and it smells as if you're outside by the grill, 3 to 4 minutes longer. Transfer to a small bowl and set aside.

Allow the skillet to cool for 5 minutes and then wipe it out. Add the coconut oil to the skillet and place over medium heat. Add half the scallions, the garlic, and ginger. Season with salt and cook, stirring, until the scallions are soft but not browned, about 3 minutes. Add the remaining uncooked corn. Cook, stirring occasionally, until the kernels have become brighter in color, 2 to 3 minutes. Stir in the turmeric so it coats the corn, then pour in the coconut milk and turn the heat to low. Simmer until the coconut milk has slightly reduced and thickened, 4 to 6 minutes.

Pour the coconut creamed corn into a shallow bowl and top with the charred kernels, hazelnuts, and chile flakes. Serve garnished with cilantro, the remaining scallions, and lime wedges on the side for squeezing.

WHILE I HAVE YOU . . . GRILLED CORN, PERSIAN STYLE

The way that my parents grilled corn was how it is done on the streets in Iran: grilled until the kernels became almost molasses-like in color with an aroma of burnt sugar. Then the cooked cobs were plunged in a salty hot-water bath to season the crisp corn. Here's how to do it.

Preheat your grill to medium-high heat. While the grill heats, in a pitcher, mix 10 cups water with ½ cup salt. The water should be very salty. When the grill is hot, arrange the shucked cobs on it and cook, using tongs to rotate the cobs every 2 to 3 minutes until they have charred in most spots, 8 to 12 minutes total. One by one, submerge the cobs in the salted water for at least 1 minute or up to 3 minutes. The longer you leave the cobs in the water, the saltier the corn will be.

BLACK PEPPER AND GINGER ASPARAGUS STIR-FRY

Can we all admit that asparagus can be fussy and, often, overrated? The flaw in nature's design is that the tip cooks before the rest of the stalk. My solution to this problem is to have the whole spears kiss the heat without getting into that unfortunate army-drab territory. Cutting the spears on an exaggerated diagonal also helps the asparagus cook faster. And it looks angular and modern.

With such a delicate, here-for-a-minute ingredient, less is more. I try not to drown it in butter and soy sauce, but those ingredients complement asparagus's sweet green flavor and remind you that life is about balance. Then the ginger and scallion and a tingle of black pepper come in, and it's downright confusing how good this dish is.

SERVES 4

1 small bunch scallions

1½ pounds thick asparagus

1 tablespoon neutral oil (such as grapeseed)

2-inch piece ginger, peeled and finely chopped

Kosher salt

1 tablespoon unsalted butter, cut into pieces

1 tablespoon soy sauce

1 tablespoon water

Freshly ground pepper

Thinly slice the scallions on a steep diagonal, keeping the green parts and white parts separate.

Snap off or trim the woody ends of each asparagus spear, usually about 2 inches from the bottom. Thinly slice the spears on a steep diagonal into about 2-inch-long pieces.

Place a wok or large skillet over medium-high heat for about 5 minutes, so the pan is ripping hot. Pour in the neutral oil and wait until you see a whisper of smoke. That's when you know it's go-time. Add the asparagus, scallion whites, and ginger to the wok. Season with salt and cook, tossing or stirring often, until the asparagus begins to lightly brown around the edges, 2 to 3 minutes. Add the butter, soy sauce, and water to the wok and cook, still tossing, until the butter melts and the sauce coats the asparagus; this happens in seconds. Turn off the heat and add at least five cranks of pepper. Give everything one final toss.

Transfer the asparagus to a platter, scatter the scallion greens on top, and serve.

ASPARAGUS RULE NUMBER-ONE

Do not come around here with that floppy, thin, pencil-size asparagus. The thicker stalks have snap, a sense of freshness. The thin stuff tends to overcook and become flaccid—something you never want in life.

PEAS WITH BIG HUNKS OF FETA AND ZHOUG

Once in your life, maybe twice, buy a bag of fresh English peas, split the pods, and use your thumbs to push out the petit pois. All that work! So little yield! The rest of the time, buy them frozen. Organic frozen peas are picked at their peak freshness and, to me, are more reliable than the fresh ones, which can sometimes be starchy and so hard to find. I like to treat the simple peas elaborately. A spicy Yemeni zhoug for green-on-green intensity, plus big hunks of fatty, salty feta, make this a dish I want to shovel into my mouth with the biggest spoon I own.

SERVES 4

2 tablespoons extra-virgin olive oil

1 large shallot, thinly sliced into rings

2 cups shelled fresh or frozen and thawed English peas

¼ cup water

Kosher salt

Freshly ground pepper

½ cup Zhoug (page 49)

4 ounces feta cheese (blotted dry if you have the time)

Pour the olive oil into a skillet and place it over medium-high heat. Add the shallot and cook, stirring now and then, until the shallot starts to soften and get a little browned, 4 to 6 minutes. Add the peas and water to the skillet (or just a splash of water if you're using frozen peas, which are already mostly cooked). Season with salt and pepper and cook, stirring occasionally, until the peas are tender, 4 to 6 minutes for fresh and about 1 minute for ones that have been thawed. Turn off the heat and scrape in the zhoug, stirring until each little pea is flecked with it. Taste a spoonful and adjust the seasoning with more salt and pepper.

Spoon the peas into a shallow bowl. Slice the feta into large shards and toss it on the peas before serving.

OTHER PEAS

The sweet English pea is ideal with the extra-hot zhoug, but you can also go with sugar snaps or snow peas (except you're not getting a pass to use frozen for those). Buy them fresh and thinly slice before cooking.

FENNEL BURIED IN CREAM

In my professional cooking experience, fennel has been an ingredient that is somewhat polarizing for so many. I fall under the category of, "will eat fennel in any way." I love it raw (see the salad on page 139), roasted until it's almost jammy, or when I get to use up the dill-like fronds and make a green sauce. It's actually a pretty perfect vegetable. It doesn't seem to be the texture that bothers people but, rather, the sweet anise flavor. So I set out to develop a fennel recipe that would unite the haters and the lovers, because we need more unity in the world, and this is my very, very tiny contribution. The results: a dish that falls under the gratin category, a category that has near-universal appeal because, well, to be gratinated is to be covered with buttered crumbs or melted cheese. (How I'd like to be buried when I pass.)

SERVES 4

2 shallots, trimmed and quartered through the root end

4 garlic cloves, smashed

2 cups heavy cream

1 tablespoon thyme leaves, plus more for serving

1½ teaspoons kosher salt

Freshly ground pepper

3 large bulbs fennel

1 ounce Parmesan, finely grated (about 1 cup)

In a small saucepan over low heat, combine the shallots, garlic, cream, thyme, salt, and 1 teaspoon pepper and bring to a simmer. Cook, stirring and watching carefully to make sure the cream doesn't boil over (which happened to me nearly every time when I was testing this recipe), 15 to 20 minutes. You want the shallots and garlic to become soft and jammy. Let cool slightly, then transfer to a blender and blend until smooth.

Place oven racks in the top and center positions and preheat the oven to 350°F.

Cut the tough stalks and the fronds from the fennel. Halve the fennel lengthwise through the core, then cut each half into 1-inch wedges. Put the fennel in a large cast-iron skillet or 2-quart baking dish and pour the garlicky cream over the top (not all of the fennel will be buried under the cream, but that's okay). Bake on the center rack until the fennel is tender, the edges are starting to brown, and the cream has reduced, 40 to 50 minutes.

Remove the skillet from the oven and turn on the broiler. Sprinkle the Parmesan over the fennel and return the skillet to the oven, this time on the top rack. Broil until the top is browned, lacy, crispy, and perfect. Please watch carefully because each broiler is different and I don't know how your broiler works. So it could take as little as 2 minutes or up to 5 minutes.

Pull the skillet out of the oven and sprinkle with some thyme leaves and more pepper. Give it 5 minutes for the hot cream to set and thicken before diving in, but also so you don't burn the roof of your mouth. I'm looking out for you.

DO AHEAD

The gratin can be baked, without the cheese, 1 day ahead. Cover and chill. Bring to room temperature before adding the cheese and broiling.

SPECIAL SAUCE

Typically, you'll see stock, a roux, and too much whisking involved when making the sauce for a gratin. But what gives this dish that extra oomph is the infused cream sauce, which may sound fussy at first, but it's really just adding delicious things, like shallots, garlic, and thyme. You let all that gently simmer before pureeing and, now, you have a luscious sauce that has a lot more going on than straight fat. Once you make this, and have the infused-cream technique down, you can swap the fennel for other vegetables and roots. It would be equally delicious with sliced cauliflower or sweet onion wedges, or go classic with thinly sliced potatoes (but leave the peels on!).

CHOOSING SQUASH

Even though winter squash are in the same family as cucumbers and melons, and planted around the same time, they take all summer to ripen. I look for squash that are a manageable size for cutting into. The super-big butternuts are not only a pain to slice but that's when they start getting starchy. I favor delicata, honeynut, kabocha, and red kuri. Each of these, and other varieties, has its own distinct flavor, but they all benefit from being roasted or added to soups and stews. When choosing, make sure the squash has no soft spots, still has its stem, and is heavy (which means it hasn't dried out in storage). Look for fun varieties. See those green-splattered, wobbly, and ungainly squash? Try those too.

SWEET-AND-SOUR CARAMELIZED SQUASH WITH PISTACHIO ZA'ATAR

Come November and December, when you usually get tired of all the squash, you won't get tired of this. Here's why: The roasted squash gets oh-so-sweet, crisp on the outside, and as tender as butter inside. Then it gets a bit of acid to tame that sweetness, and plenty of texture to keep you guessing with each bite. That's where the agrodolce comes in, a sweet-tangy syrup made with vinegar, raisins, and honey. The fresh za'atar, with pistachios, thyme, sumac, and lemon zest, adds the crunchy texture the dish needs.

SERVES 4

1 (2- to 2½-pound) winter squash (such as delicata, honeynut, kabocha, or red kuri)

4 shallots, skins left on

¼ cup extra-virgin olive oil, or as needed

Kosher salt

Freshly ground pepper

¾ cup red wine vinegar

¼ cup runny honey

3 tablespoons golden raisins

½ cup Pistachio Za'atar (page 42)

Preheat the oven to 425°F.

Halve the squash lengthwise (it'll be training wheels for splitting wood) and use a spoon to scoop out the seeds and any stringy bits. Cut each half into 3- to 4-inch pieces. Halve the shallots lengthwise through the root end.

On a rimmed baking sheet, toss together the squash, shallots, and olive oil. Season with salt and pepper and toss once more. Spread out the squash and shallots so they have some room to breathe and get that deep golden brown color underneath. (If they're on top of one another, they'll just steam.) Roast, flipping the squash and shallots after 20 minutes, and continue cooking until nicely browned and tender, 30 to 40 minutes total.

While the squash roasts, in a small saucepan over medium heat, combine the vinegar, honey, and raisins and bring to a simmer. Cook, stirring occasionally, until the raisins have plumped and the mixture has reduced to a syrup, 6 to 8 minutes. The syrup (aka agrodolce) should be thick enough to coat the back of a spoon but not so thick that it doesn't pour off easily.

Arrange the squash and shallots on a platter or large plate and spoon over the agrodulce. Sprinkle the pistachio za'atar on top and serve.

CRISPY MUSHROOMS WITH BUTTERY SOY AND RUNNY YOLKS

I can think of countless ways to celebrate *all* the mushrooms (minus portobellos), but I figured it's best to focus on the technique that will change the way you cook your mushrooms rather than tailor a recipe to any specific type. What I've learned over the years, working in restaurants and for magazines, is that people get confused by these fungi. I think it's because of their high water content, which makes them tricky to deal with when it comes to browning, plus the fact that they shrink and soak up so much oil when cooked. Should you add more oil? (Maybe a bit.) Do you need to add the mushrooms in batches? (Unnecessary.) *Just let them be.* Yes, they will soak up all the oil at first, but it'll soon release, along with their water and then the process of browning will begin. It takes some patience, but the reward is huge. And don't worry about the barely cooked egg yolk (salmonella usually resides on the shell, not inside the egg). Its richness takes the dish to full-blown indulgence.

SERVES 4

1½ pounds mixed mushrooms (I like shiitake, oyster, trumpet, and maitake; but if you find any freaky ones at the farmers' market, go for it)

¼ cup neutral oil (such as grapeseed), or as needed

Kosher salt

2 garlic cloves, crushed

3 tablespoons unsalted butter

2 tablespoons soy sauce or tamari

2 teaspoons sherry vinegar, or 1 lemon wedge to squeeze over

Freshly ground pepper

2 tablespoons finely chopped chives

1 or 2 egg yolks (from a happy chicken)

Using a kitchen towel, wipe off any dirt from the mushrooms. Give a slight trim to the tough stem ends, or to the base if it's a cluster. Tear or cut into large pieces. They don't need to be all the same size. Preferably they shouldn't be, so your finished dish will have a range of textures.

Set a large cast-iron or stainless-steel skillet over medium-high heat. Add the neutral oil and heat until it gets quite hot, almost smoking. Add the mushrooms (they will pile up), season lightly with salt, and give them a toss until all the oil is absorbed. At first, the mushrooms will steam as they release their water. Cook, without fussing, until the mushrooms have browned deeply underneath and have gotten wonderfully crispy around the edges, 3 to 4 minutes. Using tongs, give the mushrooms a toss or flip and cook until they are deliciously browned, tossing or flipping again, if needed, 7 to 9 minutes more. If the pan looks dry, add another 1 tablespoon oil.

Turn the heat to medium and add the garlic, butter, and soy sauce to the skillet. Let the butter melt and foam up (this will happen in seconds) and toss the mushrooms so they soak up the soy butter.

Slide the skillet off the heat and add the vinegar. Season with lots of pepper and give the mushrooms a toss once more. Taste and see if they need more salt (the soy will have reduced and concentrated, so likely not, but always good to check).

Transfer the mushrooms to a large plate and sprinkle with the chives. Gently nestle an egg yolk or two into the top of the mushrooms to finish the dish (they'll cook *juuuuust* a bit from the heat of the mushrooms) before serving.

GLOSSY BARBECUED EGGPLANT WITH PEANUT SALAD

Bondage. Leather. Eggplant. Those were the notes I made for myself about this recipe. Not exactly cryptic. When you grill eggplant, it looks like it's wrapped in a leathery, tight casing. There's something kinky about it. Or is it just me?

You'll notice that I am going to ask you to get up close and personal with your eggplant by making slits into its flesh. That's not only for a cool patterned effect. Eggplant is like a sponge and you want the flesh exposed so that the hot, sticky, vinegary glaze can sneak into all the spots and make the eggplant glisten under the spotlights.

SERVES 4

4 large Japanese eggplants (this is not a time for globe eggplants)

Kosher salt

⅓ cup runny honey

⅓ cup unseasoned rice vinegar

⅓ cup low-sodium soy sauce

3 tablespoons hot chile paste (such as sambal oelek)

2 tablespoons neutral oil (such as grapeseed)

½ small white or red onion, thinly sliced into rings

⅓ cup coarsely chopped cilantro

¼ cup toasted peanuts, with skins or without, or cashews (see page 24), coarsely chopped

1 lime, cut into wedges

Get your grill going to medium heat.

Starting at the base of each eggplant, halve lengthwise through the stem. Score the flesh in a ¼-inch crosshatch pattern with the tip of a paring knife. (It gives you more control than your chef's knife.)

Place the eggplants on a rimmed baking sheet and sprinkle 1 teaspoon salt onto the cut sides. Let the eggplants rest for 15 minutes, so they soak up the salt and release some of their water.

In a small skillet over medium-high heat, combine the honey, vinegar, soy sauce, and chile paste. Simmer and stir (it'll bubble) until reduced by half (just shy of syrupy), 5 to 7 minutes. Transfer this glaze to a small bowl to cool.

Blot the eggplants dry with a kitchen towel (or paper towel, if you must). It may not look like much water, but it'll make a difference when you're grilling the eggplants. Brush both sides of the eggplants with the neutral oil, then grab the glaze and head to the grill.

Grill the eggplant, cut-side down, until you see the skin beginning to develop a deep burnished color around the edges, about 4 minutes. Using tongs, turn the eggplants over and let the second side cook for 3 to 4 minutes. While the eggplants cook, using a pastry brush, coat the eggplants with some of the glaze (save some glaze for the finish). Squeeze the side of the eggplants with your tongs to check for doneness. They should be squishy and custardy. Turn the eggplants over one more time, so the glaze can caramelize, about 1 minute.

Transfer the eggplants to a platter and drizzle with some of the reserved glaze or serve it on the side. Scatter the onion, cilantro, and peanuts over the eggplants and squeeze a few lime wedges over the top. Serve with the remaining lime wedges on the side for squeezing.

THE MISUNDER-STOOD EGGPLANT

Some people hate eggplant. And, truthfully, eggplants don't taste like much. But I prize them for their meaty flesh and their ability to absorb flavor. At the height of their season (the hottest months of the year), eggplant can be squat and pear-shaped or quite long and phallic, almost snakelike, in shades of pink, purple, white, and a striped variety called graffiti. The rumor that you need to salt eggplant to rid it of any bitterness is false. Eggplant has been bred to omit bitterness. I still season it ahead of time to expel some water, which helps it absorb more flavor.

Craving Cardoons

When I first encountered cardoons in a restaurant kitchen, they looked like angry celery. They have these long, wide stalks covered in an ashy white web and prickly leaves. When you first see one, you would never think, *I could eat that.* And you should never try a *raw* cardoon—it would be super-astringent and unpleasant. Maybe these traits are the reason we just don't see cardoons often at the farmers' market, or at all in the grocery store. But I love them.

They're in the thistle family, a cousin to artichokes, and beloved in Italy. So it makes sense that Italian restaurants, like Via Carota in Greenwich Village, are the only places I've found them on menus, or off-menu (always worth an ask at Via Carota). Why? To eat them, you have to trim off nearly 40 percent before cooking. Once they're painstakingly prepared, their webby leaves removed and stalks shaved, the flavor is like a concentrated artichoke. Delicious. Unlike an artichoke, they have an even texture, like a celery stalk. They're perfect when lightly fried and served with a squeeze of lemon juice. If you see them on a menu, you must order them!

I wonder, are they really that good? Or do I love them because of their rarity, their specialness? I love serving cardoons because I get a chance to surprise people, and that makes me happy. (I think a lot of chefs feel this way; we love to boast about having cardoons on the menu.) When I find them at the market, maybe one week in fall, I take photos with one, as if it's a giant pumpkin or a furry alpaca. I have photos of myself holding bundles of cardoons. Yeah . . .

Maybe you can't find them. That's fine. This excitement isn't about the cardoons exclusively, but about the feeling of discovery, of newness, when you buy and cook something that you've never cooked before. Maybe that's a red carrot, or an ugly squash, or a long breakfast radish, or spicy dandelion greens. I was conflicted about; which vegetables to include in this book, thinking practically about what's readily available. If there isn't demand for high-maintenance cardoons, for example, markets aren't going to carry them, and farmers aren't going to grow them. Perhaps we should make a fuss over getting them. To me, it's about challenging the sameness of the way we eat, cook, and shop in this country.

Maybe you *can* find them. In that case, put on some gloves and trim 3 inches from the root end, as you would celery, then trim 1 inch from the top. Pull off all the leaves. Using a paring knife, trim the sides to remove the bristly spiky edges. Fill a large bowl with water and squeeze in the juice of 1 lemon. Take a damp kitchen towel and rub off the webby ashy exterior. Drop the cardoons in the lemony water to keep them from browning. Bring a large pot of salted water to a boil over high heat. Drop the stalks into the water and cook for at least 15 minutes. This is where the process gets annoying (ha). Fish out a stalk. Trim off an inch and taste it. It should be tender and not at all bitter. Return the stalk to the pot and keep cooking and tasting every 5 minutes until it's tender, but not mushy, and tastes delicious. (The smaller stalks cook faster.) Drizzle them with good olive oil and season with grated Parm, salt, pepper, and a squeeze of fresh lemon juice. See what I mean?

CARAMELIZED SWEET POTATOES WITH BROWNED BUTTER HARISSA

My Iranian family LOVED sweet potatoes the old-school Thanksgiving way: mashed with brown sugar, maple syrup, and butter and baked with a marshmallow topping. I hated it. Too many types of sweet flavors piled up on one another. Then I had a revelation as a teenager, when I made a beautifully roasted sweet potato with hot sauce and butter. Now it's hard for me not to eat them year-round. That's the idea behind this harissa brown butter—it's incredibly savory and just a bit spicy to counter the sweet potato's sweetness. Very few things in life are better than hazelnuts browning in butter, but you can use another nut (or seeds!) if you like.

You'll find the regular ol' (but consistent) jewel and garnet varieties of sweet potato at grocery stores. Both have a deeply orange and creamy flesh but keep your eye out for Japanese sweet potatoes, which have an almost fluffy interior.

SERVES 4

6 small to medium sweet potatoes

3 tablespoons neutral oil (such as grapeseed)

Kosher salt

½ lemon

1 cup full-fat Greek yogurt

1 tablespoon water (optional)

½ cup raw hazelnuts, coarsely chopped

¼ cup unsalted butter

1 tablespoon harissa paste

1 tablespoon runny honey

Flaky sea salt

Preheat the oven to 425°F.

Halve the sweet potatoes lengthwise and place them on a rimmed baking sheet. Drizzle the neutral oil all over and season with kosher salt. Give the sweet potatoes a toss until coated in the oil, then flip them so the cut side is facing down.

Roast the sweet potatoes until you can almost see a sticky ring around the edges, 25 to 30 minutes. It may take longer if your sweet potatoes are on the thick side.

Using a Microplane, finely grate the zest of the lemon half into a bowl and then squeeze the juice from it, catching any seeds with your other hand. Add the yogurt, season with kosher salt, and stir. If the yogurt you're using is on the thick side, stir in the water to reach your desired consistency.

When the sweet potatoes are almost done, put the hazelnuts and butter in a small skillet and place it over medium-low heat. Cook, stirring frequently, until the hazelnuts have become toasty and the butter begins to turn an amber brown, 4 to 6 minutes. Slide the pan off the heat and add the harissa and honey, stirring until the mixture looks speckly and smells fragrant, 20 seconds. Season the harissa butter with kosher salt.

Using a metal spatula, separate the sweet potatoes from the baking sheet (some may have stuck, but caramelized sugar is a good thing). Spread the yogurt sauce on a platter or plate and arrange the sweet potatoes on the sauce, cut-side up. Spoon over the harissa butter, sprinkle with plenty of flaky sea salt, and serve.

CHOOSING HARISSA

Harissa varies wildly from brand to brand. Some are much spicier than others or heavier on the tomato or red pepper or cumin. For these sweet potatoes, we need harissa *paste*, which comes in a tube (sold in a box) and is the most common form you'll find in North Africa, where harissa originates. The paste format is great for blooming—to wake things up!—which is what we do with the butter sauce. Harissa in a jar is more of a condiment for spooning over roasted fish or meats.

TANGY ROASTED BEETS WITH MINT AND SESAME SPRINKLE

When just picked, fresh beets smell like sweet dirt. I love that. They need to be gently cooked, so their natural sweetness begins to open up. Here, a splash of water added to the roasting pan creates a steam bath for the beets, concentrating their natural sugars while also preventing them from drying out. When they're done steam-roasting, the tough skins should come off like a slip dress. From my holey white T-shirt to my bare hands to the lemony yogurt, they'll stain anything they touch. So keep them separate if that bothers you, or let them be tie-dye. Don't worry, it'll wash off.

When the beets are cooked and still warm, I cut them into different shapes and toss them with vinegar right away so they soak it up. You're going for an almost pickled beet flavor. At this point, you can store them and use them throughout the week. (They're begging to be paired with something bright, rich, or bitter—think citrus, blue cheese, or bitter greens.) But it doesn't get more delicious, to me, than pairing these tangy beets with creamy yogurt and lots of sesame seeds and mint.

SERVES 4

2 pounds beets (between golf ball– and tennis ball–size)

1 lemon

¼ cup extra-virgin olive oil, plus more to finish

Kosher salt

3 tablespoons unseasoned rice vinegar, red wine vinegar, or white wine vinegar

2 tablespoons finely chopped mint

1 tablespoon toasted sesame seeds (see page 24)

1 cup full-fat Greek yogurt, labneh, or ricotta

Preheat the oven to 400°F.

Trim the beet tops, leaving about 1 inch left on. (I prefer to sauté the greens separately in olive oil and garlic.) Give the beets a scrub and toss them in a roasting pan with about an inch of water—they can sit snug among one another. Thinly slice half the lemon, removing the seeds, and add the slices to the water in the pan. Save the other lemon half for later.

Pour the olive oil over the beets and season with salt. Give the pan a shake, so the beets are nice and coated, then cover tightly with foil. Roast, giving the pan a shake halfway through, until the beets are tender, 50 to 60 minutes. You'll know they're done as you do with potatoes, when a paring knife slips in easily.

Remove the foil from the pan and let the beets cool. Using a kitchen towel, slip the skins off the beets. Cut the beets into wedges, rounds, obliques, or whatever makes you feel like Michelangelo. (I like big, graphic pieces.) Place the beets in a medium bowl and douse them with the vinegar. Season with a generous amount of salt and toss.

Using a Microplane, finely grate the zest of the reserved lemon half into a small bowl. Add the mint and sesame seeds to the bowl and mix with your fingers until the mixture isn't clumpy.

Put the yogurt in another small bowl along with a big pinch of salt. Squeeze the juice of the naked lemon half into the yogurt, catching any seeds with your other hand, and stir together.

Swoosh a spoonful of lemony yogurt on a plate and top with the beets. They'll immediately begin to wonderfully stain the yogurt. Scatter the minty sesame seeds on top and serve.

DO AHEAD

Beets can be roasted, peeled, and cut into pieces up to 1 week ahead. Store in an airtight container in the fridge.

ROASTED CARROTS WITH HOT GREEN TAHINI

Size matters. Especially when it comes to carrots. The peeled "baby" carrots sold in plastic bags should be avoided at all cost. For this recipe, we want them on the bigger side (but not the ones that look like they should be reserved for horses). Look for carrots with their green tops attached to ensure their freshness. I always leave the peel on for looks but also, hey, nutrients.

Like the others in the sweet, orange veg category, carrots can take a lot of heat, almost to the point of burning. And I like them that way. If you don't like charred and slightly smoky flavors, then cook them for less time. Roasting the carrots with the spices will allow you to skip toasting the spices separately, and give a crackling seedy texture. The carrots will get a nice chew but remain soft and almost creamy at the center, while the tip of the carrot gets extra crisp. The hot green tahini helps counter the carrots' sweet flavor and make for a creamy pool for the carrots to lay on top of.

SERVES 4

1 teaspoon coriander seeds

1 teaspoon cumin seeds

1½ pounds carrots, scrubbed

1 red onion, skin left on, cut into 1-inch-wide wedges

¼ cup extra-virgin olive oil

Kosher salt

1 cup Hot Green Tahini (page 48)

Preheat the oven to 450°F.

In a mortar and pestle, crush the coriander seeds and cumin seeds until they're coarsely ground, or use a spice mill or the bottom of a mug to do the job. Don't crush them finely because you want the spices to bring some texture to the carrots.

Halve the carrots lengthwise, then throw them and the onion onto a rimmed baking sheet and add the olive oil, coriander seeds, and cumin seeds. Season with salt and toss until everything is well dressed.

Roast the carrots, shaking the pan halfway through, until they have browned in spots and the ends are starting to get frilly, 20 to 25 minutes.

Spread some of the tahini on a platter or spoon it into a bowl to serve on the side. Arrange the carrots and onions on the platter and finish with a spoonful of oil from the baking sheet before serving.

DO AHEAD

While these are very good served hot, the carrots are quite delicious at room temperature and can be roasted 3 hours ahead.

CRISPED POTATOES WITH ROMESCO

One night at the dinner table, my boyfriend turned to me out of nowhere and said, "Eh, I don't need potatoes." As if he'd thought it over and decided, if he had to give up one vegetable, it would be the potato. I was appalled. I had some opinions forming about him (which I had kept to myself) and this just added to that. You see, I have never met a potato I didn't like. Thankfully, the comment wasn't prompted by a potato dish I had cooked, or we'd probably have ended things right then and there. But live without potatoes? Never.

The potatoes in this recipe go through a two-step cooking process: boiling and then roasting. Make the romesco while the potatoes cool after boiling. Boiling them first allows the outsides to get soft enough to then become very crisp in a hot oven. The result is out of this world, which, thankfully, isn't running out of potatoes anytime soon.

MAKES 4 SERVINGS

2 pounds golf ball–size baby Yukon gold potatoes

Kosher salt

⅓ cup extra-virgin olive oil

Crunchy Romesco (page 52)

Preheat the oven to 450°F.

Drop the potatoes in a medium pot and add water to cover by 2 inches, along with a handful of salt (about ¼ cup), and bring to a boil. Lower the heat to maintain a simmer and cook until the potatoes are just cooked through and easily pierced with a paring knife, 10 to 15 minutes (the time will vary depending on the size of your potatoes). Be careful not to overcook the potatoes or they will fall apart when smashed. Drain the potatoes and let cool in the pot.

Using your hands, smush the potatoes so that their skins start to tear and the flesh is slightly exposed. You can flatten them with the bottom of a coffee mug if you must but I'm into adult hot potato fun. Toss the potatoes on a rimmed baking sheet with the olive oil and season with salt.

Roast the potatoes, flipping after 15 to 20 minutes, until they are shatteringly crisp and golden brown, 35 to 40 minutes total. Transfer the potatoes to a platter, dot with the romesco, and serve with more romesco on the side.

DO AHEAD

You can boil the potatoes 1 day ahead and store them in the fridge. They are actually easier to crisp up when cold.

THE ALWAYS DEPENDABLE YUKON

More often than not, in North America, you're likely to encounter only a handful of potato varieties that have been found to be commercially successful in grocery stores, whereas in some countries, like Peru, potato varieties exist in the hundreds. (Yay, capitalism!) You have your russets, which are extremely starchy and ideal for frying. Next, you have your fingerlings and Red Bliss, which fall on the opposite side of the spectrum—waxy and ideal for boiling or roasting, where they can retain their shape. Yukon golds fall smack in the middle, making them ideal for developing a crisp, caramelized outside, while still having a buttery, fluffy inside.

BUTTERED POTATOES WITH SALTED LEMON

While it's hard to refuse a potato that has been crisped up in the oven or fried into perfect stackable fries, I want to reiterate that a tiny, thin-skinned, golden-fleshed potato getting boiled until the insides become so fluffy and creamy is a very good and very delicious thing. It also helps when butter gets involved. Here, preserved lemons add acidity to the potatoes while the salty brine seasons them. Since preserved lemons can vary on how salty they are, taste the potatoes before adding more salt to the finished dish.

SERVES 4

2 pounds small, waxy potatoes (such as peewees, fingerlings, or new potatoes)

1 preserved lemon, seeds removed, finely chopped, plus 2 tablespoons (or more) brine

½ cup unsalted butter, cut into pieces

1 small bunch chives, or 3 scallions, thinly sliced

1 cup coarsely chopped dill

Freshly ground pepper

Kosher salt

Place the potatoes in a large pot of salted water and bring to a boil. Cook until they are very tender and can be easily pierced with a paring knife, 10 to 15 minutes (the time will vary depending on the size of your potatoes). Drain and let cool for 10 minutes. Lightly crush the potatoes with your hands, or by pressing with the bottom of a small bowl, and transfer the potatoes to a serving bowl.

Add the preserved lemon, brine, and butter to the bowl. Toss until the butter has completely melted and the potatoes have soaked up the dressing and become extremely lemony. Add the chives, dill, and lots and lots of pepper. Give another toss. Taste a spoonful. It should be well seasoned and lemony. Adjust with more brine, salt, and/or pepper, if needed, and serve warm.

FEELING DAIRY-FREE?

Since we're working with butter, which sets at room temperature, this is best served warm. That being said (because I want you to live freely), you can swap out the butter for ⅓ cup extra-virgin olive oil and serve it at room temperature as a potato salad. It will become the favorite side dish for your summer gatherings.

FALL-APART CARAMELIZED CABBAGE SMOTHERED IN ANCHOVIES AND DILL

My love for cabbage runs deep, as deep as my love for Diana Ross's 1983 iconic Central Park concert in the rain (it's a YouTube must-watch). And yet, this recipe was never supposed to be in this book. I did a pop-up dinner one night and, at the last minute, decided to add this dish to round out the menu. The cabbage gets seared hard on the stove top before it goes into the oven to soften to an almost melty texture. While still warm, the cabbage is spooned with an intense garlic-anchovy sauce made with so much dill. The sauce drapes the cabbage and sneaks into its every layer. The dish ended up becoming my favorite one that night. The pistachio cake (see page 319) that I made for dessert was a close second. When you make this dish (not *if*), you'll be shocked that you might eat the whole thing in one sitting.

SERVES 4

1 head basic green or purple cabbage or fancy savoy

¾ cup extra-virgin olive oil

Kosher salt

4 oil-packed anchovies, drained and finely chopped

1 garlic clove, finely grated

1 cup coarsely chopped dill

½ cup toasted walnuts (see page 24), finely chopped

2 teaspoons finely grated lemon zest

1 tablespoon fresh lemon juice

Freshly ground pepper

Preheat the oven to 350°F.

Halve the cabbage through the core. Cut each half into three wedges, keeping the core intact.

Set a large cast-iron or stainless-steel skillet over medium-high heat. Add ¼ cup of the olive oil and heat until it is hot and shimmering. Season the cabbage with salt and then place it in the skillet. Cook, using tongs to press down on the cabbage, so it becomes deeply charred and kind of tender (it'll soften more in the oven), 3 to 5 minutes per side. If your skillet isn't large enough to brown all the pieces at once, do it in batches.

Remove the skillet from the heat and carefully cover it with aluminum foil (the pan will be hot!). Transfer the skillet to the oven and roast until the cabbage is very tender, 30 to 40 minutes. When it's ready, a paring knife should slide in and out of the cabbage core like butter.

While the cabbage is in the oven, in a medium bowl, stir together the anchovies, garlic, dill, walnuts, lemon zest, lemon juice, and remaining ½ cup olive oil. Season with salt and plenty of pepper. If you let it sit for 10 minutes, the flavors will soften and meld.

Once the cabbage is done, arrange the pieces on a platter and spoon the sauce all around and between the melty layers. Sprinkle with more pepper and serve.

CHOOSING CABBAGE

Green and purple cabbage are interchangeable here; they're both firm and dense, intensely crunchy, consistent when raw but even better grilled or roasted to death. And cheap! Love 'em. Napa cabbage has a longer ovular shape with a crunchy base and tender leafy tops; I like it for quick stir-fries, or torn up, massaged slightly, and eaten raw. It's juicy and light, not as dense as those other guys. Savoy is harder to find—it's the Cabbage Patch Doll cabbage—with dramatic beautiful leaves straight from a Caravaggio painting. I use it the same way as conventional cabbage, like in this caramelized cabbage recipe. It makes everything you cook worthy of a still-life painting.

184

LONG BEANS WITH CREAMY SESAME SAUCE

In the height of summer, you'll find me picking through the overflowing bean pile at the market. From the svelte haricots verts, which I rarely cook, as they're near-perfect raw, to the reliable green beans, which deserve a kiss of smoke, either blistered in a hot pan or charred on the grill until their once-snappy texture disappears. The wider, flatter Romano, or pole, beans are sturdier and beg to be braised until they're nearly falling apart. I always grab a few of each variety whenever I find them.

Here, the beans are simply boiled in what may seem like overly salted water. But trust me, they are only in this salty bath for a few minutes, which will deeply season them and bring out the vibrant green color we're after. Drag them through the creamy sesame sauce—which can be paired with nearly any vegetable: broccoli, carrots, cucumbers, steamed greens, or frozen spinach you forgot in the freezer until just now—and you'll experience them in an entirely new light.

SERVES 4

Kosher salt

1½ pounds green beans or Romano beans (ends trimmed if you feel like it)

¼ cup tahini

1 teaspoon finely grated lemon zest

3 tablespoons fresh lemon juice

2 tablespoons white miso

2 tablespoons extra-virgin olive oil

1 teaspoon runny honey

1 teaspoon peeled, finely grated ginger

1 teaspoon toasted sesame oil

2 to 3 tablespoons water

½ cup coarsely chopped cilantro

Freshly ground pepper

Bring a large pot of water to a boil and throw in two large handfuls of salt (about ½ cup). You want the water to be overly salty because this is truly the only chance for the beans to get seasoned deeply.

While the water comes to a boil, fill a large bowl with ice and add enough water so that the green beans will be submerged. Set the bowl close to the pot of boiling water.

Drop the beans into the boiling water and cook until they are bright green and tender, 3 to 5 minutes, depending on how thick your beans are. I prefer them on the soft side but not limp. If you like them still a tad crunchy, cook for only 4 minutes. Using tongs or a slotted spoon, transfer the green beans to the ice bath and let them chill out for 10 seconds, which will stop them from continuing to cook and turning to mush.

Drain the beans and lay them out on a clean kitchen towel. You want to get them as dry as possible, so they don't carry water that dilutes the dressing.

In a small bowl, whisk the tahini, lemon zest, lemon juice, miso, olive oil, honey, ginger, sesame oil, and 2 tablespoons of the water until smooth. If the sauce is stiff, stir in the remaining 1 tablespoon water to loosen. Taste for salt; you may need to add just a pinch.

Spoon some of the sauce on a platter. Place the beans onto the sauce and top with more. Scatter the cilantro over, finish with pepper, and serve.

CHARRED BRUSSELS SPROUTS WITH CREAMY NUOC CHAM

A moment of silence for all who have consumed overcooked, boiled, or steamed brussels sprouts. Truthfully, I think the tiniest member of the cabbage family didn't enter my life until I was an adult in New York and every restaurant seemed to fetishize deep-fried brussels sprouts. The key to getting these sprouts perfectly crispy without overcooking them (or buying a deep fryer) is to bake them on the bottom rack of a very hot oven. Then you take them to the point of utter deliciousness (a place worth going) by dousing them with a cashew sauce spiked with fish sauce.

SERVES 4

1½ pounds brussels sprouts

¼ cup neutral oil
(such as grapeseed)

Kosher salt

Creamy Nuoc Cham (page 57)

½ cup coarsely chopped cilantro

Place an oven rack in the bottom position and preheat the oven to 450°F.

Trim and discard the stem end from each sprout. Halve each sprout lengthwise and place on a rimmed baking sheet. If you find some sprouts to be on the small side, leave them whole so all will cook evenly. Toss with the neutral oil and season with salt. Spread out the sprouts and flip them so that the cut side is facing down.

Roast the sprouts until the tops have puffed slightly and become crisp and deeply brown underneath, 25 to 30 minutes.

Remove the sprouts from the oven and transfer to a large bowl. Pour a few large spoonfuls of the nuoc cham over and give it a lazy toss. Sprinkle with the cilantro before serving. Some bites will be more crunchy and others will be more sauced. Keeps your mouth guessing.

PERFECT CAULIFLOWER WITH SPICY COCONUT CRISP

I wish you could press a button on this page and hear the sound effects of how I feel about this recipe. This cauliflower is THAT GOOD. You cut slabs of cauliflower into, yes, cauliflower *steaks*, before snapping off the florets. The technique serves a purpose: the flattened sides of the cauliflower get caramelized all over, whereas it only browns in spots when you keep the stalk round. After the steaks are roasted, you break them into pieces so they're more practical for the home cook but still manage to get that high-priced vegetarian main-course effect seen in restaurants. Aesthetically, I like it, too. Remember to collect any crumbly bits, cores, and leafy parts, which add dimension and different textures to the finished dish. To bring the caramelized cauliflower back to life after roasting, it gets a sprinkling of toasted, spicy crunchy coconut with plenty of lime zest and juice to seduce you. Or whoever you're cooking for.

SERVES 4

1 head cauliflower or romanesco (keep any green leaves or stems that come with it)

⅓ cup melted coconut oil or extra-virgin olive oil

2 garlic cloves, finely grated

½ teaspoon ground turmeric

Kosher salt

SPICY COCONUT CRISP

2 tablespoons melted coconut oil or extra-virgin olive oil

2 serrano or jalapeño chiles, thinly sliced

1 cup unsweetened coconut flakes

1 teaspoon finely grated lime zest

Kosher salt

½ cup coarsely chopped cilantro (leaves, stems, and all)

2 limes, cut into wedges

Place an oven rack in the bottom position and preheat the oven to 450°F.

If the outer leaves of the cauliflower look fresh and not brown, pull them off and give them a coarse chop. Trim the bottom core of the cauliflower so it can stand on its stem. Cut the cauliflower into 1-inch-thick slabs (you'll probably get four or five pieces), then snap off the florets from the slabs.

In a large bowl, combine the ⅓ cup coconut oil, garlic, and turmeric and stir to mix. Throw in the cauliflower pieces and leaves, season with salt, and then toss with a large metal spoon or rubber spatula. (Skip using your hands this time to avoid turmeric stains.)

Spread the cauliflower on a rimmed baking sheet and roast, flipping the pieces after the first 15 minutes, until deeply golden brown on both sides, 25 to 30 minutes total.

To make the coconut crisp: When the cauliflower is almost ready, in a small skillet over medium heat, combine the coconut oil, chiles, and coconut flakes. Cook, stirring occasionally, until the coconut flakes are golden brown in most spots and smell sweet, 2 to 4 minutes. Remove the skillet from the heat and stir in the lime zest. Season with salt and stir again.

Transfer the cauliflower to a platter and crumble the coconut crisp over it. Scatter the cilantro on top and squeeze the juice from a few lime wedges over. Serve with the remaining lime wedges on the side for squeezing.

CHOOSING COCONUT FLAKES

Always buy unsweetened coconut so you can control the sweetness. (We associate coconut's flavor with sweetness, but that comes from its aroma, not its actual flavor.) I buy flakes or shreds, depending on my mood. The big flakes are graphic and cool, but everything goes faster with shreds—from toasting to incorporating into a dish. Once you open the package, keep it in the fridge to preserve freshness.

BROCCOLINI WITH WARM ANCHOVY DRESSING

Hear me out on steaming broccolini/broccoli: Hard-roasted broccoli can get stringy, fibrous, and hard to eat. I want broccoli as bright green as the Jolly Green Giant. Steaming not only cooks broccoli fast (remember that steam is hotter than boiling water), but it also softens the broccoli, giving it the ability to soak up flavor, like this dressing with a ton of anchovies, parsley, and whole-grain mustard. This dish is, basically, a better version of the side of broccolini you'd get at an Italian restaurant. The warm anchovy-mustard-parsley situation would also work very well with other leafy green veg, like broccoli rabe, mustard greens, and Tuscan or curly kale. (Note that those greens are less dense than broccoli and will soak up more water during cooking, so squeeze out the water after they've taken a bath.)

SERVES 4

2 bunches broccolini, or 2 heads broccoli

Kosher salt

⅓ cup extra-virgin olive oil

1 large shallot, thinly sliced into rings

5 oil-packed anchovies, drained

4 garlic cloves, thinly sliced

1 fresh red chile, thinly sliced

⅓ cup coarsely chopped parsley

2 teaspoons grainy mustard

Freshly ground pepper

Lemon wedges for squeezing

Prep your broccolini by trimming off 1 inch from the stems to get rid of the woody ends. If the stalks are on the thick side, halve them lengthwise. If you're using broccoli, trim the ends and peel off the leathery outer layer of the broccoli stems to reveal the more tender inside. Cut the broccoli into 5-inch-ish-long spears (like you're faking broccolini).

Fill a large heavy pot fitted with a steamer basket with 2 inches of water and bring to a boil. Add the broccolini and season with salt. Cover the pot and steam the broccolini until bright green and crisp-tender, 3 to 4 minutes. Using tongs, transfer the broccolini to a platter or plate.

In a small saucepan over medium heat, combine the olive oil, shallot, anchovies, and garlic. Cook, stirring occasionally, until the shallot and garlic are beginning to crisp up and the anchovies have disintegrated, 7 to 9 minutes. Turn off the heat and stir in the chile, parsley, and mustard, which may pop and sizzle. Season with salt and pepper.

Spoon the warm dressing over the broccolini and squeeze some lemon juice over the top, leaving the other wedges for your guests.

DO AHEAD

The broccolini can be cooked and dressed a few hours ahead, then kept loosely covered at room temperature.

PERFECTLY ROASTED BROCCOLI/SO, YOU'RE NOT INTO STEAMED BROCCOLI

Preheat the oven to 425°F. On a rimmed baking sheet, toss the broccolini or broccoli with 3 tablespoons extra-virgin olive oil. Season with salt, making sure everything is evenly coated. Roast, tossing after 10 minutes, until lightly charred on the stems and florets, 15 to 20 minutes total. Proceed as directed.

CRISPY ROASTED ARTICHOKES

This recipe is loosely inspired by a great Italian dish called carciofi alla giudia, in which artichokes get deep-fried in olive oil until they resemble the dried flowers that my sister used to hang on her walls. I wanted to have crispy artichokes while skipping the deep-frying (a New York studio apartment and a pot of hot oil never will seem like a good idea to me). There is some prep involved when dealing with artichokes, which may sound annoying, but once you've done that (I've got you—see the following), it's a matter of oven-steaming the artichokes until they're tender, then tossing them in oil and blasting in the oven until their leaves are as crispy as potato chips. And if that isn't delicious enough, dredge each bite in a spoonful of doctored-up Parmesan mayonnaise.

SERVES 4

4 large artichokes

4 garlic cloves, unpeeled

¼ cup extra-virgin olive oil

4 thyme sprigs

Kosher salt

⅔ cup mayonnaise

½ cup finely grated Parmesan

2 tablespoons finely chopped parsley or basil

1 tablespoon Dijon mustard

2 teaspoons finely grated lemon zest

1 tablespoon fresh lemon juice

Freshly ground pepper

Lemon wedges, for squeezing

Place an oven rack in the bottom position and preheat the oven to 425°F.

Working with one artichoke at a time, cut 1 inch from the top of the leaves and ½ inch from the stem. Pluck off the hard green leaves until you get to the pale-golden inner leaves (the tender ones that feel like tulip petals). The stem is a little tough, like a broccoli stem, so remove its outer layer with a vegetable peeler; shave it like a carrot. Split the artichoke in half lengthwise and you'll notice the heart at the base of the artichoke, which is the almost-white part, and a deep magenta-fuchsia "choke," which is those spiky bits. Take a spoon and go right above where the heart is and scoop out the bristly purple choke.

Arrange the artichokes in a roasting pan, cut-side down, and throw in the garlic. Pour in 1½ to 2 cups water (just enough to come ½ inch up the sides of the artichokes). Tightly cover the pan with aluminum foil, so the artichokes get a nice steam bath.

Bake the artichokes until a paring knife slides easily through the center, 15 to 20 minutes. Remove the roasting pan from the oven and crank up the temperature to 500°F (or as high as your oven goes). Slip off the foil, carefully pour out any excess water, and set aside the steamed garlic cloves, leaving the artichokes in the pan.

Pour the olive oil over the artichokes and add the thyme. Season with salt and toss gently, so the artichokes are coated in oil. Flip the artichokes so the cut side is facing down again. Roast, uncovered, flipping the artichokes after 10 minutes, until the bottoms are deeply browned and crisp and the tops are golden, 10 to 15 minutes total.

While the artichokes crisp, squeeze the reserved garlic cloves from the skins into a small bowl. Add the mayonnaise, Parmesan, parsley, mustard, lemon zest, and lemon juice. Season with salt and pepper and stir. Dip in your pinkie and taste. You're excited, right?

Arrange the artichokes in a shallow bowl and serve with the garlic mayonnaise and lemon wedges.

GRAINS, PASTAS, CHEAP HAPPINESS

198

The grains and pasta recipes here aren't filler, and they aren't sides. They're dinner.

Lately, my diet has leaned more vegetable and grain heavy than meat based, so these dishes take center stage. Most recipes in this chapter are quick and easy enough for weeknights, like the creamy Chickpea Cacio e Pepe with Caramelized Lemon (page 226), my current default pasta. I became more confident cooking pasta while working in restaurants and test kitchens, and I'll teach you my secrets (see page 210). (And it's not just butter. Well, there is *some* butter.) Though I don't think pretending to be Italian helped make me any better at tomato sauce. Or, did it?

For a healthful moment, make the farro bowl with melty zucchini on page 209. It only gets better as it sits. We'll take a deep dive into the ritual that is Persian rice on page 202 and how to achieve tahdig, the burnt bottom crust of the rice. If you crave a project—and dairy—go straight to the ricotta dumplings on page 222, which aren't technically a grain but a pasta cousin, and I absolutely had to include them. Those little pillows . . . oh my god. Where to begin? Make them when you want to impress someone—or yourself.

BUTTERY NORI-SPECKLED RICE

My goal here is to show you how to make a perfect pot of rice—something that's simple for some cooks, and a source of kitchen insecurity for others. An ingredient as ancient as rice needs extra care and patience to reveal how special and delicious it can be. If you love your rice cooker, great, but I do believe knowing how to cook rice in the ol' pot is an essential skill to have (sorry for the peer pressure).

This rice will be perfect on its own, a little sticky and nutty, and if that's how you want to enjoy it, then leave it be. But I couldn't help myself from giving it something more in the form of nori and butter. The nori blooms in the butter and creates this vibrant deep-sea green while extracting the salty flavor of the nori into the fat. As you fold it into the rice, you'll see how each grain gets coated in the speckled butter, and then you're ready to dive in.

SERVES 4

1½ cups short-grain rice

1 sheet toasted nori

¼ cup unsalted butter

1 teaspoon flaky sea salt

Put the rice in a medium bowl and fill with lukewarm water. Run your fingers through the rice, gently swooshing the grains around to loosen the starch. The water will quickly become murky. Dump out as much water as you can and repeat until the water runs slightly more clear (another three or four rinses). Drain well because you don't want any excess water going into the pot, which will cause mushy rice. Don't want that.

Transfer the rice to a small to medium saucepan (with a diameter no wider than 8 inches) that has a tight-fitting lid. Pour in 1¾ cups fresh cold water and bring to a boil over medium-high heat. Give the rice a stir to help keep it from sticking to the bottom of the pan. As soon as you see a bubble or two, give the rice one more stir, then cover the pan and turn the heat to low. Cook until the water has evaporated and the rice is tender, 16 to 18 minutes. You have to trust me on this and not lift the pot lid to peek, please. I'll know if you do. Remove the pot from the heat and let it sit (leave that lid on tightly!) for 10 minutes, so the grains can absorb any excess water.

While the rice rests, tear the nori sheet into small-enough pieces to fit in a spice mill or blender. Finely grind the nori until it becomes a powder. Set aside.

Set your smallest skillet or saucepan over medium heat and add the butter. Once the butter is completely melted and beginning to foam, turn off the heat and sprinkle in the nori powder. Stir so the nori blooms and stains the butter.

Fluff the rice with a fork, pour in the nori butter, and stir gently until each grain is coated. Then put the lid back on for 5 minutes. (Trust!) Uncover, sprinkle with salt, and stir before serving. Every bite will be delicious, but the occasional bite with flaky salt will make you lose your mind.

KODA FARMS

I wouldn't say I'm a brand loyalist to that many food products (that's reserved for my skincare routine). Koda Farms, however, is one brand that will be in my life forever. It's one of the oldest rice farms in California. I swear by their Kokuho Rose, an heirloom Japanese rice variety that is incredibly toothsome, with an almost sweet finish.

CHELO BA TAHDIG

This is, by far, the longest recipe in this book, even though the ingredient list is quite short. My goal is to guide you to make this dish with each grain separate, magnificently fluffy, and gorgeously stained from the saffron. And, yes, there is the tahdig, the scorched crispy rice on the bottom, a prize I still fight my dad for.

What I hope you also take away from this recipe is a deeper understanding and respect for the traditions of Iranian culture and the ritual of making Persian rice. To feel the sensations behind the lines of the recipe. To take your time to run your hands through the grains. To watch the saffron transform the water into a color only nature can make. And to smell the rice as it soaks in the water, as you boil it, after it has been steamed, and again when the bottom has formed that caramelized crust.

Chelo means "plain steamed rice" in Farsi, whereas *polos* are rice dishes with other ingredients folded in, like pilafs—I included a few variations of these.

If there's one piece of equipment you'll see in every Persian household, it's a nonstick pot. Although I almost never use nonstick cookware, for this recipe, it's essential. It makes life easy when you want to serve the rice on a platter, or flip and invert it for easy release. Trust me and pay the money to invest in that peace of mind.

SERVES 4 TO 6

3 cups basmati rice

Kosher salt

1 large pinch saffron threads
(a heaping ½ teaspoon)

3 tablespoons hot water

¼ cup neutral oil
(such as grapeseed)

3 tablespoons full-fat plain yogurt

3 tablespoons unsalted butter,
cut into pieces

Place the rice in a large bowl and add lukewarm water to cover by 1 inch. Submerge your hand in the bowl and get intimate with your rice, agitating the grains until the water becomes cloudy. Tip out as much water as you can into the sink without letting any grains escape. Refill the bowl with water and repeat three more times, until the water is almost clear.

Cover the rice again with water and sprinkle in 2 teaspoons salt. Soak the rice for at least 20 minutes or up to 2 hours. This step will begin to hydrate the grains, which will shorten the cooking time but also help the grains keep their shape during cooking.

Grab a medium nonstick pot with a tight-fitting lid. Fill the pot three-fourths full of water (about 3 quarts) and place it over high heat. Bring to a boil and season the water with ¼ cup salt. You want that water very salty because the grains will soak up the seasoned water more while cooking than during soaking.

When the water boils, turn the rice into a colander to drain, and then add it to the pot. Grab a wooden spoon and give the rice a few stirs for the first minute of cooking to prevent it from sticking to the bottom of the pot.

You'll notice the water will stop boiling when you add the rice. Wait and watch until the water begins to boil again. This can take as few as 3 minutes or as many as 6 minutes. Once the rice comes back to a boil, the grains will have nearly doubled in size. These are the indicators that the rice is now al dente (which is what you want) and ready to be drained.

Working quickly, drain the rice in a colander and rinse it with cold water, shaking the colander so the rice gets cooled evenly and to prevent it from overcooking. Set your parboiled rice and pot aside while you get things going for the tahdig.

Place the saffron threads in a mortar and pestle with a tiny pinch of salt. The salt will help break down the saffron into a powder. Use the pestle to crush the saffron until you have fine flecks of saffron. Transfer to a small bowl, pour the hot water over the saffron, and let it steep for 1 minute.

In a medium bowl, whisk together the neutral oil, yogurt, and 1 tablespoon of the saffron water. Scoop out about 1 cup of the rice and scatter it over the saffron yogurt. Use a spoon to gently toss the rice until every grain is coated. Grab your nonstick pot again and spread the saffron-yogurt rice on the bottom of the pot into one, even layer.

Using a wooden spoon, gradually pile the remaining plain rice on top of the yogurt rice, so it forms a mound like the shape of a mountain. This gives the rice room to expand while steaming. Using the end of the wooden spoon handle, poke six holes in the rice (without hitting the bottom of the pot), to allow the steam to rise to the top.

Cook the rice over medium-high heat, covered, until you start to hear a sizzle, 6 to 8 minutes. That's how you know the tahdig is starting to form. Turn the heat to medium-low and continue to steam the rice, covered, until it is fluffy and fragrant, 30 to 35 minutes. Turn off the heat and slide the pot off the burner.

Uncover the pot, add the butter, and drizzle in the remaining 2 tablespoons saffron water. Using the wooden spoon, gently mix and fluff the rice, melting the butter and allowing the saffron water to stain all the grains, without disturbing the bottom layer. Place the lid back on the pot and set it aside to cool for 5 minutes. This step ensures that the tahdig releases easily from the bottom of the pot.

Now you have two options: First, you could place a large plate or platter over the pot. With confidence and gratitude, invert the pot. The rice should—it will!—plop out in one piece, like a cake, revealing the tahdig. If you're too nervous to flip and invert the pot (this is a safe space here), go with the second option. Just transfer the rice to a platter without disrupting the tahdig. Then, using your wooden spoon, break the tahdig from the bottom of the pot in large pieces and arrange it on top of the rice or on the side.

CONTINUED

CHELO BA TAHDIG, CONTINUED

MORE TAHDIG AND RICE ADVENTURES

There are endless customizations, and here are several special ones.

Bread Tahdig: Tear 1 large piece, or multiple pieces, of lavash until you have enough to cover the bottom of the pot. Pour ¼ cup neutral oil into the pot, along with 1 tablespoon of the saffron water. Arrange the lavash on the bottom of the pot, making sure no pieces overlap. Place the parboiled rice on top and continue with the recipe.

Lettuce Tahdig: Tear 4 to 6 pieces of the dark green leaves from a head of romaine lettuce. Pour ¼ cup neutral oil into the pot, along with 1 tablespoon of the saffron water. Arrange the lettuce leaves on the bottom of the pot, making sure no pieces overlap. Place the parboiled rice on top and continue with the recipe. (This is my favorite.)

Morasa Polo (Jeweled Rice): In a large skillet over medium heat, melt ¼ cup unsalted butter with 1 tablespoon neutral oil. Add 1 large onion (diced) and cook until very soft and golden brown. Stir in ⅔ cup mixed chopped dried fruit (raisins, currants, cherries, and apricots are my go-tos) and ⅔ cup chopped toasted nuts (pistachios and almonds work best). Toss the parboiled rice with the fruit and nuts. Proceed to steam.

Sabzi Polo (Herbed Rice): Toss the parboiled rice with 2 cups finely chopped herbs (a mix of parsley, dill, and cilantro is my preference) and 1 bunch scallions, thinly sliced. Proceed to steam.

FARRO WITH MELTY ZUCCHINI AND SUMAC

This salad works with any grain, so use your favorite, speltheads. Barley boys. Freekeh freaks. I cook them all the same way, like I cook pasta: Fill a big pot with water, bring it to a boil and salt it, then drop in the grains and cook until they're as plumped and chewy as you desire. But remember that, like dried beans, the grains soak up flavor as they cook, so flavor that water as you see fit. Throw in a garlic head, a lemon peel, an onion, a few glugs of olive oil. It's only going to make it more delicious. Nicely seasoned water is a good start.

To go with the grains, I went with a mostly tasteless, watery, somewhat seedy, rarely attractive vegetable: zucchini. I don't *hate* it; I just think we can all agree no one gets very excited for zucchini. With this treatment, however, I learned to kind of, maybe, sort of, love it. Like other vegetables with high water content, you want to get that water out, so they can take on some color (and flavor). But beyond that, I did something you're often told never to do with zucchini: overcook it. It'll break down and start to almost tear and get jammy and a little sweet, while it bathes in garlic sizzled in olive oil.

SERVES 4

Kosher salt

1½ cups farro or spelt

5 garlic cloves, thinly sliced

½ cup extra-virgin olive oil

3 zucchini or other summer squash, any color, thinly sliced

1 teaspoon mild chile flakes (such as Aleppo), plus more for sprinkling

1 cup green olives (such as Castelvetrano),

½ small red onion, thinly sliced

¼ cup red wine vinegar

2 teaspoons ground sumac, plus more for sprinkling

1 teaspoon finely grated lemon zest

Freshly ground pepper

2 cups coarsely chopped mixed herbs (such as basil, mint, parsley, and/or tarragon)

Bring a large pot of water to a boil and throw in a handful of salt (about ¼ cup). Add the farro and boil, skimming off any foam that may rise to the top, until the grains are al dente, 25 to 35 minutes, but do take a spoonful and taste a few before pulling the pot off the heat. That is the true way to know when the farro is ready.

While the farro boils, in a large skillet over medium heat, combine the garlic and ¼ cup of the olive oil. Cook the garlic, stirring occasionally, until just barely golden brown around the edges, about 2 minutes. Add the zucchini, season with salt, and cook, tossing and stirring occasionally, until the zucchini begins to break down. The pan may feel overcrowded at first, but the zucchini will release its water and start to shrink. Once you notice the zucchini begin to stick to the skillet, continue to cook, stirring occasionally, until it becomes very soft and almost jammy, 12 to 15 minutes total. Remove the skillet from the heat, sprinkle in the chile flakes, and toss to distribute evenly.

Using the side of a chef's knife or the bottom of a mug, crush the olives to break them into large craggy pieces. Toss out the pits. Put the olives in a large bowl and add the onion, vinegar, sumac, and lemon zest. Season with salt and pepper and toss to combine. If you can spare 5 minutes, let the mixture sit so the onion slightly pickles and mellows out.

Add the farro to the olives, along with the remaining ¼ cup olive oil. Season with salt and pepper and toss to coat and combine. Taste a spoonful; it should be pretty tasty at this point. Add the zucchini and herbs and toss once more. Sprinkle with more sumac or chile flakes to finish.

DO AHEAD

The grains can be cooked 3 days ahead. Let them cool to room temperature, then cover and refrigerate. The salad (without the herbs) can be made 2 days ahead and refrigerated. Assemble just before serving.

PASTA LESSONS

Salting

Everybody tells you that your pasta water should taste like the ocean. Well, I think it shouldn't. Don't get me wrong—it should be salty. That salt will season your otherwise flavorless pasta. But you don't want pasta water so salty that a splash of it in your sauce ruins it. So fill a pot with water, and when it boils, toss in a small handful of kosher salt, about ¼ cup for every 4 quarts of water. (You add it when the water boils to keep the salt from causing pockmarks on the bottom of your pan as it heats. Look it up.)

Fresh versus Dried

Some people want their pasta so al dente it's crunchy. I want "bite," and you can only get that from dried pasta—fresh is too delicate and silky. When you're cooking dried pasta, take the timing on the box as a suggestion. If it says 8 to 10 minutes, I start checking the noodles at the 6-minute mark and recheck every minute after that until it's just right. For pasta that will keep cooking in a sauce, I want it not-quite-ready; maybe I'll even see a white speck of raw pasta when I bite off a piece of bucatini. For pasta that's getting tossed with pesto or carbonara, it needs to be ready to go since you're assembling the pasta with those sauces off the heat. Depending on the shape, some dried pastas can take 15 to 16 minutes, but fresh pasta will be ready in 1 to 3 minutes (so fast). For fresh pasta, rich with egg yolks, keep the toppings minimal. Mascarpone and lemon zest, butter and mushrooms, or, if you're Martha Stewart, truffles.

Avoiding Stickage

This isn't about what you do after you've drained your pasta, it's about what you do before. First, you need enough water in the pot for the pasta to dance and flow and feel itself. When you drop the pasta in, stir it, so it doesn't stick to the bottom, and then stir it another three or four times while it cooks. It's not rice; it'll be fine if you mess with it. Smaller shapes are more likely to get stuck at the bottom, so get your wooden spoon in there and rescue them.

A Good Sauce Always Includes Pasta Water

Some of the greatest restaurants in the world have a vat of starchy liquid that's like the mother pasta water pot; chefs add ladlefuls to their sauce to bind it with the slippery noodles. And it's just as essential at home. Pasta water allows the pasta and sauce to properly become one. Otherwise, you have two separate entities. There is no pasta dish I've made that doesn't require pasta water. Even if the sauce is pesto or carbonara, the pasta water helps emulsify the sauce so it will cling to the noodles. Scoop out the water with a glass measuring cup a few minutes before the pasta's ready, so you don't pour all your pasta water down the sink when you drain your pasta. I almost always save 1½ cups of water, knowing I'll rarely use that much, but I want to feel sure I'll have enough.

But If You Accidentally Threw Out the Pasta Water

Use 1 cup of hot water with a teaspoon of salt stirred in and hope the starch on the noodles helps your imposter pasta water emulsify and get the job done.

This Is a Two-Pot Operation

You'll have your pasta boiling in one big pot, but the second pot, for sauce, needs to be able to hold the pasta too. So get out a Dutch oven or another pot big enough for the amount of pasta you're cooking—usually a pound, right? Don't try it in a skillet, you'll have sauce all over the stove top, and the only person you can blame is yourself.

Finish with Butter

This is absolutely why restaurant pasta is so good. And it's only a tablespoon or three, not half a stick! The milkfat in the butter helps emulsify the sauce; it also gives the pasta a glossy finish. And if other things in the sauce are intense—spicy garlic or assertive tomato or grassy olive oil—a tiny smidge of butter tones things down, so the ingredients mellow out. I have a not-so-traditional habit of adding a knob of butter to pesto when that raw, robust, in-your-face sauce needs to be taken down just a notch. Add the butter 1 tablespoon at a time, and make sure it's cold so it doesn't separate.

COLD SOBA
WITH LEMONY
PEANUT AND
CRUNCHY VEG

On the hottest days of the year, I find myself having intense cravings for something cold and slippery, fresh and crunchy. I want nothing more than cold soba. It is, perhaps, the only noodle I can think of that actually tastes better to me cold than hot. It has a distinctly nutty flavor, and its slightly rough texture makes sauce stick to it like Velcro.

My craving is less of a noodle need and more of a noodle salad-y yearning, with an ideal ratio of noodle-to-crunchy veg of 50:50, but I'll let you choose how much you'd like to add. I tend to favor superbly crunchy, watery vegetables, such as bean sprouts, celery, cucumbers, and radishes. The sauce is a riff on a peanut sauce, but more spicy and vinegary, without being *too* creamy.

SERVES 4

⅓ cup peanut butter, cashew butter, or tahini

3 tablespoons soy sauce

2 tablespoons black vinegar or unseasoned rice vinegar

2 teaspoons finely grated lemon zest

1 tablespoon fresh lemon juice, or as needed

2 teaspoons peeled, finely grated ginger

2 teaspoons granulated sugar

2 teaspoons toasted sesame oil

Kosher salt

14 ounces dried soba noodles

Thinly sliced scallions for serving

Sliced cucumber for serving

Cilantro sprigs, with as much stem as possible, for serving

Sliced fresh chiles for serving

Crushed toasted peanuts or cashews (see page 24) and/or sesame seeds for serving

Bring a large pot of water to a boil. While you're waiting, in a medium bowl, combine the peanut butter, soy sauce, vinegar, lemon zest, lemon juice, ginger, sugar, sesame oil, and salt to taste and whisk until a smooth sauce forms.

When your water boils, drop the noodles into the pot, give them a stir, and cook until barely tender, about 5 minutes (refer to the package directions just to be sure). Drain and rinse under cold water to stop them from cooking. Drain again.

Divide the noodles among four bowls and spoon the sauce on top. Scatter each serving with scallions, cucumber, cilantro, chile, and crushed nuts and serve.

BIG SHELLS WITH SPICY LAMB SAUSAGE AND PISTACHIOS

If shells make you think of ricotta-stuffed, tomato sauce–coated, baked pasta, I feel that. My aunt made a mean version of it. I haven't had those stuffed shells in decades, but I miss the giant shell pasta shape. So let's use them to make a less labor-intensive pasta and BRING BACK jumbo shells. Here, lamb sausage browns and makes its way into the pockets of the shells, so every bite is an adventure. The bitter broccoli rabe cuts through the sausage party, while raw—not toasted—pistachios bring a buttery, fresh crunch. This is one of those sauces that tastes like it's been cooking for much longer than it has been; it's sneaky like that.

SERVES 6

Kosher salt

1 bunch broccoli rabe

3 tablespoons extra-virgin olive oil

1 pound spicy lamb or hot Italian pork sausage, casings removed

1 pound jumbo shells or paccheri

4 garlic cloves, thinly sliced

Freshly ground pepper

2 tablespoons unsalted butter, cut into pieces

1 teaspoon finely grated lemon zest

2 tablespoons fresh lemon juice

⅓ raw pistachios, coarsely chopped

Finely grated Parmesan for serving

Bring a large pot of water to a boil, then throw in about ¼ cup salt.

Trim the thick stems from the broccoli rabe and reserve for another use (a stir-fry!). We want the leafy greens and tender stems only, not the intense crunch from the thicker parts. Run your chef's knife through the greens and stems two or three times to give them a very coarse chop. Set aside.

In a large heavy pot over medium-high heat, warm the olive oil. Using your hands, grab small clumps of the sausage (you're going for rustic meatballs, about the size of a golf ball) and add to the pot. Cook, casually turning each piece as it becomes crusty, until deeply golden brown all over, 3 to 4 minutes.

Using a slotted spoon, transfer the sausage to a plate, leaving behind all that good lamb fat. Remove the pot from the heat (we'll come back to that later). If it looks like the sausage has given off a lot of fat, tip some of the fat into a bowl, so you're left with about 2 tablespoons in the pot. Save the rest for another use (like fried eggs).

Meanwhile, drop the pasta into the boiling water and give it a couple of stirs. Cook, stirring occasionally, until the pasta is just shy of al dente, about 1 minute *less* than the package suggests (it'll finish cooking in the sauce). Scoop out 1½ cups pasta water and then drain the pasta.

Return the pot with the lamb fat to the stove top over medium-low heat and add the garlic. Cook, scraping any browned bits stuck to the pot and stirring, so the garlic cooks evenly, until the garlic has softened slightly, about 2 minutes. Add the broccoli rabe, season with salt and pepper, and continue cooking, stirring, until the greens have wilted and are bright green, 3 to 5 minutes. Add the sausage to the pot along with any juices that have collected on the plate. Using a wooden spoon, smush the sausage to break into smaller, but still coarse, pieces.

214

Add the pasta and butter to the pot, along with ¾ cup pasta water. Cook, tossing often and adding more pasta water a tablespoon or two at a time, if needed, to create the sauce, until all the shells are coated in the sauce, 2 to 3 minutes. Turn off the heat, add the lemon zest and lemon juice, and toss the pasta to coat.

Sprinkle the pasta with the pistachios and Parmesan. Set out the pot for people to serve themselves, or take control and assemble each bowl, making the perfect pasta-to-sausage ratio for yourself.

A QUICK WAY TO MAKE FRESH SAUSAGE

In case you can't find a high-quality sausage, here is my ratio for making it at home: Combine 1 teaspoon kosher salt, 1 teaspoon sweet paprika, ¾ teaspoon crushed or ground fennel seeds, and ½ teaspoon red pepper flakes in a bowl. Add 1 pound ground meat and 2 finely grated garlic cloves. Using your hands, mix it all together until everything is evenly integrated.

HOW TO
SCRUB CLAMS

Even if I buy them from my most trustworthy fishmonger (Hi, Josh!), I'm always going to scrub my bivalves (clams, cockles, mussels, oysters, scallops). Take a gnarly stainless-steel scrubber (or bristly brush, or sponge) and scrub each individual clam under cold water, placing them in a large bowl afterward. Cover the clams in the bowl with cold water and let them soak for 10 to 15 minutes to extract the sand. Drain and rinse once more. If they're still dirty after the first soak (you see a lot of sand at the bottom of the soaking bowl), give them a second bath. Better to be safe than to have a gritty sauce.

FREGOLA WITH BUTTERY CLAMS AND YUZU KOSHO

Fregola is a tiny, Sardinian, beadlike pasta that comes in a range of sizes. It's perfect with clams because pieces of fregola make their way into the open clams like another treasure to find inside. I like to use the clam shells to scoop and scrape out the meat, and then use them as spoons for the fregola. My mother's probably rolling her eyes. (I have terrible table manners.)

The sauce is silky and buttery, a classic lemon–white wine combination that brings out the brininess of the clams and tastes like the beach. But I couldn't stop there. I played around with adding yuzu kosho, a fermented Japanese condiment made of yuzu citrus zest, chiles, and salt that's always in my fridge. It's intensely fruity, salty, and fiery. There's no substitute for it. The otherwise ho-hum usual white wine–clam sauce gets transformed with the hit of yuzu kosho. That's the extent of how much I can hype it up until you make it yourself and see.

SERVES 4

Kosher salt

¼ cup extra-virgin olive oil, plus more for drizzling

3 garlic cloves, thinly sliced

½ cup dry white wine (avoid anything overly oaky or sweet; like the unloved Pinot Grigio someone brought to your last party)

2 pounds (about 24) smallish littleneck clams or (about 36) cockles, scrubbed well

1 cup fregola

¼ cup unsalted butter, cut into pieces

1 tablespoon yuzu kosho

2 large handfuls (about 1 small bunch) basil leaves

Bring a large pot of water to a boil, then season lightly with about 2 tablespoons salt. (The clams will release their briny liquid and the yuzu kosho has plenty of salt in it, so no need for the pasta water to be heavily seasoned here.)

While the water comes to a boil, in a large heavy pot with a lid, combine the olive oil and garlic and place over medium heat. Cook for a minute or two, stirring, until the garlic begins to take on a light golden color. You want that sweet garlic flavor rather than a deep toasty one, so keep it on the lighter side and avoid having it go brown. Quickly stir in the wine and let simmer until reduced by half, about 2 minutes. Add the clams and shake the pot around so they can get comfortable. Place the lid on the pot and steam, shaking the pot occasionally, until the clams open and release their juices. I check mine after the first 3 minutes, but it depends on the size of your clams, plus there are always a few stragglers that need another minute or two. As the clams open, use tongs to transfer them to a bowl, leaving their juices behind. If there are some that refuse to open, chuck them, as this means they started out dead.

Once most of the clams have opened, go ahead and add the fregola to the boiling water and stir a few times so nothing sticks to the bottom of the pot. Cook, stirring occasionally, until very al dente, about 2 minutes *less* than what the package suggests. The pasta will finish cooking in the sauce.

When the fregola is at the very al dente stage, scoop out 1½ cups pasta water and then drain the pasta. Add ¾ cup pasta water, the fregola, and butter to the pot of wine sauce. Turn the heat to medium-high and cook until the sauce is rich, thick, and glossy and the pasta is cooked through, about 2 minutes. Turn off the heat and stir in the yuzu kosho. Taste a spoonful of the sauce to see if it needs a touch more salt. Add the basil and return the clams to the pot, tossing them with the tongs to reheat them.

Spoon the fregola and clams into shallow bowls. Drizzle with olive oil and serve, setting out an empty bowl for guests to put their shells in.

219

RICOTTA DUMPLINGS

I don't tend to make as much fresh pasta as I used to, but these will scratch anyone's itch for a pasta project. The proper name for these dumplings is *gnudi*, which translates to "ravioli without the wrapper" in Italian. Why isn't the English language as clever?

These little cheesy orbs have been by my side for some time now. Fatty, creamy, light, and bouncy. I learned this recipe from Ignacio Mattos at Estela, who learned it from Judy Rodgers at Zuni Café, who learned it from a chef in Florence, who learned it from god knows where. It goes way back. A mixture of ricotta and flour is shaped into these delicate, but not fragile, pillows.

This is a technique-heavy recipe, so I kept the ingredients minimal. Although this would be a good time to sneak in whatever green vegetables you've got on hand (such as asparagus, green garlic, or peas). A spoonful of pesto stirred into the sauce at the end is also delicious—just try to avoid drowning these beauties in an overly rich meat sauce or a tomato sauce that wants to steal the spotlight.

SERVES 4

2 cups full-fat ricotta, drained

1 cup finely grated Parmesan (use a Microplane!), plus more for serving

1 egg, plus 1 egg yolk

1½ teaspoons kosher salt

½ cup all-purpose flour, or as needed

2 cups Drinkable Chicken Broth (page 232) or good chicken stock

3 tablespoons cold unsalted butter, cut into pieces

2 tablespoons finely chopped chives

Freshly ground pepper

In a food processor, combine the ricotta, Parmesan, egg, egg yolk, and salt. Pulse until the mixture becomes very smooth and thick. Sprinkle in the flour and pulse just until smooth. Transfer the batter to a medium bowl.

Line a baking sheet with parchment paper and dust it with flour. (I use a fine-mesh sieve, but you can use your hand.)

From this point you have two choices: Go casual and form the dumplings by the spoonful, or shape them into tiny, delicate, crescent moons. No judgment. It really just depends on how much time you have.

For the easy shaping option: Using two large spoons, shape heaping tablespoonfuls of batter into small mounds and place them on the prepared baking sheet. Dust with more flour.

For the slightly advanced shaping option: Using a large spoon, scoop up about 1 tablespoon of the batter. Scrape the spoon against the lip of the bowl at a 45-degree angle to smooth the mixture. Using the side of your index finger, push the batter off the spoon and let it drop onto the baking sheet, forming a rustic crescent in the process (this may take a few tries). Repeat until you've used all of the batter. Dust the tops with more flour.

Place the baking sheet with the dumplings in the freezer for 20 minutes to firm them up.

Bring a large pot of lightly salted water to a simmer over medium heat. Once the water is simmering, one by one, add the dumplings and cook, using a spoon to gently turn them over occasionally until they have puffed up, almost doubled in size, and are cooked through, 3 to 4 minutes.

While the dumplings cook, in a large skillet over medium heat, bring the chicken broth to a simmer. Once the dumplings are cooked, use a slotted spoon to transfer them to the simmering broth. Add the butter and cook, gently swirling the skillet. Cook until the butter melts and the sauce is slightly thickened, 3 to 5 minutes. Just know this is not the time to toss or stir vigorously. We want those dumplings to retain their shape.

Spoon the dumplings and some of the sauce into shallow bowls. Sprinkle with the chives, pepper, and more cheese and serve.

DO AHEAD

The dumplings can be formed up to 1 month ahead. After forming them, place the baking sheet in the freezer until they are frozen solid, then transfer them to a resealable plastic bag and store in the freezer. Drop the frozen dumplings into the boiling water and cook for about 6 minutes.

CHOOSING RICOTTA

You need crumbly ricotta that's on the drier side. If you can find ricotta that's strained, buy that. If there's liquid in the container, you need to strain it, pressing down with a spatula to express as much liquid as possible (but no need to get out the cheesecloth). And, as with all dairy, always use full fat!

SPICY CAULIFLOWER RAGÙ WITH LEMONY BREADCRUMBS

I've developed four or five Bolognese variations, and I hold my recipe for classic Bolognese dear to my heart (find it at bonappetit.com). But it's this cauliflower recipe that takes the top spot for me. Breaking the cauliflower into tiny bits in a food processor lets the veg retain its shape while also, somehow, developing an almost velvety texture—not unlike slow-cooked ground meat—as it cooks.

I tend to crave denser pastas to go with the sauce that gets all the yummy things: anchovies, onion, and garlic and a healthy amount of olive oil. A squeeze of tomato paste makes it taste like a sauce that has been bubbling all day.

SERVES 4 TO 6

Kosher salt

1 head cauliflower

3 tablespoons extra-virgin olive oil, plus ¼ cup

¾ cup panko breadcrumbs

1 teaspoon finely grated lemon zest

Freshly ground pepper

1 large red onion, or 2 large shallots, very thinly sliced

6 garlic cloves, thinly sliced

8 oil-packed anchovies, drained

1 teaspoon red pepper flakes, or 1 red chile, thinly sliced

½ cup tomato paste

1 pound bucatini, spaghetti, or rigatoni

2 tablespoons unsalted butter

¼ cup finely chopped parsley

Bring a large pot of water to a boil, then throw in a handful of salt (about ¼ cup).

Break off the florets from the cauliflower and coarsely chop the stems. In a food processor, and working in batches, pulse the cauliflower until the pieces are the size of lentils (some smaller and some larger ones are fine), transferring the cauliflower to a bowl as you go. (If you don't have a food processor, just finely chop the cauliflower and it'll still be delicious.)

Meanwhile, pour the 3 tablespoons olive oil into another large pot and place over medium heat. Add the breadcrumbs and gently fry, stirring often, until they have become crisp and deeply golden brown, 3 to 5 minutes. Stir in the lemon zest and season generously with salt and ground pepper. Transfer to a bowl and set aside.

Wipe out the pot, pour in the remaining ¼ cup olive oil, and place over medium heat. Add the onion and garlic and season with salt. Cook, stirring occasionally, until the onion and garlic are almost jamlike, and lightly caramelized, 12 to 15 minutes.

Add the anchovies to the pot and sprinkle in the red pepper flakes. Cook until the anchovies have completely melted into the onion and garlic, about 2 minutes. Plop in the tomato paste and season with salt. Cook, stirring, until you have a thick, deeply red paste, 2 to 3 minutes. Add the cauliflower and cook, stirring, until it has cooked down slightly and begins to stick to the bottom of the pot, 6 to 8 minutes. Season with salt, then keep warm over low heat.

Drop the pasta into the boiling water and cook until very al dente, about 2 minutes *less* than what the package suggests (it'll finish cooking in the sauce). Just before the pasta is al dente, scoop out 2 cups pasta water. Using tongs, transfer the pasta to the sauce, along with the butter and 1 cup pasta water. Simmer over medium heat, tossing the pasta around, until the sauce has thickened and clings to the pasta, about 3 minutes. If the sauce looks too thick, add more pasta water, 1 tablespoon at a time, to thin.

Turn off the heat, add the parsley, and quickly toss with the tongs to evenly distribute. Divide the pasta among the bowls, sprinkle the breadcrumbs over the top, and serve.

CHICKPEA CACIO E PEPE WITH CARAMELIZED LEMON

There are many recipes for pasta e ceci (aka pasta with chickpeas). The majority that I've encountered are brothy, almost souplike. This recipe emphasizes both the chickpeas and the pasta but is equally comforting and a lot creamier than the usual versions.

Much of the magic of this dish lies in crushing the chickpeas, so they release their starches and transform the pasta water into a creamy sauce. Some of the chickpeas retain their shape, whereas others turn to delicious mush, and the caramelized lemon lends some chewy tang and brings the pasta back to life post-boiling. It's incredibly satisfying. If I still need to convince you to make this, know that it was the first meal that I made for my boyfriend, and he has been attached to me ever since.

SERVES 4 (PLUS, MAYBE, SOME LEFTOVERS, THOUGH I DOUBT IT)

Kosher salt

¼ cup extra-virgin olive oil

1 small Meyer or regular lemon, thinly sliced, seeds picked out

1 (15-ounce) can chickpeas, drained and rinsed

1 large shallot, finely chopped

1 rosemary sprig, or 4 thyme sprigs

Freshly ground pepper

1 pound tubular pasta (such as calamarata, paccheri, or rigatoni)

¼ cup unsalted butter, cut into small pieces

½ cup finely grated Parmesan cheese, plus more for serving

Bring a large pot of water to a boil, then throw in a handful of salt (about ¼ cup).

While the water is doing its thing, set a separate large pot or Dutch oven over medium heat and pour in the olive oil. Add the lemon and cook, using tongs to flip the slices until they begin to lightly brown and shrivel up, 6 to 8 minutes. Using the tongs, transfer the caramelized lemon slices to a bowl, leaving the oil in the pot.

Dump the chickpeas into the oil and let them get a little crisp and golden, stirring occasionally, 5 to 7 minutes. Add the shallot and crush the rosemary to release its oil and drop it into the pot. Season with salt and lots and lots of pepper and give everything a stir. Cook until the shallot is beginning to soften, 3 to 5 minutes.

Meanwhile, add the pasta to the boiling water and cook until almost al dente, about 2 minutes *less* than what the package suggests (it'll finish cooking in the sauce).

Just before the pasta is al dente, scoop out 2 cups pasta water. Add 1½ cups pasta water to the pot with the chickpeas and bring to a simmer, still over medium heat. (This may seem like a lot of liquid, but it will thicken once the remaining ingredients are added.) One piece at a time, stir in the butter until the pasta water and butter have become one.

Using a slotted spoon, transfer the pasta to the sauce. Cook, stirring often and sprinkling in the Parmesan a little at a time. (Don't add the cheese all at once, as that can make the sauce split and turn grainy.) Keep stirring until the cheese is melted and the sauce is creamy and clings to the pasta, about 3 minutes. If the sauce looks too thick, add more pasta water, 1 to 2 tablespoons at a time to thin (but know that saucier is ideal because it will thicken as it cools). Turn off the heat and fold in the caramelized lemon. Sprinkle with an almost ridiculous amount of pepper and more Parmesan before serving.

SOUP
OBSESSED

Wait! If you're about to skim past this chapter because soups and stews seem as sexy to you as a pair of old socks, don't.

I have high soup standards, and I brought my A game to these recipes. These are soups with big, explosive flavors that you'll want to serve at dinner parties. Even the word "soup" undersells how great these dishes are—as if we're talking about oyster crackers reluctantly plopping into a bowl of microwaved Campbell's chicken noodle.

I don't think of soup making as throwing everything in a pot and calling it a day. My recipes are about more than a bunch of stuff bubbling on the stove. A good soup is about layering, building flavors. Like in my

Ginger Chicken and Rice Soup with Sizzled Black Pepper (page 244), you'll see that I don't think it's enough to cook chicken and rice together in one fabulous mush. That mush is arguably pretty good, but the crispy chicken skin and scallion oil on top take it to a totally different place (that place: a restaurant, in your home). Ash Reshteh (page 236), a traditional Persian soup, has it all—legumes *and* noodles, three types of greens, and all the toppings to play with. Coconut chowder (see page 243) is so rich and savory and garlicky that I'd tell everyone to make that one first.

DRINKABLE CHICKEN BROTH

It has been a practice for thousands of years for us humans to make consistently outrageous claims about the medicinal benefits of the food we eat. This can certainly be said about simmering animal bones in water. We—food people, people who love food—fetishize broth. Like it's this witchy healing potion that only gets better over time. But I disagree. That broth is ready after 3 hours. At that point, you have everything you need; get on with life. (Yes, I've enjoyed bone broth and realize certain animal bones take a lot longer than 3 hours to properly release all that goodness, but I have little desire to be doing that in my kitchen.)

This chicken broth is so flavorful on its own that, sure, you can drink it, but it's not so potent that it overpowers the dish you cook with it. The key to this balance is using both raw and roasted chicken wings. The raw chicken makes a light, delicate broth, while the roasted chicken wings bring that intense, chicken-y flavor. So this is the best of both worlds.

MAKES 2 QUARTS

4 pounds chicken wings

1 large yellow onion, skin left on, quartered

1 garlic head, unpeeled, halved crosswise

3 celery stalks, chopped

½ bunch parsley

2 fresh bay leaves, or 4 thyme sprigs

6 ounces shiitake mushrooms, stems left on

3 quarts cold water

Preheat the oven to 425°F.

Spread out half of the chicken wings on a rimmed baking sheet. Roast until the skin is deeply golden brown, 40 to 50 minutes.

Using tongs, transfer the roasted chicken wings to a large pot, scraping and adding as much of the browned bits stuck on the baking sheet as you can. Add the remaining chicken wings, onion, garlic, celery, parsley, bay leaves, and mushrooms and pour in the water. Place the pot over medium-high heat and bring to a strong simmer. As soon as this happens, turn the heat to medium-low so the broth barely simmers. The more fiercely you simmer a broth, the cloudier it becomes, so let it go low-and-slow for now.

As the broth simmers, skim any foam that rises to the top but leave all of that good fat (there will be plenty) in there, until the volume has reduced by one-third, 2½ to 3 hours. Turn off the heat, then strain the broth into a large heatproof bowl, but do not press down on the solids because that makes for a cloudy broth. Compost the solids; they've given everything they've got at this point.

You can either season the broth and drink it, use it to start your stew or soup project, or ladle it into a few nonreactive containers to freeze for later use. If using the broth right away, skim off some (definitely not all) of the fat. I find a ladle does a decent job of this. You can also chill the broth, which will solidify the fat on top, making it easy to remove. The broth will keep, covered, in the fridge for up to 1 week or for 3 months in the freezer.

WHY WINGS?

Chicken wings have fat, cartilage, and bone, so they add a lot of flavor and body to your broth. You want a stock that gelatinizes when chilled, that has a jiggle to it. That doesn't happen with lean chicken parts. Drumsticks, thighs, the neck, and backbone are all great alternatives to wings.

COOL BEANS

I have cooked countless pots of beans and can safely say they are very difficult to mess up. The only thing that could go wrong is, well, if you don't cook them fully and if you don't add enough salt. No one wants their beans al dente and tasting like nothing. Even if they split and fall apart, it's not the end of the world. Some bean varieties are just more likely to do so.

When it comes to flavoring the beans and their broth, I tend to always add some kind of onion-y thing, fat, salt, and herbs. Other ingredients, like cured meat, tomatoes, and cheese rinds, will only add more flavor, so go ahead and add what you have. Bear in mind that once you have a pot of beans, you can it eat as is, but why stop there? Wilt in some hardy greens, like kale or mustard greens, in the last few minutes or serve over fried bread (see page 113) with lots of shaved Parm and olive oil on top.

SERVES 6

½ cup extra-virgin olive oil

1 yellow onion, skin left on, halved

1 garlic head, skin left on, halved crosswise

1 pound beans white beans (such as cannellini, corona, or gigante)

1 small fennel bulb, halved

4-ounce slab salami or mortadella

1 small bunch mixed herbs with stems (such as parsley, dill, and/ or basil), plus more for serving (optional)

4 strips lemon peel

Kosher salt

Aioli (see page 61) for serving (optional)

Chile flakes or freshly ground black pepper for serving (optional)

Breadcrumbs (see page 45) for serving (optional)

Add ¼ cup of the olive oil to a Dutch oven or large pot and place over medium heat. Add the onion and garlic, cut-side down, and cook until caramelized and golden brown, about 3 minutes. Add the beans, fennel, salami, herbs, lemon peel, remaining ¼ cup olive oil, and water to cover by 2 inches. Season with salt and bring to a boil.

Turn the heat to medium-low, and simmer, uncovered, stirring and tasting a bean or two occasionally, until, well, the beans are done. Depending on the size, they can take as few as 50 minutes to 1½ hours (maybe even more!) to finish cooking. The goal is to gently cook the beans so that they plump up, are creamy inside, and hold their shape. If you notice the liquid is reducing and the beans are not done, add more water to keep them submerged.

Taste a spoonful of broth and a few beans. They both should be very delicious. Adjust the seasoning, adding more salt if needed. Ladle the brothy beans into individual bowls and dress with a dollop of aioli, some herbs, a pinch of chile flakes, breadcrumbs, or all of them—however you like—before serving.

WHAT'S ONION SKIN DOING IN HERE?

It's not out of laziness. Keeping the onion skin on is a chef's trick for making a golden-colored broth. Natural food dye, baby.

ASH RESHTEH

Ash is a category of thick soups in Iranian cuisine and ash reshteh is the most well-known, filled with all kinds of legumes, a mountain of greens, and reshteh, the thin, flat noodles that resemble linguine. Usually, we eat the soup on Charshanbe Suri, also known as the Festival of Fire. It falls on the eve of the Wednesday before Nowruz, the Iranian New Year. On that night, you're supposed to have a bowl of ash reshteh and jump over multiple little fires to get rid of bad spirits. Yes, it works (thanks for asking).

The soup gets garnished with a much-loved Iranian dairy product called kashk (think of it as funky sour cream), along with sizzled mint and crispy onions. Kashk can be assertive. It's more sour and salty than yogurt or sour cream. If you find it, try it, please. But because it's hard to find, I mimicked it with yogurt thinned with lemon juice. The sizzled mint has a toasty, earthy flavor and an emerald-green color. I normally never break my noodles, ever ever ever, but here you do. Iranians don't have patience for long noodles like the Italians do.

SERVES 6 (PERSIANS; 8 FOR PERSIANS)

10 tablespoons extra-virgin olive oil

2 large onions, thinly sliced

4 garlic cloves, thinly sliced

½ cup dried green or brown lentils, rinsed

¼ cup dried cranberry or navy beans, soaked overnight, and drained

¼ cup dried chickpeas, soaked overnight, and drained

1 teaspoon ground turmeric

2 quarts water, or as needed

8 ounces linguine

2 bunches mature spinach, trimmed, coarsely chopped

1½ cups finely chopped parsley

1 cup finely chopped dill

Kosher salt

Freshly ground pepper

2 tablespoons dried ground mint

⅓ cup full-fat yogurt (not Greek)

2 tablespoons fresh lemon juice

In a large pot over medium heat, warm 3 tablespoons olive oil. Add half the onions and all the garlic and cook, stirring occasionally, until the onion softens and becomes deeply browned in spots (a few charred spots are welcome), 10 to 12 minutes. Add the lentils, beans, chickpeas, and turmeric and cook, stirring, until the turmeric has coated everything, about 1 minute. Pour the water into the pot and bring to a boil. Then turn the heat to medium-low and let things happen at a gentle simmer, skimming off any foam that may rise to the top, until the beans and chickpeas are halfway cooked (they should still be very al dente), 30 to 40 minutes, but it may take longer depending on the age of your beans and whether or not you soaked them.

Break the linguine in half and add to the pot. Cook, stirring occasionally, until the beans are creamy but still hold their shape and the noodles are tender, 20 to 25 minutes. The soup might look thick at this point, resembling a chili. You want this!

Add the spinach, parsley, and dill to the pot and cook until just wilted and slightly darkened, 4 to 6 minutes. Season with salt and pepper. The greens should have released some water and loosened things up but, if the soup looks so thick that it will be a workout to stir, thin it with more water.

While the soup simmers, pour 3 tablespoons olive oil into a skillet and place it over medium heat. Add the remaining onions and cook, stirring often, until deeply golden brown and jammy, 12 to 15 minutes. Transfer the onions to a paper towel to drain the excess oil and then season with salt.

Carefully wipe out the skillet, return it to medium heat, and add the remaining 4 tablespoons olive oil. Add the mint and cook, stirring often, until the mint oil is fragrant and slightly darkened, about 1 minute. Transfer to a small bowl.

When you're ready to serve, mix the yogurt and lemon juice and season with a big pinch of salt. (It should have the consistency of heavy cream.) Add a spoonful of water to loosen more, if needed.

Divide the soup among bowls and top each with some of the lemon-yogurt, a drizzle of mint oil, and a handful of jammy onions (in that order) to serve.

HOT-AND-SOUR GARLIC SOUP WITH SHIITAKE AND CELERY

This is a tribute to my favorite soup of all time. I love hot-and-sour soup so much that my family has an origin story about it. When my mother was in labor with me, her closest friend brought quarts of hot-and-sour soup to give to everyone in the family who had gathered. They say its scent has stayed with me ever since.

Anyway, I wanted this soup to echo those flavors, to be lip-smacking, peppery, hot, and sour. The base is your best chicken broth enhanced with tons of garlic and ginger, while a few teaspoons of pepper bring the heat and rice vinegar brings the sour. Crispy browned mushrooms are for topping—which will make you wonder why you don't garnish every soup you make with them. (For a traditional hot-and-sour soup, I recommend the recipe from *Mastering the Art of Chinese Cooking* by Eileen Yin-Fei Lo. Every recipe in that book is truly exceptional.)

SERVES 4

1 pound silken tofu

3 tablespoons neutral oil (such as grapeseed), or as needed

1 pound shiitake, maitake, and/or oyster mushrooms

Kosher salt

8 to 10 garlic cloves, thinly sliced

3 tablespoons peeled, finely chopped ginger

2 teaspoons freshly ground pepper

6 cups Drinkable Chicken Broth (page 232) or good chicken stock

4 celery stalks, thinly sliced, plus all the leaves

¼ cup unseasoned rice vinegar

3 tablespoons soy sauce or tamari

2 teaspoons toasted sesame oil

3 scallions, thinly sliced

½ cup coarsely chopped cilantro

Open the package of tofu and drain off any water. Gently pat the tofu dry, then cut it into 1-inch pieces.

Set a medium pot over medium-high heat. Add 2 tablespoons of the neutral oil and heat until hot and glossy. Tear the mushrooms into big, craggy pieces. If using shiitakes, remove and toss out the knobby, dense stems. Drop the mushrooms into the hot oil and let them be until they get crisp and brown underneath, about 3 minutes. Season with salt, then give them a toss and continue cooking until they're browned all over and crisp in most spots, another 2 minutes. Using a slotted spoon, transfer half the mushrooms to a plate and set aside, leaving the remaining mushrooms in the pot.

Add the garlic, ginger, and pepper to the pot. Cook, stirring, until the garlic has slightly softened and some pieces have become toasty and golden, 2 to 3 minutes. If the pot looks dry and some of the garlic begins to stick, that's okay, add the remaining 1 tablespoon neutral oil to loosen things up. Pour in the chicken broth, season with salt, and bring to a boil. Once you see bubbles, turn the heat to medium and bring the soup to a gentle simmer. Drop in the celery (but not the leaves, they come later) and cook until almost tender, about 2 minutes.

Stir the vinegar, soy sauce, and sesame oil into the soup, then turn off the heat and slip in the tofu.

Ladle the soup into bowls and top with the scallions, cilantro, celery leaves, and reserved crispy mushrooms to serve.

MY FAVORITE (EASY-TO-FIND) SOY SAUCE

I haven't tried every soy sauce out there, and there are so many varieties, some of which age like fine wines. But the one I buy and use regularly is Gold Mine Natural Food Co.'s nama shoyu soy sauce. Sometimes commercial soy sauce brands have an almost acrid aftertaste and an assertive saltiness. You want sweet, nutty flavor from the soybeans in soy sauce. Nama shoyu has a more equal wheat-to-soybean ratio, which gives it a nuanced, well-rounded flavor that doesn't taste too salty. It isn't labeled "reduced salt," but the sodium content seems on par with other reduced-salt options. Store it in the fridge after opening.

MASOOR DAAL WITH SALTY YOGURT

Like most Indian dishes, daal is highly regional and you can find hundreds of variations of it when you're recipe hunting. This is masoor daal, which translates to "red lentils." The stewed lentils are topped with tempered spices, called tadka. Those spices, which open up when they bloom in oil, hit your senses bite after bite. The creamy lentils beneath can only be described as intensely comforting. This is my favorite way to eat lentils.

SERVES 4

2 tablespoons ghee, virgin coconut oil, or neutral oil (such as grapeseed), plus ¼ cup

1 red onion, finely chopped

2-inch piece ginger, peeled and finely grated

4 garlic cloves, thinly sliced

2 teaspoons ground coriander

1 teaspoon ground turmeric

2 cups masoor daal
(dried red lentils), rinsed

7 cups water

Kosher salt

2 teaspoons black mustard seeds

1 or 2 bird's eye chiles, thinly sliced (seeded, if you're heat sensitive)

2 teaspoons cumin seeds

1 teaspoon Kashmiri powder or smoked paprika

Plain (not Greek) yogurt for serving

Cilantro sprigs for garnishing (optional)

Lime wedges for squeezing

Steamed basmati rice
(see page 202) or Fluffy (and Crisp) Flatbread (page 111)
for serving

In a large saucepan over medium heat, melt the 2 tablespoons ghee. Add the onion and cook, stirring occasionally, until lightly charred around the edges and tender, 10 to 12 minutes. Add the ginger, garlic, coriander, and turmeric and cook, stirring to bloom the spices and let the turmeric stain the other ingredients. This will only take 10 seconds or so.

Add the lentils to the pot and stir to coat with the onion and spices. Pour in the water, turn the heat to high, and bring to a boil. Then turn the heat to medium-low, add a pinch of salt, and cook, stirring occasionally, until the lentils have split and collapsed into the broth in a golden mush, 20 to 25 minutes.

Meanwhile, in a small skillet over medium heat, melt the remaining ¼ cup ghee. When the ghee is glossy and hot, add the mustard seeds and cook, swirling the pan around until you can hear the mustard seeds begin to crackle, about 2 minutes. Add the fresh chile(s), cumin seeds, and Kashmiri powder and stir until the ghee is completely red from the chile powder, about 20 seconds. Immediately remove the skillet from the heat and set aside. This is your tadka.

Ladle some daal into each bowl, then spoon some yogurt over, along with the tadka. Garnish with cilantro, if you like, squeeze lime juice over, and serve with rice or flatbread.

MILLIONS OF MUSTARD SEEDS

Indian cooking frequently uses black mustard seeds, which are pungent and more mustardy tasting than yellow mustard seeds—those have a more mellow flavor. Frying the black mustard seeds takes that pungency down a notch, but the flavor is still deliciously mustardy with a fun little crunch. Be careful not to overdo the frying; they can taste rancid if overcooked.

SPICY COCONUT CHOWDER WITH TOASTED GARLIC

This is a creamy soup that you can easily make vegan (skip the fish sauce and use water). Fulfill your clam chowder dreams and add 2 pounds of clams before you add the potatoes (fish out the clams when they've opened, finish the soup, and then return them to the pot before serving). Or, you know, make it as-is, which is how I like it. The coconut milk–chicken broth base is fragrant with lemongrass and ginger, the buttery Yukon gold potatoes melt in your mouth and help thicken the soup, and a simple chile oil with toasted garlic tops things off with a bit of flair—and crunch.

SERVES 4

6 garlic cloves, sliced

2 chiles (such as Fresno, Holland, or serrano), thinly sliced

¼ cup neutral oil (such as grapeseed), plus 2 tablespoons

1 yellow onion, or 2 medium shallots, thinly sliced

2 lemongrass stalks, bottom third only (about 6 inches long), tough outer layers removed, finely chopped

2 tablespoons peeled, finely chopped ginger

Kosher salt

1 pound baby Yukon gold potatoes, sliced into ½-inch rounds

2 teaspoons ground coriander

2 (13.5-ounce) cans full-fat coconut milk

2 cups Drinkable Chicken Broth (page 232) or good chicken stock, or water

3 baby bok choy, coarsely chopped

1 tablespoon fish sauce, or as needed

1 tablespoon fresh lime juice, or as needed

1 cup coarsely chopped cilantro and/or Thai basil

Freshly ground pepper

In a large heavy pot over medium heat, combine the garlic, chiles, and ¼ cup neutral oil. Cook, stirring occasionally, until the garlic is pale golden and starting to crisp, 2 minutes. Transfer this garlic-chile oil to a small bowl and set aside.

Pour the remaining 2 tablespoons neutral oil into the pot and return it to medium heat. Add the onion, lemongrass, and ginger and season with salt. Cook, stirring occasionally, until the onion has softened slightly but has not browned, 6 to 8 minutes. Add the potatoes and coriander and stir to coat the potatoes with the onion and oil.

Stir the coconut milk and chicken broth into the pot, turn the heat to medium-high, and bring to a simmer. Simmer, stirring occasionally, until the potatoes are very soft and nearly falling apart, 25 to 30 minutes. Grab a wooden spoon and mash down a few of the potatoes to help them release their starch, which will thicken the soup and make it even more creamy. Add the bok choy and simmer until just crisp-tender, 2 to 3 minutes. Turn off the heat and stir in the fish sauce and lime juice. Taste and add more of each, if you'd like.

Ladle the soup into bowls. Scatter the cilantro over the top, drizzle with the reserved garlic-chile oil, finish with a few cranks of pepper, and serve.

CHOOSING COCONUT MILK

The best coconut milk should be unsweetened, without any gums or preservatives. I'm not talking about the stuff in the refrigerated section of the grocery store (that's watered down for coffee and smoothie use). I like Native Forest brand organic coconut milk, which I can always find at Whole Foods and, according to some googling, doesn't use monkey labor (look it up—it's horrifying). Shake the can before using to mix up the fatty cream and the more liquid part of the milk.

GINGER CHICKEN AND RICE SOUP WITH SIZZLED BLACK PEPPER

If you're under the weather, with one sip of this soup you'll feel instantly better (or at least fool yourself into thinking that). The broth is flavored simply with chicken, ginger, and plenty of garlic, and the starch from the rice thickens the soup, giving it a creamy consistency without cream. The healthy amount of pepper will open up your sinuses. It's also topped with crispy chicken skin, which is what you *really* need on a sick day. I think the soup is beyond perfect as-is, but if you're a meddler, go ahead and throw in a handful of greens, a jammy egg, sliced sweet potato, or that jalapeño that's getting wrinkly in the produce drawer. Make this recipe your own.

SERVES 4

4 bone-in, skin-on chicken thighs (about 1½ pounds)

3 tablespoons neutral oil (such as grapeseed)

Kosher salt

3 scallions, thinly sliced

1 tablespoon freshly ground pepper

6 garlic cloves, thinly sliced

2 tablespoons peeled, finely chopped ginger

½ cup jasmine rice, rinsed

6 cups water

1 tablespoon fresh lemon juice, or as needed

Bear with me here, as I'm about to tell you to rip the skin off those chicken thighs. But first, pat the chicken thighs dry, so it's easier to grip the skin. Peel the skin off each thigh and lay it flat on the bottom of a heavy pot. (Set the naked thighs aside for the soup.) Pour the neutral oil over the chicken skin.

Set the pot over medium heat and allow the chicken skin to gently release some of its fat and shrivel up, 3 to 5 minutes. Continue to cook, flipping occasionally, until the skin is crisp all around and golden brown, another 3 to 5 minutes. Using tongs, transfer the chicken skin to a small bowl, leaving the fat behind. Season the skins with a bit of salt while still hot.

In a medium bowl, combine the scallions and pepper, then carefully tilt the pot with the chicken fat over the scallions and pepper. They will immediately sizzle and the scallions will wilt. Season with salt and stir. Set aside.

Return the pot to the stove and drop in the garlic, ginger, reserved chicken thighs, and rice. Pour in the water, turn the heat to high, and bring to a boil. Season with salt and turn the heat to medium-low. Gently simmer the soup, skimming off any foam that accumulates on the surface, and stirring to prevent the rice from sticking to the bottom of the pot, until the chicken is cooked through and the rice is very tender and has thickened the soup to an almost creamy consistency, 25 to 30 minutes.

Using tongs, remove the chicken thighs and set aside until cool enough to handle. Shred the meat with your fingers or two forks and then return to the pot. Pour in the lemon juice and taste. It should be very chicken-y, with bites of ginger and some brightness. Adjust with salt and more lemon juice, if needed.

Ladle the soup into bowls and spoon some of the scallion oil on top. Use your fingers to crush and scatter the crispy chicken skin over the top for the grand finale before serving.

248

When I was a kid in the '90s, I was absolutely entranced by Red Lobster commercials.

I couldn't look away from the dramatic close-ups of fire engine—red lobster tails getting dunked in bowls of melted butter in slow motion. At home, we didn't eat much seafood because neither of my parents had a big craving for it. The only fish that I grew up eating was my mother's salmon, and I still can't shake how good it was (see page 258). To satisfy my curiosity back then, I began ordering different fish at every restaurant my family went to. I think my first was tempura shrimp at a sushi spot. When I worked in restaurants in New York, one of my first gigs was as an oyster shucker. (I love the small, soothing tasks required to prepare seafood— deveining shrimp, cleaning clams, filleting fish.) Now I cook fish or seafood almost as much as I make vegetables (my truest love).

The recipes in this chapter show a range of ways to prepare fish, from slow roasting to grilling a whole fish, and, I hope, if you're at all intimidated by cooking fish, that my instructions are thorough enough to convince you to keep working at it. You know what? I never did make it to Red Lobster. But I did have lobster at Varney's out on Long Island and, with butter running down my fingers and a bowl full of demolished shells in front of me, I took a claw and in *slooow* motion, dunked it in more melted butter. Bliss.

CLAMS WITH CRISPY HAM AND BUTTER BEANS

It's hard to screw up clams when you're adding, a big splash of white wine, crusty bread, and aioli. While not essential, I suggest you fry the bread as you do for the toast on page 113. Place the toasts in the serving bowls before topping them with the clams and they will soak up some of that broth. I don't even use utensils for this meal. I get in there with my hands and end up with clam broth all over my beard. Worth it.

SERVES 4

¼ cup extra-virgin olive oil

6 slices serrano ham or prosciutto

3 spring onions, or 1 large shallot, thinly sliced

6 garlic cloves, thinly sliced

2 tablespoons tomato paste

2 teaspoons smoked paprika

1 cup dry white wine (plus a lot more for drinking)

4 pounds (about 40) small-ish clams (such as littleneck or manilla), scrubbed (see page 218)

1 (15-ounce) can butter, cannellini, or other white beans, drained and rinsed

1 cup coarsely chopped parsley

1 cup aioli (see page 61)

4 thick slices crusty bread, toasted

Line a plate with a paper towel and place it near the stove.

Place a large pot over medium heat, add the oil, and, when it's shimmering, arrange half the ham in a single layer in the pot to avoid overcrowding. Cook the ham, turning once or twice, until shriveled up and crisp, about 3 minutes. Transfer to the prepared plate to drain, leaving behind any fat in the pot, and repeat with the remaining ham.

Add the onions and garlic to the pot and cook, stirring occasionally, until slightly softened but not browned, 3 to 4 minutes. Stir in the tomato paste and paprika and cook until the tomato paste has taken on a deep brick-red color, about 2 minutes.

Pour the wine into the pot and let reduce by half, 2 to 3 minutes. Add the clams and cover, shaking the pot occasionally, until they begin to open, 3 to 7 minutes, depending on how large your clams are. As the clams open, use tongs to transfer them to a bowl.

Turn the heat to medium-low and add the beans to the pot. Stir, letting the beans soak up some of the clam broth and warm through for a minute or two. Return the clams to the pot. Turn off the heat, sprinkle in half the parsley, and toss to distribute thoroughly.

Slather the aioli on top of the toasts and place one in each of four bowls. Spoon the clams, beans, and broth over the bread. Sprinkle with the remaining parsley. Crush the crispy ham, sprinkle over the bowls, and dig in.

250

SCALLOPS WITH GRAPEFRUIT– BROWN BUTTER

I think one of the most luxurious orders at a restaurant is "I'll have the scallops." You know you've made it when you're saying that. At home, scallops don't need much work to prepare other than a close eye to make sure they don't overcook. You want a sear that gives them a serious crust. My strategy is to place them in the pan in a clockface formation so you can keep track of when it's time to flip them. The grapefruit-butter pan sauce comes together as you whisk, and a handful of raw radishes brings a fresh, crunchy contrast.

SERVES 4

16 dry-packed sea scallops

Kosher salt

3 tablespoons extra-virgin olive oil, plus more for drizzling

6 tablespoons unsalted butter

¾ cup fresh grapefruit juice

1½ teaspoons finely grated grapefruit zest

2 small radishes, thinly sliced

1 teaspoon mild chile flakes (such as Aleppo)

Flaky sea salt

Remove the side muscle from each scallop. (It's the little rectangular tag of tissue on the side of the scallop. It has a slightly chewy texture that some people don't care for.) Pat each scallop dry with a paper towel and season all over with kosher salt.

Pour the olive oil into a large stainless-steel skillet (there should be enough oil to coat the surface of the pan) and place over medium-high heat. Once the oil looks glossy and you see the first wisp of smoke, about 3 minutes, use tongs to arrange the scallops in a clockwise rotation, starting at twelve o'clock. Press lightly but don't move them around; let them be. Watch until you see the edges are getting deeply golden brown, 3 to 4 minutes. Flip them over so the other side can brown, another 2 to 3 minutes.

Transfer the scallops to a platter or among plates and set aside. Pour out the excess oil and let the skillet cool off for a minute.

Drop the butter into the skillet and set over medium heat. Once the butter has completely melted, using a wooden spoon, scrape loose any brown bits left over from searing the scallops, which will give the sauce more flavor. After about 1 minute, the butter will smell toasty and will have browned.

Add the grapefruit juice to the skillet and cook, whisking often, until the sauce begins to reduce and thicken, 2 to 3 minutes. Remove the pan from the heat and add the grapefruit zest and season with kosher salt.

Pour the sauce over the scallops and scatter the radish slices on top. Sprinkle with the chile flakes and drizzle with olive oil. The scallops should be bathing in a pool of citrus sauce and olive oil. Now you know why you've made it.

WHY ONLY DRY-PACKED SCALLOPS?

Salt water–packed scallops have a bouncy texture and can taste a little soapy. Dry-packed scallops will sear better. If the scallops at your shop aren't labeled, ask the fishmonger how they were packed.

STICKY, SPICY BASIL SHRIMP

I developed a habit of eating the entire shrimp when I was a kid. I don't mean sucking on the heads. I put whole shrimp in my mouth, shell and everything, and let my body absorb it. If that's too much for you, tear these shrimp apart, lick your fingers, and get messy with someone you love who'll never judge you. Don't even bring out the cutlery. Remove the head, slurp away, and get that concentrated sweet shrimp flavor. Then eat the body.

This intensely garlicky, spicy, and sweet marinade will truly make anything delicious. Boneless, skinless chicken thighs for the grill. Pork chops. Smothered on cauliflower and roasted. But it's particularly good with shrimp, the sweetest meat you can have. Shrimp can take this sticky-spicy sauce like a champ. The marinade is aggressive but, when it cooks down in the hot pan, it mellows the raw flavor of the garlic and chile. Have plenty of beer on ice when you serve this one.

SERVES 4

4 Fresno chiles, coarsely chopped

8 garlic cloves, smashed

2-inch piece ginger, peeled and thinly sliced

½ cup granulated sugar

3 tablespoons fish sauce

2 teaspoons kosher salt

¼ cup neutral oil (such as grapeseed), plus 2 tablespoons

2 pounds head-on (flavor!), shell-on shrimp (or prawns)

3 cups basil leaves

Lime wedges for serving

Sliced cucumbers for serving

In a blender, combine the chiles, garlic, ginger, sugar, fish sauce, salt, and ¼ cup neutral oil and blend until very smooth. Pour this marinade into a medium bowl and add the shrimp. Give the shrimp a toss and let them sit in the marinade for 15 minutes.

In a large cast-iron or nonstick skillet over medium-high heat, warm the remaining 2 tablespoons neutral oil. When the oil feels hot and you just start to see a wisp of smoke, use tongs to arrange the shrimp in the skillet, discarding the excess marinade. Cook the shrimp until lightly charred around the edges, 2 to 3 minutes. Flip and cook on the second side until the shrimp are pink and cooked through, another 2 minutes. Turn off the heat, add the basil, and toss vigorously until the basil is wilted and your mouth begins to salivate.

Transfer the shrimp to a large plate or platter. Arrange the lime wedges and cucumber slices around the edge and serve. Encourage guests to squeeze the lime over and munch on the cucumbers to offset the heat from the chile.

DO AHEAD

The shrimp can be marinated a day ahead. Cover and refrigerate until ready to use.

SALT-AND-PEPPER COD WITH TURMERIC NOODLES

When I visited Hanoi, I only scratched the surface of all the foods I wanted to try. Cha̕ cá lã vọng was high on my list. Its flavors sounded so similar to ones used in Iran—fish with turmeric and dill—that I wondered how different the Vietnamese dish would taste. At one famous restaurant, this dish is all they serve. I sat down in a dark mahogany chair from where I could see the chefs at work, searing white fish on a tiered metal skillet, adding spices, and finishing it off with scallion greens and dill. But what took it to another place was the nuoc cham, rice noodles, so many herbs, fresh chiles, and ice-cold beer that went with it. My mind was blown.

This is a slight riff on that dish. I still cook the cod with ginger, garlic, salt, and pepper, and the noodles still get flavored with the turmeric (but bloomed in butter). The ginger and ground pepper almost make a crust, so you will cook the first side hard to get it to caramelize.

SERVES 4

1 bird's eye, serrano, or Fresno chile, thinly sliced

3 garlic cloves; 1 crushed, 2 finely grated

¼ cup water

2 tablespoons fish sauce

2 tablespoons fresh lime juice

1 tablespoon granulated sugar

¼ cup neutral oil (such as grapeseed)

2 teaspoons peeled, finely grated ginger

2 teaspoons freshly ground pepper

1½ pounds boneless, skinless white fish (such as cod, hake, or haddock)

Kosher salt

6 ounces dried vermicelli noodles

4 scallions, thinly sliced

1 cup coarsely chopped dill

3 tablespoons unsalted butter

1 teaspoon ground turmeric

Fresh herbs (such as mint, cilantro, and more dill) for serving Lime wedges for squeezing

In a medium bowl, combine the chile, crushed garlic, water, fish sauce, lime juice, and sugar. Stir until the sugar has completely dissolved. (The garlic is only meant to flavor the sauce, so don't let anybody bite into it when you serve.) Taste the sauce—this is your nuoc cham; it should hit on multiple senses. Set aside.

In a medium bowl, stir together 3 tablespoons of the neutral oil, the ginger, pepper, and grated garlic. Slice the cod into about 2-inch pieces, then add to the bowl and season with salt. Using a spoon, toss until each piece is evenly coated. Set aside.

Bring a medium pot of water to a boil. Turn off the heat and drop in the noodles. Give them a stir every minute or so until they've become soft and silky, 4 to 5 minutes but follow the times on the package. Drain and set the noodles aside on a plate. I typically give the noodles a few snips with a pair of shears to tame their wild strands and make them easier to eat. Hold on to the pot for later.

Set a large nonstick skillet over medium-high heat. Add the remaining 1 tablespoon neutral oil, and, when the oil is hot, lay the pieces of cod in the pan and fry the fish until lightly golden underneath, 2 to 3 minutes. Flip the fish and then scatter the scallions and dill over and watch them sizzle and wilt rapidly. Don't stir, so that the fish doesn't fall apart, can brown underneath, and cooks through, another 2 minutes.

In the reserved medium pot over medium heat, melt the butter and then add the turmeric. Once the turmeric begins to sizzle, add the drained noodles and toss with tongs until each strand is stained gold and warmed through, about 1 minute.

Set everything out on separate serving plates if you're going family style. Alternatively, divide the noodles among bowls and spoon some fish into each bowl. Tear some of the herbs into pieces and sprinkle over the fish. Spoon the nuoc cham over the fish. Squeeze lime juice over the top. Eat a fistful of herbs between each bite.

MOM'S SALMON

In the '90s, salmon was *the* fish to cook. It was the only fish my mother prepared. It showed up on our dinner table every two or three weeks, always made the same way—under a blanket of dill. Even during Nowruz, the Persian New Year, when Iranians typically eat smoked or fried white fish or white fish with herby saffron buttered rice (see page 202), Mom's salmon always took its place. Salmon has a high fat content and thrives when it's drowned in more fat plus dill and garlic, but feel free to use other herbs, spices, and citrus instead. This low-roasting technique can be used on other types of fish, such as cod or halibut, but there is no substitute for the saffron. That's what makes it Mom's Salmon!

SERVES 4

1 teaspoon saffron threads

Kosher salt

2 tablespoons warm water

2 bunches Swiss chard or other leafy greens (such as lacinato kale)

¾ cup extra-virgin olive oil

1 Meyer or regular lemon, thinly sliced, seeds removed

4 green garlic stalks, halved lengthwise, or 4 garlic cloves, thinly sliced

1½ pounds skinless salmon fillet (preferably center-cut)

⅓ cup coarsely chopped dill

Preheat the oven to 325°F.

In a mortar and pestle, crush the saffron threads and a pinch of salt into a fine powder. Dump the ground saffron into a small bowl and pour in the water. Set aside.

Pull the chard leaves off the stalks. Roughly tear the leaves, set them aside, and finely chop the stalks.

In a large skillet over medium-high heat, heat ¼ cup of the olive oil. Toss in the chard stalks and cook, stirring occasionally, until tender, about 3 minutes. Add the chard leaves, half the lemon slices, and half the green garlic and stir a few times until the leaves just begin to wilt, about 2 minutes. (They will continue to wilt and cook in the oven. You're just giving them a head start.) Slide the skillet off the heat.

Season the salmon with salt on both sides and lay on top of the chard in the skillet. Pour the saffron water over the salmon and then top with the remaining lemon and green garlic. Scatter the dill all over and pour in the remaining ½ cup olive oil. Transfer the skillet to the oven.

Roast the salmon until it is opaque and easily flakes off with a fork around the thickest part, 25 to 30 minutes. Serve the salmon from the skillet or tear into large pieces using two forks and transfer to your preferred fancy serving platter. Spoon the greens around the fish and bathe both in all the lovely, lemony-scented fat from the pan. Then call your mother and tell her you love her.

GRILLED SNAPPER WITH CHARRED LEEK SALSA VERDE

I won't fool you, grilling a whole fish is a task that can make even a professional cook a bit squeamish. If you have done it before and succeeded, yay for you. If you haven't mustered up the courage to do so or have failed miserably, listen up. You want to stick with fish that are on the smaller size (less than 2 pounds). They're more manageable to work with and easier to flip. No heavy lifting by the grill allowed. Also, and this is just my opinion, I avoid layering all kinds of flavors and spices on the fish until *after* it has been grilled. I love a sticky glaze and all the spices, but I don't want to risk any moments of stickage or overly burnt ingredients. The skin will show you when it's ready to be flipped and that's when a large metal spatula (the one you might often use for flipping patties) is your friend.

You're using the whole leek for the salsa verde. The dark green leafy parts give texture and the rest of the leeks transform on the grill; becoming almost black and ashy on the outside. But they have the most soft, creamy sweet flesh that goes with the lime juice and chiles.

SERVES 4

2 medium leeks

2 serrano chiles

½ cup finely chopped cilantro

2 tablespoons fresh lime juice

½ cup neutral oil (such as grapeseed), plus more for rubbing

Kosher salt

2 (1½-pound) whole fish (such as snapper or small black bass), gutted and scaled

Thinly sliced red onion for serving

Thinly sliced radishes for serving

Sliced avocado for serving

Corn tortillas for serving

Lime wedges for serving

Preheat your grill to medium-high.

Cut off the dark tops from the leeks. Thoroughly wash the tops and leeks to remove any dirt or sand inside and pat dry with paper towels. Set the tops aside (we're going to use them later). Arrange the chiles and leeks directly on the grill grates and grill, turning with tongs every few minutes, until they are blackened in most spots, about 3 minutes for the chiles and 8 to 12 minutes for the leeks. Transfer both to a rimmed baking sheet and set aside for 5 minutes to cool. Keep the grill on.

Finely chop the reserved dark leafy part of the leeks, the grilled chiles, and the grilled leeks. Drop all of that into a medium bowl and stir in the cilantro, lime juice, and ⅓ cup of the neutral oil. Season with salt and set this salsa verde aside.

Pat the fish dry with paper towels, season inside and out with salt, and then rub with neutral oil. Now pour some neutral oil into a bowl; grab a few more paper towels, a pair of tongs, a metal spatula, and your fish; and head back to the grill. Using the tongs, dip a paper towel in the oil and clean the hot grill and oil the grates by swiping it on the grates. Repeat twice.

Lay the fish on the grates with the backbones facing you and let cook without fussing with them until you can see that the skin is crisped and beginning to puff up and become charred, 8 to 10 minutes. Using the metal spatula, flip the fish away from you. If the skin is still sticking, it's not quite ready, so just leave it alone for another minute or so and then try again. Once the fish ready, flip and continue cooking until the second side is crisped and the fish is fully cooked, another 8 to 10 minutes.

Transfer the fish to a platter and serve with the salsa verde, onion, radishes, avocado, tortillas, and lime wedges.

DO AHEAD

The salsa verde can be made up to 1 day ahead, covered, and stored in the fridge. Bring to room temperature before using.

SEARED SQUID WITH JUICY TOMATOES AND PISTACHIO DRESSING

I want you all to be cooking more squid at home. It's sustainable, cooks quickly, is versatile (it's good grilled, braised, and, obviously, fried), and also happens to be delicious. I love squid prepared all the ways, but the easiest (and most delicious) is dressed in olive oil with plenty of garlic and then seared hard. The trick when cooking is to sear the squid in batches since it will release some liquid at first, but the liquid will eventually (I promise) evaporate and a nice, caramelized exterior will form.

For the dressing, try to chop the pistachios finely so that they thicken and integrate into the sauce and are not just a crunchy addition. Tomatoes up to medium size will work, as long as they're super-sweet and in season. As with 99 percent of my seafood recipes, I want a ton of puckery citrus, so I make the dressing mostly out of lemon zest and juice. Aioli is not a must but, damn, it takes this dish over the edge.

SERVES 4

2 garlic cloves, finely grated

5 tablespoons extra-virgin olive oil, plus more for drizzling

1 pound cleaned squid bodies and tentacles

1 small shallot, finely chopped

1 teaspoon finely grated lemon zest

2 tablespoons fresh lemon juice

2 tablespoons pistachios, finely crushed or chopped

Kosher salt

12 ounces small to medium tomatoes, halved or quartered

⅓ cup oregano leaves

Chile flakes (your favorite kind), for sprinkling

Aioli (see page 61) for serving (optional)

In a medium bowl, whisk together the garlic and 3 tablespoons of the olive oil. Add the squid and toss to coat in the garlic oil.

In a large bowl, stir together the shallot, lemon zest, lemon juice, pistachios, and remaining 2 tablespoons olive oil. Season this pistachio dressing with salt and set aside.

Set a large cast-iron skillet over high heat for 5 minutes. You want it roaring hot to quickly cook the squid. Working in batches (do not overcrowd the pan; I also like to keep the bodies and tentacles separate because they often cook at different rates), arrange the squid in the pan and cook, turning occasionally, until lightly charred in spots and cooked through, 3 to 4 minutes. Transfer the squid to a cutting board and cut the tubes in half or in rings. Season with salt.

Add the tomatoes and oregano to the bowl with the pistachio dressing and season with salt. Give the tomatoes a toss and arrange on plates or a large platter and top with the squid. Drizzle with more olive oil and sprinkle with chile flakes. Serve with aioli on the side, if you like.

BUTTER-SLATHERED WHOLE FISH WITH JAMMY FENNEL

You can smear a whole chicken with butter, so why not fish? Let's face it, the crispy skin is more important than the silky flesh inside, but that's crucial, too, and cooking fish in the oven, as I do with this recipe, makes it easy to have both. Please don't be afraid of cooking a whole fish. There are two reasons to do it: (1) It's cheaper than fillets. (2) You get tons of crispy skin. Money in the bank! The fennel seeds in the butter perfume the fish while the butter browns. Why aren't we doing this all the time?

SERVES 4

3 large fennel bulbs

¼ cup extra-virgin olive oil, plus ⅓ cup

Kosher salt

2 teaspoons fennel seeds

6 tablespoons unsalted butter, at room temperature

3 garlic cloves, finely grated

2 (1-pound) whole branzino, small black bass, or trout, scaled and gutted

¾ cup Fresh and Puckery Lemon Sauce (page 36)

Place an oven rack in the bottom position and preheat the oven to 425°F.

Trim and discard the long stalks and fronds from the fennel bulbs, then trim each root end and remove any outer layers that look a little brown. Sit the fennel bulbs upright and cut it into about ½-inch-wide planks. Transfer to a rimmed baking sheet and pour in the ¼ cup olive oil. Season with salt and toss until each piece is coated. Spread out the fennel planks so they have room to brown rather than steam (which happens when they're all piled up). Roast the planks until they have formed a golden brown crust underneath, 12 to 15 minutes.

Meanwhile, in a mortar and pestle, crush the fennel seeds until finely ground, or pulse in a spice mill or finely chop using a chef's knife. Options! Put the butter, garlic, and ground fennel in a small bowl and, using a fork, mash and mix up everything.

Place the fish on a cutting board and pat dry thoroughly with paper towels. Smear the fennel butter all over the skin and dot a few pieces inside the tummies. Season the fish generously inside and out with salt.

Remove the fennel from the oven and flip each plank. Scoot the shrunken and caramelized fennel pieces to the corners of the baking sheet and lay the fish in the center. Roast the fish until it is opaque and flakes when pressed gently with a fork, and the other side of the fennel has become soft and jammy, 15 to 18 minutes.

Using a metal spatula, transfer the fennel and the fish onto a large platter. Spoon some of the lemon sauce over the fish and serve the rest alongside.

MEATY
THINGS

My meat philosophy (I'm supposed to have one?) is to eat really good meat, and not a lot of it.

"Really good" doesn't mean expensive; it means knowing where your meat comes from, supporting farms in your area who treat their animals right—you've heard all of this before. I think of meat as a special-occasion food, and so the recipes in this chapter reflect that. You'll find pared-down options that highlight a good cut, like A Proper Steak (Plus Brown Butter–Fried Onion Rings) on page 298, and then the party meats, like the braised lamb on page 282. You'll also learn plenty of techniques along the way, like how to achieve juicy white chicken meat (see page 270).

I prefer meat with its bone in, skin on, and as much marbling as possible, which all contribute to flavor and character. (So, if you're looking for boneless, skinless chicken breasts, you won't find them here.) I've found that the challenge for people learning to cook meat is fear and discomfort. The chicken is slimy, the muscles tough to cut, the blood, oh the blood! And the only way to get over it is to face it—or be vegetarian. Nothing wrong with that (just turn to page 153).

JUICY CHICKEN BREAST AND ANTIPASTO SALAD

For most of my life as a carnivorous human on planet Earth, I sneered at chicken breasts. If I were to eat them, I wanted them breaded and fried (tomato sauce on the side, please!). Truth is, chicken breasts are a low success–rate cut of meat because they have very little fat, which typically results in them being dry, tough, and reserved for bodybuilders and sad people. The way to get around this and be a happier juicy, white meat–eating person is to go for chicken breasts with their skin and bones intact, because they act as a kind of armor that prevents the meat from drying out while it's quickly seared and then roasted. I almost always want something briny, wet, and crunchy with my protein, and this lighter version of an Italian antipasto salad also gives me an excuse to buy a jar of those neon-colored pepperoncini that I can't live without.

SERVES 4

2 large bone-in, skin-on chicken breasts

Kosher salt

2 tablespoons extra-virgin olive oil, plus ¼ cup

1 cup castelvetrano olives

6 celery stalks, thinly sliced, plus any leaves!

1 cup parsley leaves

1 cup pepperoncini, plus 2 tablespoons pepperoncini brine

½ small red onion, thinly sliced, rinsed

1 cup toasted walnuts (see page 24), coarsely chopped

3 tablespoons red wine vinegar or sherry vinegar

Freshly ground pepper

3 ounces Parmesan, shaved (about 1 cup)

Preheat the oven to 425°F.

Pat the chicken dry with paper towels, season it all over with salt, and then set aside for 15 minutes for the salt to absorb.

In a large ovenproof skillet over medium-high heat, heat the 2 tablespoons olive oil. Arrange the chicken, skin-side down, in the skillet and cook, using tongs to press it down occasionally, until the skin is deeply golden brown and crisp, 4 to 6 minutes. Turn the chicken over and immediately transfer the skillet to the oven. Roast the chicken until the thickest part of the breast registers 145°F on an instant-read thermometer, 20 to 25 minutes. Using tongs, transfer the chicken to a cutting board and let cool for 10 minutes.

While the chicken rests, using the side of a chef's knife or the bottom of a mug, crush the olives to break them into large craggy pieces. Toss out the pits. Place the olives in a large bowl and stir in the celery and leaves, parsley, pepperoncini and brine, onion, walnuts, and vinegar. Pour in the remaining ¼ cup olive oil and season with salt and lots of pepper. Give the celery a taste. It should be plenty seasoned and vinegary. (Celery is the wateriest ingredient, and if that tastes good, everything else will taste good.)

Carve the chicken breast away from the bone, then cut it into thick slices, ¼ to ½ inch wide. Divide the chicken and salad among four plates, garnish with the pepper and Parm, and serve.

DO AHEAD

The chicken can be made 2 days ahead but CANNOT be reheated. Bring it to room temperature or slice and serve it cold.

SPICY CHICKEN AND TOMATO CONFIT

It makes sense to me that the little gay boy who loved to cook had a fascination with the term *confit*. It's French (which I thought sounded fancy) and, although it was originally a method for preservation, now it's a lesson in excess—and how luxurious that can be. Chicken legs cook slowly in a bath of olive oil until they develop a shreddy, barely-able-to-hold-on-to-the-bone texture. The other ingredients added to the mix benefit from all that fat as well. Shallots and garlic become sweet and jammy. The lemon perfumes the oil while becoming so soft you could eat the whole fruit. The chiles add a zap of heat. And those tomatoes, well, they're perfect. They shrink up, forcing their sugars to concentrate, giving them a juicy jamminess you won't forget.

SERVES 4

4 whole bone-in, skin-on chicken legs or 2½ to 3 pounds bone-in, skin-on drumsticks and thighs

Kosher salt

1 pound small tomatoes, halved lengthwise

3 shallots, skins left on, halved lengthwise

2 garlic heads, unpeeled, halved crosswise

1 lemon, quartered and seeded

8 jarred Calabrian chiles, or 3 fresh red chiles, halved lengthwise

4 rosemary sprigs

1½ cups extra-virgin olive oil

Sherry or red wine vinegar for splashing

Preheat the oven to 325°F.

Season the chicken all over with salt and let sit for 15 minutes for the salt to absorb.

Put the chicken into a 9 by 13-inch baking dish or a shallow braising dish. Scatter the tomatoes, shallots, garlic, lemon, chiles, and rosemary around the chicken; things will likely be very snug and that's more than okay. Pour in the olive oil so everything is mostly submerged in the fat.

Place the baking dish in the oven and roast the chicken until the meat is almost falling off the bone, the tomatoes have shriveled up, and it smells very delicious, 1½ to 2 hours. Let cool for 10 minutes.

Scoop up about 3 tablespoons of the oil from the baking dish, pour it into a large well-seasoned cast-iron or nonstick skillet, and place over medium-high heat. Using tongs, transfer the chicken legs to the skillet, skin-side down, and cook, pressing down on the legs and moving the skillet around so the skin browns evenly, 2 to 3 minutes.

Transfer the legs to a large plate or platter. Using a slotted spoon, scoop the goodies from the baking dish, including some of the oil, and add to the chicken on the platter. Splash a tablespoon or two of vinegar over everything and serve.

DO AHEAD

The chicken can be cooked a few hours, or even 1 day, ahead. It's very delicious at room temperature.

GOOD FAT

The schmaltzy leftover fat can be strained into an airtight container and refrigerated for up to 1 month. Use it to fry up some eggs, crisp up potatoes (see page 180), or fold into a pot of rice.

STICKY-SWEET ROAST CHICKEN

This chicken is inspired by the well-named "Famous Garlic Aromatic Crispy Chicken" at Wu's Wonton King in New York City. The key to the perfect texture, browned skin, and shreddable meat is starting at a super-high heat and dropping the temp the second that the bird goes into the oven. The glaze requires a few rounds of shellacking before it sticks, so, uh, stick with it. And because you have this sticky chicken skin, you need *exxxxxtra* crunch for textural contrast in the form of fried shallot, garlic, and ginger.

SERVES 2 (HUNGRY PEOPLE OR
4 MODERATELY HUNGRY)

1 (3½- to 4-pound) whole chicken

Kosher salt

Freshly ground pepper

¼ cup packed light brown sugar

¼ cup unseasoned rice vinegar

3 tablespoons low-sodium
soy sauce or tamari

2 tablespoons neutral oil
(such as grapeseed), plus ¼ cup

1 large shallot, thinly sliced
into rings

6 garlic cloves, thinly sliced

2 tablespoons peeled,
finely chopped ginger

Lots of chopped cilantro
for topping

Thinly sliced scallions for topping

Pickled ginger for topping

Buttery Nori-Speckled Rice
(page 200) or cooked short-grain
rice for serving (optional)

Preheat the oven to 450°F.

Season the chicken inside and out with salt and pepper, really getting into all of the crevices. Let the chicken hang out for at least 1 hour at room temperature, which will help the meat absorb the salt. If you can season a few days in advance and let rest, uncovered, in the fridge, even better.

In a small skillet over medium heat, combine the brown sugar, vinegar, and soy sauce and stir to incorporate. Bring to a simmer and cook until you see lots of big bubbles and the mixture has thickened just enough to coat the back of a spoon, 5 to 7 minutes. Pour this glaze into a small bowl and set aside. Wipe out the skillet and set aside for later.

If you notice any beads of water on the chicken skin that may have released after you seasoned it, pat it dry with a paper towel to help it brown. Place the chicken in a large cast-iron skillet and rub it all over with the 2 tablespoons neutral oil.

Slide the skillet onto the oven's center rack, so the chicken legs are facing toward the back (this is the hottest part of the oven and will help the legs cook before the breast dries out) and turn the temperature to 325°F. Roast the chicken, brushing with the glaze two or three times, until the skin is glossy, sticky, and the flesh is cooked through, 80 to 90 minutes.

Meanwhile, pour the remaining ¼ cup neutral oil into the reserved skillet and add the shallot rings, garlic, and chopped ginger. Place the skillet over medium heat and cook, stirring to make sure everything is crisping evenly, until the shallot and garlic are golden brown and crisp and the ginger has slightly darkened, 7 to 10 minutes. Using a slotted spoon, scoop out the crispy bits from the oil and scatter them over a paper towel to drain. Season with salt while it's still hot.

Pull the chicken from the oven and let rest for 20 minutes, so the juices can redistribute (nonnegotiable). Carve the chicken and place it on a platter, topping it with the crispy bits plus cilantro, pickled scallions, and pickled ginger. Serve with rice on the side.

TANGY POMEGRANATE CHICKEN

Fesenjan is a controversial Persian stew. (Maybe, I guess, they all are?) Whether you make it sour or sweet is the biggest point of contention. For me, it shouldn't be sour and it shouldn't be sweet. It should be perfectly both, and with a little tingle. Walnuts, pomegranate molasses, and chicken are the core trio (hundreds of years ago that meat would have been peacock). My fesenjan recipe will be in my Persian cookbook one day, along with all of my other Persian secrets, but for now, here's more of a chicken braise with a good amount of atypical lime juice, all inspired by fesenjan but definitely not a version of it—not at all.

SERVES 4

4 whole bone-in, skin-on chicken legs, or 2½ to 3 pounds bone-in, skin-on drumsticks and thighs

Kosher salt

1 tablespoon neutral oil (such as grapeseed)

1 yellow onion, finely chopped

1 cup raw walnuts, coarsely chopped

½ teaspoon ground turmeric

¼ teaspoon ground cinnamon

¾ cup water

½ cup pomegranate molasses

¼ cup fresh lime juice

1 large handful herbs (such as basil, cilantro, and/or dill)

Preheat the oven to 325°F.

Pat the chicken dry with paper towels, season all over with salt, and let sit for 10 to 15 minutes for the salt to absorb.

Pour the neutral oil into a large ovenproof skillet and place over medium-high heat. Lay the chicken legs in the skillet, skin-side down, so they are snug and lying flat. Cook, using tongs to press down on the chicken, so the skin makes contact with the bottom of the pan to encourage browning, until the legs are surrounded by their own fat and the skin underneath is deeply browned, 5 to 7 minutes. Transfer the chicken to a plate, skin-side up, leaving that golden chicken fat behind.

Let the skillet cool for a few minutes, then return it to medium heat. Add the onion and cook, stirring and scraping any brown bits that may have stuck to the bottom of the pan, until the onion is lightly charred around the edges, 6 to 8 minutes. Add the walnuts and continue to cook until they smell nutty and the onion is deep golden brown in most spots, another 3 to 5 minutes. Sprinkle in the turmeric and cinnamon and stir, so the spices can bloom.

Pour the water, pomegranate molasses, and lime juice into the skillet and season lightly with salt. Nestle the chicken back into the skillet, skin-side up, and spoon some of the sauce over each leg. Transfer the skillet to the oven, uncovered, and bake the chicken legs until the sauce has thickened and the flesh is begging to be torn away from the bone, 50 to 60 minutes. Scatter the herbs on top, or on the side, of the chicken legs and serve.

CHILE AND CITRUSY YOGURT-BRINED ROAST CHICKEN

This recipe is evidence of my wishing that I could have a tandoor in my tiny New York kitchen. But when I have a house in the country with a brick-oven tandoor, a massive collection of cast iron, and a man who'll love me forever . . . I'll cook over the fire. But enough fantasy. In reality, this is a rigged version that isn't even close to a real tandoor. Get the oven going at high heat and pretend with me. The yogurt marinade adds tang and helps the chicken tenderize. When the chicken skin is dark, burnished, and puffing up, you're done.

SERVES 4

1 yellow onion, coarsely chopped

6 garlic cloves, crushed

4 serrano or jalapeño chiles, halved, seeded, and coarsely chopped

1½ cups full-fat yogurt (not Greek)

2 tablespoons extra-virgin olive oil, plus ¼ cup

2 tablespoons finely grated lemon and/or grapefruit zest

Kosher salt

1 teaspoon ground turmeric

1 (3½- to 4-pound) whole chicken

1½ pounds tiny potatoes

Freshly ground pepper

In a blender, combine the onion, garlic, chiles, yogurt, 2 tablespoons olive oil, citrus zest, 2 tablespoons salt, and turmeric and puree until you have a silky-smooth brine.

Pat the chicken dry with paper towels and put it in a large bowl. Pour in the yogurt brine. Using your hands—or tongs, if you must—flip the chicken so it is dressed all over. If the chicken isn't fully submerged in the brine, weigh it down with an inverted plate. Transfer the bowl to the fridge to brine the chicken for 12 to 24 hours, flipping the chicken after the first 6 to 12 hours. (No big bowl? No room in your apartment fridge for a big bowl? Brine the chicken in a gallon-size resealable plastic bag.) Remove the chicken from the fridge 1 hour before you plan to roast it.

Preheat the oven to 425°F.

Lift the chicken from the brine, letting any excess drip off, and place, breast-side up, on a rimmed baking sheet.

In a medium bowl, toss the potatoes with the remaining ¼ cup olive oil and season with salt and pepper, then arrange them around the chicken.

Place the baking sheet in the oven so the chicken legs face the back. Roast, without peeking or fussing, until the potatoes are tender and the chicken skin is deeply golden brown and seems to have puffed up (this usually happens, but not always) and the thickest part of a breast registers 150°F on an instant-read thermometer, 50 to 60 minutes.

Remove the baking sheet from the oven and let the chicken rest for 15 minutes. Transfer the chicken to a cutting board (but don't clean that baking sheet) and carve it. Arrange the chicken on a platter with the potatoes, pour any juices that remain on the baking sheet over the potatoes, and serve.

SHAWARMA-SPICED LAMB CHOPS WITH PICKLE SALAD

Although these chops beg to be grilled on an open fire, you can skip that and sear them in an oiled cast-iron pan for 3 minutes per side. The shawarma spice is my way of trying to re-create the smell and flavor from the New York City halal carts that I survived on in college. Stir it with yogurt and it becomes a marinade that is delicious on these chops, but I've also spread it on pork chops, chicken wings, and beef short ribs. The pickle salad is pure pucker. You need something bright and acidic to cut the fatty lamb. I prefer the svelte, Middle Eastern–style cucumber pickles because they're saltier than they are sweet, but any pickle, cucumber or not (Radish! Okra! Turnip!), would be delicious.

SERVES 4

1 tablespoon coriander seeds

1½ teaspoons cumin seeds

1½ teaspoons black peppercorns

1½ teaspoons smoked paprika

¾ teaspoon ground turmeric

4 garlic cloves, finely grated

¼ cup full-fat Greek yogurt or sour cream

2 tablespoons neutral oil (such as grapeseed)

12 lamb rib chops (about 3 pounds)

Kosher salt

½ small white onion, thinly sliced

1 cup very coarsely chopped pickles (your favorite half- or full-sour work well here)

1 cup parsley

2 tablespoons fresh lemon juice, or as needed

Extra-virgin olive oil for drizzling

Toum (page 62) for serving

Fluffy (and Crisp) Flatbread (page 111) or a nice store-bought one, warmed for serving

In a spice mill, combine the coriander seeds, cumin seeds, peppercorns, paprika, and turmeric and pulse until finely ground. Pour the spice mixture into a large bowl and whisk in the garlic, yogurt, and neutral oil.

Sprinkle the lamb chops all over with salt and then toss them in the yogurt mixture until coated. Don't bother with tongs—they just get in the way. Use your hands and embrace the fact that you'll smell like spices and garlic for a couple of hours. Let the chops sit at room temperature for at least 20 minutes, or cover and chill for up to 12 hours.

Preheat the grill to medium-high for 10 minutes.

Once the grill grates are hot, remove the lamb chops from their marinade and arrange them on the grill. Cook, turning every minute to allow the fat to render, until the ribs have formed a beautifully caramelized crust, or until an instant-read thermometer inserted into thickest part of a chop registers 120°F for medium-rare, 6 to 8 minutes. If the fire begins to flare, move the chops to a cooler spot on the grill (usually the area on the grill closest to you). Transfer the chops to a platter and let rest for 5 to 10 minutes.

While the chops rest, in a medium bowl, toss together the onion, pickles, parsley, and lemon juice. Drizzle with a touch of olive oil, season with salt, and toss once more. Add more salt and lemon juice to taste.

Serve the chops with the pickle salad, a bowl of toum, and flatbread. Dinner isn't over 'til you've gnawed on the bones.

TO FRENCH OR NOT TO FRENCH?

The answer is *never*. *Frenched* is a term for the process of cutting away the flavorful fat and the last few inches of meat from the bone end of a rib chop (you see this often with lamb chops and bone-in rib eyes). It's purely aesthetic, making the chops, as what some people may think, more presentable and elegant, but when you french a chop, you're getting rid of some of the best parts. We want *all* the fat here.

CRUSHED ORANGE AND ROSEMARY-BRAISED LAMB WITH CRUNCHY PISTACHIO YOGURT

This is the big, showy piece of meat you've been waiting for. The green garlic, citrus, and yogurt contrast with the rich, heavy lamb, lending freshness to liven up the deep, braised flavor. And although any large cut of meat can seem intimidating to prepare, most of the work happens in the oven. The result is lamb so tender it's almost jelly-soft. You can either go bold and serve it on the bone or let it cool and tear it into shreddy shards, then toss those back into the braising liquid to warm. Important announcement: Crisp up any leftovers in a pan with neutral oil (or use the rendered lamb fat to fry a couple eggs and pop them on top) and add a crunchy salad for next night's dinner.

SERVES 8

BRAISED LAMB

1 (6- to 7-pound) bone-in lamb shoulder

Kosher salt

½ cup extra-virgin olive oil

2 red onions, quartered through the root end

6 green garlic stalks, coarsely chopped, or 2 garlic heads, sliced crosswise

4 (2-inch) strips orange peel

1 handful rosemary or thyme sprigs and/or bay leaves

2 dried chiles de árbol, or ½ teaspoon red pepper flakes

1 tablespoon fennel seeds

2 cups dry white wine (that's good enough to drink)

1 quart Drinkable Chicken Broth (page 232) or good store-bought chicken stock or water, or as needed

To make the braised lamb: Pat the meat dry with paper towels and then season all over with salt. (If you can do this a day ahead and chill the lamb, great. If not, carry on.)

Preheat the oven to 325°F.

Pour ¼ cup of the olive oil into a heavy ovenproof pot, large enough to hold the lamb comfortably, and place it over medium-high heat. Add the lamb and sear all over, waiting until the underside has become deeply brown and caramelized before turning, 4 to 6 minutes per side and 15 to 20 minutes total. You want the lamb to caramelize while rendering some of its fat. Using tongs, lift and transfer the lamb to a plate and set aside.

Carefully tilt the fat out of the pot into a small bowl. Save this! (Use a spoonful to tame the bitterness of hardy greens or to add richness to brothy beans; see page 235.)

Return the pot to medium heat and pour in the remaining ¼ cup olive oil. Add the onions and green garlic and give them a stir, so they get nicely coated in the oil. Cook, stirring occasionally, until they have taken on a golden brown color in spots (they won't be soft, but that's okay), 4 to 6 minutes.

Crush the orange peels and rosemary sprigs in your hands and scatter them over the onions and green garlic, along with the chiles and fennel seeds. Warm them a bit to release their aromas, 10 to 15 seconds, remove the pot from the stove and place the lamb back into the pot. Pour in the wine and chicken broth; the liquid should come just slightly above the halfway point on the side of the meat. If you need more, just add more broth, if you have it, or water.

Place the pot in the oven, uncovered, and braise the lamb, flipping it every 45 minutes or so to make sure it's cooking evenly, until the liquid has slightly reduced and the meat is begging to pull away from the bone, 3½ to 4 hours. Using tongs, transfer the lamb to a cutting board and let rest for 20 to 30 minutes.

CONTINUED

CRUSHED ORANGE AND ROSEMARY–BRAISED LAMB WITH CRUNCHY PISTACHIO YOGURT, CONTINUED

CRUNCHY PISTACHIO YOGURT

2 tablespoons raisins, chopped

1 tablespoon fresh lemon juice

1 garlic clove, finely grated

3 cups full-fat Greek yogurt

⅓ cup toasted pistachios
(see page 24), coarsely chopped

Kosher salt

Extra-virgin olive oil for drizzling

Strain the braising liquid into a medium saucepan, picking out and tasting a jammy onion or garlic clove that has been cooked to death but is still somehow satisfying. Give the braising liquid a taste; it will be on the oily side. The lamb will have rendered quite a bit of fat that you'll want to skim most, but not all, off. Although fat is flavor, too much fat can prevent you from tasting the other ingredients. At this point, you have a few options and I advise you to apply this technique with any braise you do. Serve the braising liquid on the side as a sauce for the lamb (as instructed here), save it for another meal, or use it as a base for a soup or stew. Find your match. I tend to reduce the braising liquid over medium heat until it just barely coats the back of a spoon (10 to 15 minutes) but you can reduce it further, by half or more. Just remember, as the liquid reduces, the broth becomes richer and more concentrated in flavor and will go from barely coating the back of the spoon to clinging onto it for dear life. Pour the reduced liquid into a small pitcher for serving.

To make the pistachio yogurt: In a medium bowl, stir together the raisins, lemon juice, and garlic. Let sit for 5 minutes to soften the raisins. Add the yogurt and pistachios and then season with salt. Give it all a stir.

When the lamb is cool enough to handle, pull or carve the meat into big shardy pieces and arrange them on a platter. Or, if you feel especially comfortable with your crowd, just put a knife and fork on the platter and let people tear into it. Pass the warm braising liquid to spoon over the lamb and the pistachio yogurt to dollop on top.

LAMB, PLEASE

I grew up eating lamb, which is a staple meat in Iranian cuisine, and most of the time, it was the shoulder, leg, or the whole head (our annual Christmas morning breakfast). These parts have stronger—yes, *gamey*—flavor and more muscle tissue, making them tricky to master. Lamb chops, on the other hand, have a milder flavor and cook in minutes.

SPICY PORK LARB WITH PLENTY OF HERBS

Every place to which I travel leaves a mark on me, especially in the way I cook and eat (I like to think that I leave a little mark on that place as well). In Thailand, I had my first taste of larb, the intensely spicy meat salad. Larb is the national dish of Laos, but it's also eaten in Thailand. Larb is, essentially, a piece of meat, maybe lamb, chicken, or fish, broken down into a very fine chop that is then seasoned with a variety of herbs and aromatics.

My version leans more Laotian as well as toward the Isan region of Thailand, which means it's heavy on the heat, the sour, and the fish sauce. Though it still has less heat than the larbs that I ate in Thailand. Serving it with crisp cabbage or lettuce cups, and steamed jasmine rice, will help tame the heat. So will an ice-cold beer.

SERVES 4

2 tablespoons fish sauce

2 tablespoons fresh lime juice

2 teaspoons granulated sugar

1 tablespoon warm water

2 tablespoons neutral oil (such as grapeseed)

4 garlic cloves, crushed

1 pound ground pork, beef, or lamb

Kosher salt

3 scallions, thinly sliced

1 large shallot, or 1 small red onion, thinly sliced

1 or 2 bird's eye chiles (depending on how hot you like it), stemmed and thinly sliced

1 lemongrass stalk, bottom third only (about 6 inches long), tough outer layers removed, thinly sliced

2 cups chopped herbs (such as cilantro, dill, mint, and/or Thai basil)

Cabbage leaves for serving

Sliced cucumber for serving

Steamed rice (see page 200) for serving

In a small bowl, stir together the fish sauce, lime juice, sugar, and water until the sugar dissolves. Set aside.

In a large saucepan over medium heat, combine the neutral oil and garlic and cook, stirring occasionally and smashing down on the garlic with a wooden spoon, until most pieces are golden brown, 2 to 3 minutes. Don't let the garlic brown too much or it'll make everything taste bitter. Add the pork, season lightly with salt, and cook, smashing the meat with the wooden spoon to break it apart, until no more pink spots remain, but it has *not* browned, about 4 minutes. (When ground meat is cooked "hard" over hot heat, it caramelizes but also becomes dry and develops a rubber band–like texture—not fun to eat. If this were a meat sauce, a Bolognese, say, the meat *should* be browned because, once you add liquid, the meat softens as the sauce simmers.)

Back to cooking. As soon as the pink disappears, toss the scallions, shallot, chile(s), and lemongrass in with the meat, and cook for another minute. Remove the pan from the heat and pour in the fish sauce mixture, add the herbs, and toss once more. Taste and adjust the seasoning with salt. The flavors should taste balanced between the chile, fish sauce, lime juice, and herbs—none should take all the attention.

Serve the larb hot or at room temp, spooned into cabbage leaves with cucumber slices and steamed rice. I highly suggest eating this with your hands.

MAKE IT VEGETARIAN

To make the larb vegetarian, swap out the meat for 1 pound torn shiitake, maitake, or any other mushrooms you like. Replace the fish sauce with 2 tablespoons soy sauce. Unlike the meat, when cooking the mushrooms you *do* want them deeply browned. If they get a bit crispy and lacy around the edges, even better.

PORK CHOPS WITH TOASTED GARLIC AND SPICY CAPERS

I don't have the patience to brine pork chops. I want them the second that I get home from the store with the groceries. One key to that crust you dream about is adding a little sugar, a trick I picked up at *Bon Appétit* (thanks, Chris Morocco). Another key is to keep flipping them as they cook, so they don't get a chance to overcook. Once the chops are good to go, let them rest and make a crispy, crunchy pan sauce-slash-warm vinaigrette to spoon over them—generously. (And, say your chops do overcook because, hey, it happens, the warm vinaigrette will restore some moisture.)

SERVES 4

1 teaspoon granulated sugar

4 (1½-inch-thick) bone-in pork rib chops

Kosher salt

2 tablespoons extra-virgin olive oil, plus ⅓ cup

¼ cup capers, drained and rinsed

4 garlic cloves, thinly sliced

1 teaspoon red pepper flakes

¼ cup coarsely chopped parsley

2 tablespoons red wine vinegar

Sprinkle the sugar evenly over the chops, then season them all over with salt. Let the chops hang out for 20 minutes at room temperature, or chill in the fridge, uncovered, for up to 24 hours.

Place a large cast-iron skillet over medium-high heat. Rub the chops with the 2 tablespoons olive oil, making sure they are completely coated. This ensures the pork chops will brown while minimizing the smoke that'll come from the skillet.

Place the pork chops in the skillet and sear them (it helps to use tongs to press down on the meat, so it makes direct contact with the surface of the hot pan, and cook) without moving the meat around, until golden brown in spots, 2 minutes. Flip the chops and continue to sear, pressing down, so the other side becomes similarly golden brown, another 2 minutes. Keep flipping and cooking the chops for 1 minute per side, until they have taken on a deep golden brown and caramelized color and an instant-read thermometer inserted into the center of the thickest chop reads somewhere between 130° and 135°F, 6 to 8 minutes, depending on the thickness of the chops. Turn the pork chops upright and sear all along the fat cap until crisp, about 1 minute.

Transfer the pork chops to a cutting board and let rest for 10 minutes while you make the sauce. Carefully wipe out the skillet. Pour the remaining ⅓ cup olive oil into the skillet and place it over medium heat. Add the capers and cook, swirling the pan often, until some of the capers begin to look like they're about to bud like a flower, 2 to 3 minutes. Add the garlic and continue cooking until pale golden and the capers have crisped up, about 2 minutes more.

Transfer the crispy bits and hot oil to a medium bowl and stir in the red pepper flakes. Then stir in the parsley and vinegar. Taste the sauce. The capers will have added their brininess, but you'll likely need another pinch of salt.

Cut the meat away from the bone, then slice it against the grain into ½-inch-thick pieces. Transfer the meat (and, for drama, the bone!) to a plate, spoon on the crispy caper garlic sauce, and serve.

KUFTEH, A DIFFERENT KIND OF MEATBALL

Supposedly, my first words were "hum hum," directed at the kufteh that my mother was tearing up and feeding me as a baby. Every time she tells the story, I feel like was a different dish. The point is, I loved food. *Kufteh* is Farsi for "meatballs," and they are made throughout Iran, in various sizes, like kufteh tabrizi, which are enormous—the size of two human fists—and with various fillings. In that spirit, these are tennis ball–size meatballs stuffed with herbs, rice, and turmeric, which get cooked in a bright, spicy tomato sauce that isn't very Iranian at all, so I'm breaking tradition.

SERVES 4

1 egg

¾ cup cooked long-grain white rice, cooled

½ cup finely chopped herbs (a mix of chives, dill, parsley, and/or tarragon), plus more for serving

6 tablespoons extra-virgin olive oil, plus more for drizzling

½ teaspoon ground turmeric

1¼ pounds ground beef, lamb, pork, or turkey (feel free to use a combination)

Kosher salt

1 yellow onion, thinly sliced

6 garlic cloves, thinly sliced

3 tablespoons tomato paste

1 teaspoon red pepper flakes

2 pints Sungold or cherry tomatoes

2 cups water

In a large bowl using a fork, beat the egg. Stir in the rice, herbs, 2 tablespoons of the olive oil, and turmeric until you have a somewhat evenly combined mixture. Add the ground meat and 1½ teaspoons salt to the bowl. Using your hands like the claw at an arcade game, mix everything until well combined. Gently roll the mixture into meatballs slightly smaller than the size of a tennis ball, but bigger than the meatballs you find at IKEA, placing each kufteh on a large plate as you roll them. You don't want to pack the mixture super-tight as you roll it; you want to keep the kufteh light.

In a large heavy pot over medium heat, warm the remaining 4 tablespoons olive oil. Add the onion and garlic and stir to coat everything in the oil. Season with salt and cook, stirring occasionally, until the onion and garlic have become soft and taken on a pale golden color, 10 to 12 minutes. Stir in the tomato paste and red pepper flakes and cook until the tomato paste starts to stick to the bottom of the pot and has slightly darkened, about 3 minutes.

Toss the tomatoes into the pot and cook, using a wooden spoon to stir and scrape any brown bits stuck to the bottom of the pot, until most of the tomatoes begin to burst their skins, 7 to 9 minutes. If the pan looks dry, add a splash of the water to loosen things up. Once most of the tomatoes have broken down, pour in the rest of the water and season with salt. Bring the sauce to a simmer and continue cooking until it has slightly reduced but is still quite brothy, 5 to 10 minutes.

Turn the heat to medium-low and, one at a time, drop the meatballs into the sauce. Cover the pot, leaving the lid slightly ajar, and simmer, occasionally spooning some sauce over the kufteh (not a must, but it's what I do), until the kufteh are cooked through and can be broken easily with a fork, 20 to 30 minutes.

Ladle meatballs and sauce into bowls or leave in the pot. Serve topped with herbs and a drizzle of olive oil.

DO AHEAD

The meatballs and sauce can be cooked 1 day ahead. Let cool to room temperature, then cover and refrigerate. Rewarm over medium-low heat.

BUTTERY BEEF AND PEANUT STIR-FRY

I get these intense cravings for stir-fries. Whether it's the hottest humid night or a blistering cold day, a stir-fry energizes me in a way that few dishes can. This one is on regular rotation in my home kitchen.

I tend to go for cuts of meat that have a healthy amount of fat on them, so they don't dry out against the intense heat of the pan. Start by popping the meat in the freezer for 10 minutes, which makes it easier to slice. Then, measure everything else, placing the ingredients in all your little prep bowls; you want every ingredient ready to go because this dish comes together fast. The leeks will become juicy (yes!) as they cook quickly in the butter-vinegar sauce. The beef gets a touch of caramelization from the sugar and assertive sherry vinegar. And once you realize how easy this recipe is, you'll be making it once a week.

SERVES 4

1 pound hanger or skirt steak or boneless short ribs

2 tablespoons neutral oil (such as grapeseed)

2 teaspoons freshly ground pepper

2 teaspoons peeled, finely grated ginger

2 teaspoons packed light brown or granulated sugar

1 teaspoon toasted sesame oil

Kosher salt

2 medium leeks

2 tablespoons unsalted butter, cut into pieces

1 tablespoon sherry vinegar or fresh lemon juice

1 tablespoon soy sauce

⅓ cup coarsely chopped toasted peanuts

Using your chef's knife, slice the beef against the grain into ¼-inch-thick strips about 2 inches long. In a medium bowl, whisk 1 tablespoon of the neutral oil, the pepper, ginger, brown sugar, and sesame oil to combine. This marinade won't be totally smooth, which is totally okay. Add the beef, sprinkle with 1 teaspoon salt, and toss to coat. Let marinate in the fridge for 20 minutes if you have the time. If not, keep moving.

Trim and discard the hairy root end and the dark green tops from the leeks. Halve the leeks lengthwise, then coarsely chop on an angle into 2-inch-ish pieces. Give the leeks a good rinse to remove any dirt and set aside.

Set a large cast-iron or stainless-steel skillet over medium-high heat. Add the remaining 1 tablespoon neutral oil and heat until very, very hot. Using tongs, add half the beef to the skillet in a single layer and cook, without stirring or tossing, until deeply brown around the edges, 2 to 3 minutes. The pieces at the edges of the pan will brown faster than the ones in the center, so flip those first. Flip and cook on the other sides until no longer pink, about 30 seconds. Transfer the beef to a plate and repeat with the remaining pieces.

Once all the beef has browned, return it to the skillet and add the leeks, butter, vinegar, and soy sauce. Season lightly with salt and cook, tossing or stirring often, until the butter is melted, the leeks have slightly wilted, and you have a smooth sauce that coats the steak, about 30 seconds. Turn off the heat and scatter the peanuts over the beef. It should look nasty good.

DO AHEAD

The beef can be marinated up to 1 day ahead. Cover it tightly and keep refrigerated until ready to use.

MISO AND CHILE-RUBBED, GRILLED SHORT RIBS

Flanken-cut short ribs—ribs cut across the bones instead of between them—are popularly used in Korean barbecue, so you can always find them at any H Mart, which are among my favorite supermarkets in the States. Their snack aisle is dangerous, to the point that I usually have a meal *before* going there. Back to the meat: The most difficult thing about cooking flanken-cut ribs is getting a butcher to cut them for you. If it were easier to get them, they might become one of your favorite cuts. They're relatively cheap, have a tremendous amount of well-marbled fat, and cook in minutes because of how thin they are. This marinade is predominantly miso with lots of garlic—it's intense, so you don't need to wait overnight to get grilling; just 30 minutes will do the trick. Once the short ribs are charred all over, and I mean *all* over, serve them ssam-style with lettuce leaves, perilla leaves, kimchi, some rice, and this vinegary scallion salad.

SERVES 4

SHORT RIBS

6 garlic cloves, crushed

4 medium-hot chiles (such as Fresno, Holland, or serrano), halved, and seeded

3-inch piece ginger, peeled and thinly sliced

¼ cup packed light brown sugar

3 tablespoons unseasoned rice vinegar

2 tablespoons white miso

2 teaspoons toasted sesame oil

3 pounds (¼- to ½-inch-thick) flanken-cut (crosscut) bone-in beef short ribs

Kosher salt

SCALLION SALAD

6 scallions

1 tablespoon unseasoned rice vinegar

2 teaspoons gochugaru

2 teaspoons toasted sesame seeds (see page 24)

1 teaspoon granulated sugar

Kosher salt

Buttery Nori-Speckled Rice (page 200)

Your favorite kimchi for serving

To prepare the short ribs: Drop the garlic, chiles, ginger, brown sugar, vinegar, miso, and sesame oil into a blender and process until you have a smooth marinade.

Spread the short ribs out on a rimmed baking sheet and season both sides with about 2 teaspoons salt. You don't need to go too heavy because the miso will add another salty layer to the ribs. Pour the marinade over the ribs and, using tongs, toss, ensuring each rib is coated with the marinade. Cover the ribs and place in the fridge to chill for at least 30 minutes or up to 4 hours.

To make the scallion salad: While the short ribs marinate, halve the scallions lengthwise, then thinly slice them on a steep diagonal. Fill a salad spinner with cold water and a few ice cubes and drop in the scallions. Let them sit for 10 minutes and watch them curl. Drain and toss out any ice cubes that didn't melt. Spin the scallions dry and set aside. In a medium bowl, whisk the vinegar, gochugaru, sesame seeds, and granulated sugar until you have something that resembles a loose paste.

Preheat the grill to high.

Arrange the short ribs on the grill grates and cook, using tongs to move them around a touch, so they get spectacularly scuffed up and lightly charred all around, about 2 minutes per side. Transfer the ribs to a platter and set aside.

Add the scallions to the bowl with the vinegar paste and season with salt. Using your hands, toss and scrunch the scallions until well coated in the dressing.

Set out the platter of short ribs, along with the scallion salad, rice, and kimchi and let people assemble the perfect bites for themselves.

DO AHEAD

The scallions can be soaked in ice water up to 1 day ahead. Store in an airtight container in the fridge until ready to use.

Three Memorable-As-Hell Steaks

I. Skinny Steak

When I was, um, trying to get in shape in high school, I put myself on the Atkins diet. (Don't judge.) My incredible, always supportive mother went out and bought a Costco bag of So. Many. Steaks. What kind of steak? Thanks for asking. They were labeled "Premium Steaks." We grilled them in a George Foreman grill. Hey, it worked better than some cooktops I've used and the steak was good enough to spark a lifelong quest. This was my introduction to cooking steak. (My Atkins phase didn't last as long as that bag of steaks in the freezer.)

II. I'll Have Diane

My favorite steak memory is from when I was a teenager eating at the Cheesecake Factory at Union Square, in downtown San Francisco. From that giant laminated menu, I ordered the steak Diane. Steak au poivre gets all the attention for its peppery cream sauce, but Diane gets that sauce *and* a pile of jammy onions on top. She's better. Eating that steak, followed by a white chocolate–raspberry cheesecake, I was one happy teenage boy.

III. Bourdain Steak

I remember watching the Paris episode of *No Reservations* as a teenager and being riveted as Anthony Bourdain gorged on an entrecôte steak (bone-in rib eye) at Chez Robert et Louise in the Marais, a dim, otherworldly restaurant. During that episode, I had the first of a thought I've had many times since: I have to go to this restaurant before I die. Three years later, I went. It was incredible. I was obsessed with everything. The fat, knobby wooden tables. The hammering of people cutting thick pieces of steak. And the steak itself. It was perfectly pink, its sear as crunchy as burnt toast. The potatoes were coarse and torn, crunchy on the outside and fluffy inside. There was a dish of gray salt on the table to sprinkle over every bite. Then and there, I realized gluttony will always be my greatest sin.

A PROPER STEAK (PLUS BROWN BUTTER–FRIED ONION RINGS)

Everybody has a dish that makes them feel fancy and special. When *I* want to feel fancy and special, I make steak. I rarely order it when I'm out because the price increase in restaurants is obscene. Making it at home doesn't have to be complicated. You don't need an intricate rub. Start with a well-marbled piece of good meat, rain it with salt, and then get that perfect contrast between a crackling brown crust and juicy pink interior in cast iron. On the stove top, you get more of the steak's surface directly in contact with the pan, rather than that space between the grates on the grill. Cast iron means a better crust. Important.

The steak alone is going to be delicious as is. But add a knob of butter, garlic and herbs and baste this infused butter over it to make even more of a crust. And we're here for the crust, remember? I don't want much with a steak. Acid in the form of a lazy salsa verde (cook parsley right in the steak fat). A dry martini. And something on the side to offer textural difference, as in, onion rings.

SERVES 2

1 (1½- to 2-inch-thick) steak, strip or bone-in rib eye

Kosher salt

1 teaspoon onion powder (optional)

1 cup all-purpose flour

1 cup buttermilk

1 large sweet or red onion, cut into ¼-inch-thick rings

2 tablespoons neutral oil (such as grapeseed)

½ cup unsalted butter, chilled

3 garlic cloves, crushed

1 small handful herbs (rosemary, sage, and thyme all work)

Freshly ground pepper

Pat the steak dry with paper towels, aggressively season it all over with salt and the onion powder and let sit for 20 minutes. If you have the time, season your steak a few hours ahead, or even a day ahead. If not, carry on.

Place the flour in a bowl and pour the buttermilk into a separate bowl. Working in batches, dredge the onion rings in the flour, shaking off the excess, then dip them into the buttermilk, letting the excess drip back into the bowl. Return the rings to the flour and toss again to coat. If the dredging looks a little uneven, that's more than okay. I promise the rings will be perfect and deeply delicious once fried. Set the rings on a plate.

Set a large cast-iron skillet or carbon-steel pan over medium-high heat and let it get ripping hot for 5 minutes. Pat the steak dry again with paper towels to ensure it gets a beautiful crust. Rub the steak with just enough of the neutral oil to coat the entire surface. Place the steak in the skillet and, using tongs, press down to encourage the meat to brown. Cook, still pressing down all over like you're learning to play the piano, until the steak is nicely colored and smells beefy, 3 to 4 minutes. Flip the steak and cook until the other side is deeply golden brown, another 3 to 4 minutes. Now, stay with me. Use the tongs to hold the steak on its side and sear around the edges (including the bone, if that's the type of steak you have) until they're beautifully crisp, about 2 minutes per edge.

Turn the heat to medium-low and add ¼ cup of the butter, the garlic, and herbs. As the butter melts and begins to foam, carefully tilt the skillet toward you and scoot the steak to the far end of the pan. Holding the skillet's handle with your nondominant hand, spoon the butter over the steak repeatedly for 1 to 2 minutes, until the internal temperature of the steak registers 120°F on an instant-read thermometer for medium-rare.

CONTINUED

A PROPER STEAK, CONTINUED

Turn off the burner and transfer the steak to a cutting board to rest for at least 15 minutes or up to 30 minutes. Using tongs, pick out the garlic and herbs and set aside for serving. Line a plate with paper towels.

Return the skillet to medium heat and add the remaining ¼ cup of the butter. Once the butter has melted, working in two batches, add the dredged onions to the skillet. Fry until golden brown and crisp, flipping the onion rings after about 4 minutes, frying 7 to 9 minutes total. Transfer the onions to the prepared plate and season with salt and pepper.

When you're ready to serve, slice the meat away from the bone (if needed), then cut slices about ½ inch thick. Serve the steak with the onion rings and reserved garlic and herbs (and a cold martini).

This short but sweet chapter reflects my sweet tooth, which, I'm sorry, isn't too long.

When it comes to dessert, I lean in fruity, tart, nutty, and not-too-sweet directions, which culminates in the anytime pistachio-plum cake on page 319. There's plenty of lemon, don't worry, just turn to page 307 to either learn, or feel nostalgic, about faloodeh, a unique Persian frozen summer dessert with crunchy rice noodles—you won't find *that* at Mister Softee, though I wish you could. Also, for peak summer, see the peach crisp on page 310 with an ingredient that brings extra crunch and extra crisp. For holidays, rely on the Apple and Tahini Galette on page 313 and repeat after me: frangipane, frangipane, frangipane.

None of these recipes calls for a stand mixer, an offset spatula, or royal icing. (You're off the hook, enjoy it.) There are absolutely NO cookies, which I happen to love— love to eat, but don't love to bake. But I admit, as a cook, my baking expertise is still growing. I'm still learning. I made my first pie just a few years ago (semi-disaster, we could only photograph half of it because the crust was so tragic). I'm still perfecting my halvah recipe. I'd love to learn how to make laminated dough so I could throw together mille-feuille, with layers of pastry and Chantilly cream. Check in with me in a year to see if I've kept my word. I might just be making apple galette after apple galette, because, well, it's that good.

FALOODEH WITH CHERRIES ON TOP

Faloodeh is one of the most famous Persian desserts. It looks out of this world: a shredded pile of fluffy ice studded with crunchy rice noodles trying to break free. It's incredibly refreshing—exactly what you want to eat on the hottest days of the year. As a kid (and, who am I kidding, as an adult), I loved it topped with sour cherry syrup. I've adapted the dessert to my favorite flavors: a tart and icy, lemony-base (similar to granita) with sour cherries on top. The contrast of textures is phenomenal; there's this crunchy, slushy, tart, cold ice plus the syrupy jamminess of the cherries and the little crunchy bites of rice noodles that have been cooked, cut, and frozen in the ice. Typically, you squeeze lime juice over everything because the rose-water base is so sweet, but because I make a very lemony version, we're skipping that. So, yeah, I've made some liberal changes to traditional faloodeh. And to my Persian aunties: Don't come after me!

SERVES 6

7 to 9 large lemons

1¾ cups water

1⅔ cups granulated sugar, plus ½ cup

1 pound pitted sweet or sour cherries, fresh or frozen and thawed

2½ teaspoons rose water

2 ounces vermicelli rice noodles

Using a vegetable peeler, remove the peel from the lemons in wide strips. Juice the lemons until you have about 1½ cups juice.

In a small saucepan (you'll be using this saucepan a few times) over medium-high heat, combine the lemon peels, water, and 1⅔ cups sugar and bring to a boil, stirring to dissolve the sugar. Turn off the heat and set the syrup aside to cool.

Once the syrup is cool, stir in the lemon juice. Strain the syrup into a square or rectangular metal baking pan and place in the freezer. (Thinly slice the candied lemon peel and save to garnish the faloodeh if you're feeling fancy or to add to seltzer to make a lazy lemonade.) Stir the icy mixture every hour or so until fully crystallized, about 4 hours. It will go from soft and slushie-like to fluffy piles of ice.

Meanwhile, wipe out the saucepan. Add the cherries and sprinkle with the remaining ½ cup sugar. Bring to a simmer over medium heat and continue cooking, occasionally stirring, until the cherries have begun to break down, 4 to 6 minutes. Turn the heat to medium-low and keep cooking until the cherries have shriveled and a thin syrup has formed, another 4 to 6 minutes. Transfer the cherry syrup to a medium bowl, stir in the rose water, and let cool.

During the final hour of stirring the ice, rinse the saucepan, fill it with water, and bring to a boil. Add the noodles, give them a stir, and cook until tender, 2 to 4 minutes. Drain the noodles and rinse under cold water. Using scissors, snip the noodles into 1- to 2-inch lengths and chill in the fridge until ready to use.

Once the fluffy ice is frozen, toss the noodles into it, stir, and return the pan to the freezer. Chill the faloodeh until the noodles are frozen and crunchy, about 20 minutes.

Before serving, fluff the ice and then scoop into glasses. Spoon on the cherry syrup. Top with the candied lemon strips and serve.

I *Will* Do Dessert.

I have always thought dessert was my Achilles' heel. I don't regret the amount of desserts I've made or haven't made. I regret that I created the narrative, internally and among my kitchen colleagues, that *Oh no, no, no, I don't do dessert*. When I have to make dessert, I love it. And I get a greater sense of accomplishment than when I sear a piece of meat or make a gorgeous salad. It's just a muscle that I have to work a bit harder.

When I was catering for my neighbors as a teenager, I'd make elaborate meals, and noticed that as the evening went on, with bubbles fizzing out and it was nearing 10 pm, guests inevitably started wondering *What's for dessert?* I *had* to serve dessert. It was a lot of fake-it "desserts" for me: Whipped mascarpone and whipped cream dusted with Microplaned chocolate and a pinch of flaky sea salt. . . . Or I'd quickly melt vanilla ice cream until it was a warm "sauce" and add dark chocolate to make this weird creamy chocolate sauce that I'd serve with fruit. At one dinner party for an intimidatingly rich woman in Sonoma, where I wasn't even allowed to see the guests, I served a cheesecake that I'd enlisted my aunt to make. "Did you make this?" the client asked me, adding, "It's really good." Of course, I lied.

Soon, I established a respectable repertoire of three desserts that I made on repeat, all easy French-ish things, none of which was overtly American (nothing frosted, and definitely no pie). There was Lindsey Shere's almond cake from the *Chez Panisse Desserts* cookbook. Chocolate pavé (a flourless, fallen chocolate cake). And olive oil cake. At some point, I got an ice-cream machine and was churning out fennel, lavender, and other bougie flavors.

Back then, I named everything to mimic the style of Chez Panisse, which helped make the simple desserts seem fancier. *Chocolate Pavé with Crème Chantilly.* (Translation: fallen chocolate cake with vanilla whipped cream.) Raspberry coulis appeared everywhere. Every salad was A Salad of Baby Greens. Everything was precious. Whereas now I have to be conscious of not overusing the word *garlicky*.

When I was in my twenties, I was embarrassed by those teenage dinners, thinking they were examples of this kid trying to get as far away from the narrative of his mom's Dodge Caravan as possible. But now, I think it's cute. As a cook, I'm so glad I had that *What's there to lose?* phase. So many cooks don't get to have that stage in their professional development.

308

And when you're a young cook with booming optimism and lofty ambitions, there are disasters. Like the time I made four olive oil cakes for a dinner that I was catering, only to have them all crumble and fall apart. So I blanketed a platter with whipped cream, broke the cake apart into hunks, tucked them into the whipped cream, and dusted it with powdered sugar. Nowadays that's intentional and fashionable, but at the time I thought it was an artsy save. (The dinner guests had to have known, right?)

Counter to all my other advice in this book, I want to offer you my admission of uncertainty. Why? I think everyone who loves food—eaters and cooks—has to challenge themselves. This chapter is evidence of me doing that. We all need those unsettling, disappointing moments when we have to rise to the occasion or give up. And we have to accept both possibilities as valid outcomes and have the motivation to try again when you mess up. I promise you'll do at least slightly better the next time. And for all the times when you're disillusioned by your progress, feel free to improvise—and steal that broken-cake trick.

PEACH AND BLACKBERRY CRISP WITH CINNAMON CRUNCH

A crisp is the ultimate dessert for people who claim they don't bake because it's impossible to mess up. I like mine with a good amount of crumb on top, in this case, inspired by Cinnamon Toast Crunch ("the taste you can see"). For extra crunch, I throw some panko in with the flour, but you could use nuts, oats, or whatever makes you happy. The berries and peaches break down and turn into luscious pie filling, and if you don't like my combo of peach and blackberries, use 3 to 4 pounds of whatever fruit you want.

SERVES 8

CINNAMON CRUNCH

¾ cup all-purpose flour

¾ cup panko breadcrumbs

½ cup packed light brown or granulated sugar

1½ teaspoons ground cinnamon

1 teaspoon kosher salt

½ cup unsalted butter, melted and slightly cooled

3 pounds ripe peaches, pitted, cut into 1-inch-thick wedges

12 ounces blackberries

½ cup granulated sugar

2 tablespoons cornstarch

1 tablespoon fresh lemon juice

1 teaspoon vanilla extract

Cold heavy cream or ice cream for serving

To make the Cinnamon Crunch: In a medium bowl, combine the flour, panko, brown sugar, cinnamon, and salt and stir to mix. Drizzle in the melted butter and work it with your fingers or a fork until there are no dry spots remaining and the mixture looks very crumbly but can hold together when squeezed. You'll have crumbles that are as small as sand and larger ones that are about the size of a quarter. Set aside in the fridge.

Preheat the oven to 350°F.

In a large bowl, toss together the peaches, blackberries, granulated sugar, cornstarch, lemon juice, and vanilla.

Pour the fruit mixture into a 12-inch cast-iron skillet or a 3-quart baking dish. Scatter the Cinnamon Crunch over the top. Bake until the crisp is lightly browned and the filling is bubbling around the edges, 30 to 40 minutes. Let cool slightly.

Put a generous scoop of the warm crisp in individual bowls, top with a spoonful of fresh cream or a scoop of ice cream, and serve.

APPLE AND TAHINI GALETTE

I'll take apple galette over apple pie any day of the week. The proportion of thinly sliced apples to flaky crust is perfect, and what takes this over the top is a tahini frangipane. We don't drop the word *frangipane* into conversation very often, do we? It sounds fussy, I know. But it's really just a matter of mixing ground nuts (or, in this case, ground seeds) with sugar, butter, and egg until it's smooth and fluffy. Spread that on the bottom of the galette crust, place apples on top, and revel in the savory, nutty flavor contrasting with the sweet apples. Serve with barely sweetened whipped cream, crème fraîche, or ice cream, if you like, but I think it's perfect on its own.

SERVES 8

GALETTE DOUGH

1½ cups all-purpose flour, plus more for rolling out

1 tablespoon granulated sugar

1¼ teaspoons kosher salt

¾ cup cold unsalted butter, cut into ½-inch cubes

4 to 6 tablespoons ice water

TAHINI FRANGIPANE

⅓ cup tahini

3 tablespoons granulated sugar

3 tablespoons unsalted butter, at room temperature

1 egg

¼ teaspoon kosher salt

APPLE FILLING

2 pounds tart, crunchy apples (such as Honeycrisp or Pink Lady), cored, thinly sliced

1 tablespoon cider vinegar or white wine vinegar

1 teaspoon vanilla extract

3 tablespoons granulated sugar

Granulated sugar for sprinkling

Heavy cream for brushing

To make the dough: In a large bowl, whisk together the flour, sugar, and salt. Dump in the butter and get your hands dirty: toss the pieces of butter so that they're lightly coated in the flour, separating any pieces that may have stuck together. Work your way around the bowl, smushing each piece once with your fingers. It's so satisfying! Don't overthink it, you just want the butter flattened like little coins coated with flour. Don't wash your hands yet.

Drizzle 4 tablespoons of the ice water over the butter-flour mixture. Rummage your hands through the mixture to combine the wet and dry ingredients. The dough may seem dry at first but it will turn into a very shaggy mass. Use your palms to knead the dough together to form a ball with no dry spots. I find it easier to do this in the bowl rather than on a work surface. You may need to drizzle in an additional tablespoon or two of the remaining water to help the dough come together but, even with the additional water, it won't be smooth or shiny.

Wrap the dough with plastic wrap and use your hands to flatten and shape into a round disk about 1 inch thick. Refrigerate for at least 2 hours or up to overnight. The dough will hydrate while it chills.

Line a rimmed baking sheet with parchment paper. Lightly flour a work surface.

Unwrap the dough and place it on the work surface. Flour your rolling pin and strike the dough with it a few times. The weight of the rolling pin will help flatten the dough. Starting from the center, roll out the dough, flipping it after three or so rolls to prevent it from sticking to the surface. (I think of it as a clock, so after I've rolled to nine o'clock, then twelve o'clock, and then two o'clock, I flip it.) Keep rolling until you have a roughly 14-inch circle. Gently gather both ends of the dough and lift and transfer to the prepared baking sheet. Cover loosely with the plastic wrap and return to the fridge to chill.

CONTINUED

APPLE AND TAHINI GALETTE, CONTINUED

To make the frangipane: In a bowl, whisk the tahini, sugar, butter, egg, and salt until you have a smooth fluffy, paste. Set aside.

Place an oven rack in the bottom position and preheat the oven to 375°F.

To make the filling: Place the apples in a large bowl and add the vinegar, vanilla, and 3 tablespoons sugar. Toss until the sugar feels like it has mostly dissolved.

Remove the dough from the fridge and lift away and discard the cling wrap. Working quickly so the dough doesn't warm up, plop the frangipane in the center of the dough and spread out evenly with a butter knife, leaving a 3-inch border. Arrange the apples in whatever manner you like. The goal is to keep each slice of apple snuggled close to the next one without stacking them on top of each other. (I have my good days and my not-so-good days with successful arranging.) Fold the edges of the dough over the apples. Brush the dough with the cream and sprinkle with the additional sugar, which will create a caramelized, crunchy crust.

Bake the galette on the bottom oven rack until the crust is deeply golden brown, the apples are tender, and the scent is irresistible, 40 to 50 minutes. Remove the galette from the oven and place the pan on a wire rack to cool for 1 hour. Cut into wedges and serve. This is best the day it is made.

FUTZING WITH FRANGIPANE

So, frangipane, the fluffy, nutty butter stuff, is usually made with almonds (think almond croissant filling—yum), but you can make it with any nut (or nut butter, to speed things up). In this recipe, use peanut or cashew butter if you don't dig tahini. They would be great too.

ORANGE BLOSSOM PANNA COTTA WITH HONEY'D STRAWBERRIES

Panna cotta is such an easy dessert once you pick up a box of gelatin at the supermarket. I wanted to mimic my favorite flavor of White Moustache yogurt (called "Kiss"—seek it out) by dropping in a bit of orange blossom water and labneh for tang. It's really simple to macerate strawberries (that means letting them sit in sugar to make their own syrup) and drizzle that on top. All of this looks and sounds fancier than it is, which is why I love it. Plus, it's easy to prepare ahead for a crowd. Just make sure the panna cotta is barely set; you want a good amount of jiggle. (Don't we all?)

SERVES 6

2¼ teaspoons (1 envelope) powdered gelatin

3 tablespoons water

3 cups heavy cream

½ cup runny honey, plus 1 tablespoon

½ teaspoon kosher salt

1½ cups labneh or full-fat Greek yogurt

4 teaspoons orange blossom water

1 teaspoon vanilla extract

1 pound strawberries, hulled and quartered

2 teaspoons fresh lemon juice

In a small bowl, stir together the gelatin and water. Let stand for 5 to 10 minutes to allow the gelatin to hydrate and get jelly-like.

Meanwhile, in a medium saucepan over medium-low heat, combine 1 cup of the cream, the ½ cup honey, and salt and stir gently until the honey has dissolved and you see no streaks, 2 to 3 minutes. Don't let the cream come to a simmer, which will kill the gelatin and we're not about murder here. Turn off the heat and gently stir in the softened gelatin, making sure it has completely dissolved.

In a large bowl, whisk the labneh, orange blossom water, vanilla, and remaining 2 cups cream until smooth. Gently whisk the gelatin mixture into the cream mixture. The texture will be silky, smooth, and pourable, like very thick cream.

Divide the panna cotta mixture into small bowls, cute cups, and/or ramekins; set on a tray; and refrigerate until set, at least 2 hours or up to 2 days.

At least 20 minutes or up to 3 hours before serving, in a medium bowl, toss together the strawberries, lemon juice, and remaining 1 tablespoon honey. Set aside to macerate, tossing whenever you feel like it, until the strawberries soften and their juices have formed a glossy syrup.

When ready to serve, spoon the strawberries over the panna cotta.

DO AHEAD

Panna cotta can be made (without the strawberry topping) up to 3 days ahead, covered, and refrigerated until ready to top and serve.

CRISPY PLUM AND PISTACHIO CAKE

This is a mash-up of two cakes that I love: Lindsey Shere's famous almond cake from *Chez Panisse Desserts* and Marian Burros's equally famous plum torte from the *New York Times*. Shere's cake comes together quickly and easily in the food processor; Burros's plops plums into a spongy, moist cake base. My spin adds a quick homemade pistachio flour that turns this cake into a distant relative of the two. It's nutty and fragrant with pistachio, while the deep-purple plum slices bake into shiny gems and sparkling turbinado sugar makes the crust crackly. A half cup of buttermilk adds tang while tenderizing the cake crumb. This isn't a show-off cake—I'm not about that—but it's so delicious it deserves to sit at the center of the table.

SERVES 8 TO 10

½ cup shelled pistachios or blanched almonds

1 cup granulated sugar

½ cup unsalted butter, at room temperature, cubed

1 egg

½ cup buttermilk

1 teaspoon vanilla extract

1⅓ cups all-purpose flour

1½ teaspoons baking powder

½ teaspoon kosher salt

1 pound plums, pitted and torn or sliced

3 tablespoons turbinado sugar (optional)

Lightly butter and flour a 9-inch springform pan. Tap out any excess flour and line the pan with parchment. (You can use a cake pan if you don't have a springform pan; but if you do so, leave an overhang with the parchment paper so you can easily lift out the cake.)

In a food processor, combine the pistachios and 1 tablespoon granulated sugar and pulse until they are a beautiful green sandy texture. Add the butter and remaining sugar and pulse until fully incorporated. Add the egg, buttermilk, and vanilla and pulse again, scraping down the sides once or twice with a rubber spatula, until the mixture is smooth.

In a medium bowl, whisk together the flour, baking powder, and salt. Add half of the flour mixture to the batter and pulse a few times. Add the remaining flour mixture and pulse just until smooth. Scrape the batter into the prepared pan and smooth out the surface with the spatula. Lightly press the plums into the batter and place in the fridge to chill for 30 minutes.

Preheat the oven to 350°F.

Scatter the turbinado sugar over the batter. Bake the cake until the edges are deeply golden brown and a paring knife inserted in the center comes out clean, 45 to 50 minutes. Set the pan on a wire rack to cool for 5 minutes before slicing and serving.

DO AHEAD

The cake can be made up to 3 days ahead. Let cool completely, cover tightly, and store at room temperature in a cool place.

Acknowledgments

This is the closest that I'll ever get to an Oscar speech, so. . . .

To my editor, Lorena Jones. I knew it was a match as soon as we had our first call. I felt that you understood me, and I was right. You went beyond what any editor could do. Thank you for your thoughtful edits, your guidance through this whole process, and your extreme patience with me. When I was riddled with self-doubt, you provided the calm that I needed, and I am forever thankful.

To the whole Ten Speed Press crew: Lizzie Allen, Jana Branson, Windy Dorresteyn, Sohayla Farman, Doug Ogan, Allison Renzulli, Kelly Snowden, Kate Tyler, Aaron Wehner, and Natalie Yera. Each of you was so excited to welcome me to the fam, and that meant the world. Thank you for all your efforts from helping with design to all the press and marketing and getting this thing out there in the world!

To my literary agent, Katherine Cowles. Eva K. told me you were the best, and going with you was one of the greatest decisions that I ever made. Thank you for all the very real-talk phone calls and lunches, for pushing me when I needed to be pushed, and for being my confidant. You've always seen the light.

To Michael Graydon and Nikole Herriott. The first decision that I made (before I even wrote the proposal for this book!) was that I wanted you two to work on this project with me. I was in awe of your brilliance from the get go (when I first met you years ago), but seeing how incredibly thoughtful and kind-hearted you each are while working on this project only made me love you both even more. This book would not be what it is without you two.

To Ryan Crouchman. Thank you for designing the hell out of this book, answering my late-night and weekend emails and texts, and bearing with me when I had some random idea and wanted to take you on that ride with me. You also have the most soothing voice that I have ever heard (which is why I always wanted us to talk on the phone rather than email!).

To Sue Li. Thank you for your beautiful food styling, checking me when I need to be checked, all the cat memes, and your invaluable friendship. And for bringing Paul into my life. I love you both.

To Rebecca Bartoshesky. You set the bar so high and this book wouldn't be what it is without your prop styling. You put me in near shock at the most incredible things you found. You will always be the silent but deadly type to me, and I love that!

To Kat Boytsova and Kaitlyn Wong. Thank you for all your hard work with much of the shopping, organizing receipts and spreadsheets, and testing and retesting. Your feedback was essential in making these recipes stand out.

To Alyssa Kondracki and Spencer Richard. Thank you both for being such damn pros on set, assisting Sue, and doing all the crazy things that food styling requires.

To Sam Williams. Thank you for bringing all the good vibes on set, exceptional playlists, and becoming everyone's crush.

To Alexis Basso and Shane Gabier. Thank you both for being so gracious and letting me use your beautiful ceramics. I feel so lucky to have your stunning work in this book.

To Juniper Tedhams. Thank you for being so generous and opening your home for the book shoot.

To Alex Beggs. Thank you for our date nights on Wednesdays, for listening to my tangents, helping me when I needed to get my scattered thoughts on paper, and being my cheerleader when I was hitting a wall. Thank you for loving skincare as much as I do. I hope to be half as good as you in life. Your heart is one of the biggest and brightest I've ever known.

To David Sabshon. Thank you for celebrating the highs of life with me but, more important, helping me get back up when I encountered the lows. Your openness and desire to do good in this world make me feel honored to have you as a friend.

To Dan Pelosi. You are the ketchup to my (Dijon) mustard. You always know how to put a smile on my face. And if my mother could adopt you, she would.

To Eric Wink, the little brother I always wanted. Thank you for being a second pair of eyes and always having such exquisite taste.

To some of the greatest cooks that I know: Carla Lalli Music, Chris Morocco, Claire Saffitz, Molly Baz, Gaby Melian, Brad Leone, and Anna Stockwell. Thank you for inspiring me daily, giving me some of the best memories, and making me a better cook.

To Julia Bainbridge, Paul Bennett, Jeremy Bennett, Christina Chaey, Todd Coleman, Dan Cingari, Jonathon Burdford, Zak Dychtwald, Emily Eisen, DeVonn Francis, John Guidi, Taylor Griggs, Trevor Himes, Elizabeth Jamie, Eva Karagiorgas, Rachel Karten, Justin Katz, Ben Mims, Nathan Needle, Eleanore Park, Jesse Rudolph, Michael Scanlon, Aria Shafa, and Emily Schultz. You all make my life sweeter and whole lot more fun.

To my big Persian family (my khalehs, amehs, dahyees, amoo, cousins, nephew) in California, Vancouver, and Iran. I love you all so much. Thank you for being so loving, over the top, and providing me with vibrant (maybe chaotic, at times) memories that have given me great material to write about

To Keith Pollock. Thank you for the countless nights talking me off a cliff, allowing me to workshop all the things out loud, and being my favorite recipe taster. Most important, thank you for seeing me completely. You have given me the greatest gift: the freedom to be who I am, and for loving me anyway. You are my rock. I love you.

To my mom, dad, and sister; don't start crying now. Thank you for trusting me and always standing by my side. I am the luckiest son and brother to have such a supportive family to the point that I think if I reheated some frozen dinners, you'd all still think that I'm a star.

Index

322

324

Library of Congress Control Number: 2021947031

Hardcover ISBN: 978-1-9848-5856-6
eBook ISBN: 978-1-9848-5857-3

Printed in China

Editor: Lorena Jones
Production editors: Doug Ogan and Sohayla Farman
Designers: Ryan Crouchman with Lizzie Allen
Typeface: Maison Neue by Milieu Grotesque
Production designers: Mari Gill and Faith Hague
Production and prepress color manager: Jane Chinn
Food stylists: Sue Li; Scarlett Lindemann (page 127)
Front cover set design: Amy Wilson
Back cover prop stylist: Rebecca Bartoshesky
Front and back cover image retoucher: Joe Tripi
Copyeditor: Mary Cassells | Proofreader: Rachel Markowitz
Indexer: Ken DellaPenta
Publicist: Jana Branson | Marketer: Allison Renzulli
10 9 8 7 6 5 4 3 2 1

First Edition